ÁNTONIA

Major Literary Characters

THE ANCIENT WORLD THROUGH
THE SEVENTEENTH CENTURY

ACHILLES
Homer, *Iliad*

CALIBAN
William Shakespeare, *The Tempest*
Robert Browning, *Caliban upon Setebos*

CLEOPATRA
William Shakespeare, *Antony and*
  Cleopatra
John Dryden, *All for Love*
George Bernard Shaw, *Caesar and*
  Cleopatra

DON QUIXOTE
Miguel de Cervantes, *Don Quixote*
Franz Kafka, *Parables*

FALSTAFF
William Shakespeare, *Henry IV, Part I,*
  Henry IV, Part II, The Merry Wives
  of Windsor

FAUST
Christopher Marlowe, *Doctor Faustus*
Johann Wolfgang von Goethe, *Faust*
Thomas Mann, *Doctor Faustus*

HAMLET
William Shakespeare, *Hamlet*

IAGO
William Shakespeare, *Othello*

JULIUS CAESAR
William Shakespeare, *Julius Caesar*
George Bernard Shaw, *Caesar and*
  Cleopatra

KING LEAR
William Shakespeare, *King Lear*

MACBETH
William Shakespeare, *Macbeth*

ODYSSEUS/ULYSSES
Homer, *Odyssey*
James Joyce, *Ulysses*

OEDIPUS
Sophocles, *Oedipus Rex, Oedipus*
  at Colonus

OTHELLO
William Shakespeare, *Othello*

ROSALIND
William Shakespeare, *As You Like It*

SANCHO PANZA
Miguel de Cervantes, *Don Quixote*
Franz Kafka, *Parables*

SATAN
The Book of Job
John Milton, *Paradise Lost*

SHYLOCK
William Shakespeare, *The Merchant*
  of Venice

THE WIFE OF BATH
Geoffrey Chaucer, *The Canterbury*
  Tales

THE EIGHTEENTH AND
NINETEENTH CENTURIES

AHAB
Herman Melville, *Moby-Dick*

ISABEL ARCHER
Henry James, *Portrait of a Lady*

EMMA BOVARY
Gustave Flaubert, *Madame Bovary*

DOROTHEA BROOKE
George Eliot, *Middlemarch*

CHELSEA HOUSE PUBLISHERS

Major Literary Characters

DAVID COPPERFIELD
Charles Dickens, *David Copperfield*

ROBINSON CRUSOE
Daniel Defoe, *Robinson Crusoe*

DON JUAN
Molière, *Don Juan*
Lord Byron, *Don Juan*

HUCK FINN
Mark Twain, *The Adventures of Tom Sawyer, Adventures of Huckleberry Finn*

CLARISSA HARLOWE
Samuel Richardson, *Clarissa*

HEATHCLIFF
Emily Brontë, *Wuthering Heights*

ANNA KARENINA
Leo Tolstoy, *Anna Karenina*

MR. PICKWICK
Charles Dickens, *The Pickwick Papers*

HESTER PRYNNE
Nathaniel Hawthorne, *The Scarlet Letter*

BECKY SHARP
William Makepeace Thackeray, *Vanity Fair*

LAMBERT STRETHER
Henry James, *The Ambassadors*

EUSTACIA VYE
Thomas Hardy, *The Return of the Native*

TWENTIETH CENTURY

ÁNTONIA
Willa Cather, *My Ántonia*

BRETT ASHLEY
Ernest Hemingway, *The Sun Also Rises*

HANS CASTORP
Thomas Mann, *The Magic Mountain*

HOLDEN CAULFIELD
J. D. Salinger, *The Catcher in the Rye*

CADDY COMPSON
William Faulkner, *The Sound and the Fury*

JANIE CRAWFORD
Zora Neale Hurston, *Their Eyes Were Watching God*

CLARISSA DALLOWAY
Virginia Woolf, *Mrs. Dalloway*

DILSEY
William Faulkner, *The Sound and the Fury*

GATSBY
F. Scott Fitzgerald, *The Great Gatsby*

HERZOG
Saul Bellow, *Herzog*

JOAN OF ARC
William Shakespeare, *Henry VI*
George Bernard Shaw, *Saint Joan*

LOLITA
Vladimir Nabokov, *Lolita*

WILLY LOMAN
Arthur Miller, *Death of a Salesman*

MARLOW
Joseph Conrad, *Lord Jim, Heart of Darkness, Youth, Chance*

PORTNOY
Philip Roth, *Portnoy's Complaint*

BIGGER THOMAS
Richard Wright, *Native Son*

CHELSEA HOUSE PUBLISHERS

Major Literary Characters

ÁNTONIA

Edited and with an introduction by
HAROLD BLOOM

CHELSEA HOUSE PUBLISHERS
New York ◇ Philadelphia

Jacket illustration: Photograph of Anna Pavelka (the model for Ántonia)
(Willa Cather Pioneer Memorial Collection, Nebraska State
Historical Society). *Inset:* Title page from the first edition
of *My Ántonia* (Boston: Houghton Mifflin, 1918)
(Courtesy of The Library of Congress).

Chelsea House Publishers

Editor-in-Chief Remmel T. Nunn
Managing Editor Karyn Gullen Browne
Picture Editor Adrian G. Allen
Art Director Maria Epes
Manufacturing Manager Gerald Levine

Major Literary Characters

Senior Editor S. T. Joshi
Copy Chief Richard Fumosa
Designer Maria Epes

Staff for ÁNTONIA

Picture Researcher Patricia Burns
Assistant Art Director Noreen Romano
Production Manager Joseph Romano
Production Coordinator Marie Claire Cebrián

© 1991 by Chelsea House Publishers, a division
of Main Line Book Co.

Introduction © 1991 by Harold Bloom

Printed and bound in the United States of America

First Printing

1 3 5 7 9 8 6 4 2

Library of Congress Cataloging-in-Publication Data

Ántonia / edited and with an introduction by Harold Bloom.
p.   cm. —(Major literary characters)
Includes bibliographical references and index.
ISBN 0-7910-0950-5.—ISBN 0-7910-1005-8 (pbk.)
1. Cather, Willa, 1873–1947. My Ántonia. I. Series.
PS3505.A87M89425   1991
813'.52—dc20
90-49709
CIP

CONTENTS

THE ANALYSIS OF CHARACTER

Harold Bloom

"Character," according to our dictionaries, still has as a primary meaning a graphic symbol, such as a letter of the alphabet. This meaning reflects the word's apparent origin in the ancient Greek *charactēr*, a sharp stylus. *Charactēr* also meant the mark of the stylus' incisions. Recent fashions in literary criticism have reduced "character" in literature to a matter of marks upon a page. But our word "character" also has a very different meaning, matching that of the ancient Greek *ēthos*, "habitual way of life." Shall we say then that literary character is an imitation of human character, or is it just a grouping of marks? The issue is between a critic like Dr. Samuel Johnson, for whom words were as much like people as like things, and a critic like the late Roland Barthes, who told us that "the fact can only exist linguistically, as a term of discourse." Who is closer to our experience of reading literature, Johnson or Barthes? What difference does it make, if we side with one critic rather than the other?

Barthes is famous, like Foucault and other recent French theorists, for having added to Nietzsche's proclamation of the death of God a subsidiary demise, that of the literary author. If there are no authors, then there are no fictional personages, presumably because literature does not refer to a world outside language. Words indeed necessarily refer to other words in the first place, but the impact of words ultimately is drawn from a universe of fact. Stories, poems, and plays are recognizable as such because they are human utterances within traditions of utterances, and traditions, by achieving authority, become a kind of fact, or at least the sense of a fact. Our sense that literary characters, within the context of a fictive cosmos, indeed are fictional personages is also a kind of fact. The meaning and value of every character in a successful work of literary representation depend upon our ideas of persons in the factual reality of our lives.

Literary character is always an invention, and inventions generally are indebted to prior inventions. Shakespeare is the inventor of literary character as we know it; he reformed the universal human expectations for the verbal imitation of personality, and the reformation appears now to be permanent and uncannily inevitable. Remarkable as the Bible and Homer are at representing personages, their characters are relatively unchanging. They age within their stories, but their habitual modes of being do not develop. Jacob and Achilles unfold before us, but without metamorphoses. Lear and Macbeth, Hamlet and Othello severely modify themselves not only by their actions, but by their utterances, and most of all through *overhearing themselves,* whether they speak to themselves or to others. Pondering what they themselves have said, they will to change, and actually do change, sometimes extravagantly yet always persuasively. Or else they suffer change, without willing it, but in reaction not so much to their language as to their relation to that language.

I do not think it useful to say that Shakespeare successfully imitated elements in our characters. Rather, it could be argued that he compelled aspects of character to appear that previously were concealed, or not available to representation. This is not to say that Shakespeare is God, but to remind us that language is not God either. The mimesis of character in Shakespeare's dramas now seems to us normative, and indeed became the accepted mode almost immediately, as Ben Jonson shrewdly and somewhat grudgingly implied. And yet, Shakespearean representation has surprisingly little in common with the imitation of reality in Jonson or in Christopher Marlowe. The origins of Shakespeare's originality in the portrayal of men and women are to be found in the *Canterbury Tales* of Geoffrey Chaucer, insofar as they can be located anywhere before Shakespeare himself. Chaucer's savage and superb Pardoner overhears his own tale-telling, as well as his mocking rehearsal of his own spiel, and through this overhearing he is emboldened to forget himself, and enthusiastically urges all his fellow-pilgrims to come forward to be fleeced by him. His self-awareness, and apocalyptically rancid sense of spiritual fall, are preludes to the even grander abysses of the perverted will in Iago and in Edmund. What might be called the character trait of a negative charisma may be Chaucer's invention, but came to its perfection in Shakespearean mimesis.

The analysis of character is as much Shakespeare's invention as the representation of character is, since Iago and Edmund are adepts at analyzing both themselves and their victims. Hamlet, whose overwhelming charisma has many negative components, is certainly the most comprehensive of all literary characters, and so necessarily prophesies the labyrinthine complexities of the will in Iago and Edmund. Charisma, according to Max Weber, its first codifier, is primarily a natural endowment, and implies a primordial and idiosyncratic power over nature, and so finally over death. Hamlet's uncanniness is at its most suggestive in the scene of his long dying, where the audience, through the mediation of Horatio, itself is compelled to meditate upon suicide, if only because outliving the prince of Denmark scarcely seems an option.

Shakespearean representation has usurped not only our sense of literary character, but our sense of ourselves as characters, with Hamlet playing the part of the largest of these usurpations. Insofar as we have an idea of human disinterestedness, we tend to derive it from the Hamlet of Act V, whose quietism has about it a ghostly authority. Oscar Wilde, in his profound and profoundly witty dialogue, "The Decay of Lying," expressed a permanent insight when he insisted that art shaped every era, far more than any age formed art. Life imitates art, we imitate Shakespeare, because without Shakespeare we would perish for lack of images. Wilde's grandest audacity demystifies Shakespearean mimesis with a Shakespearean vivaciousness: "This unfortunate aphorism about art holding the mirror up to Nature is deliberately said by Hamlet in order to convince the bystanders of his absolute insanity in all art-matters." Of *Hamlet*'s influence upon the ages Wilde remarked that: "The world has grown sad because a puppet was once melancholy." "Puppet" is Wilde's own deconstruction, a brilliant reminder that Shakespeare's artistry of illusion has so mastered reality as to have changed reality, evidently forever.

The analysis of character, as a critical pursuit, seems to me as much a Shakespearean invention as literary character was, since much of what we know about how to analyze character necessarily follows Shakespearean procedures. His hero-villains, from Richard III through Iago, Edmund, and Macbeth, are shrewd and endless questers into their own self-motivations. If we could bear to see Hamlet, in his unwearied negations, as another hero-villain, then we would judge him the supreme analyst of the darker recalcitrances in the selfhood. Freud followed the pre-Socratic Empedocles, in arguing that character is fate, a frightening doctrine that maintains the fear that there are no accidents, that overdetermination rules us all of our lives. Hamlet assumes the same, yet adds to this argument the terrible passivity he manifests in Act V. Throughout Shakespeare's tragedies, the most interesting personages seem doom-eager, reminding us again that a Shakespearean reading of Freud would be more illuminating than a Freudian exegesis of Shakespeare. We learn more when we discover Hamlet in the Freudian Death Drive, than when we read *Beyond the Pleasure Principle* into *Hamlet*.

In Shakespearean comedy, character achieves its true literary apotheosis, which is the representation of the inner freedom that can be created by great wit alone. Rosalind and Falstaff, perhaps alone among Shakespeare's personages, match Hamlet in wit, though hardly in the metaphysics of consciousness. Whether in the comic or the modern mode, Shakespeare has set the standard of measurement in the balance between character and passion.

In Shakespeare the self is more dramatized than theatricalized, which is why a Shakespearean reading of Freud works out so well. Character-formation after the passing of the Oedipal stage takes the place of fetishistic fragmentings of the self. Critics who now call literary character into question, and who proclaim also the death of the author, invariably also regard all notions, literary and human, of a stable character as being mere reductions of deeper pre-Oedipal desires. It becomes clear that the fortunes of literary character rise and fall with the prestige of normative conceptions of the ego. Shakespeare's Iago, who wars against being, may be the first deconstructionist of the self, with his proclamation of "I am not what I am." This constitutes the necessary prologue to any view that would regard a fixed ego as a virtual abnormality. But deconstructions of the self are no more modern than Modernism is. Like literary modernism, the decentered ego came out of the Hellenistic culture of ancient Alexandria. The Gnostic heretics believed that the psyche, like the body, was a fallen entity, mechanically fashioned by the Demiurge or false creator. They held however that each of us possessed also a spark or pneuma, which was a fragment of the original Abyss or true, alien God. The soul or psyche within every one of us was thus at war with the self or pneuma, and only that sparklike self could be saved.

Shakespeare, following after Chaucer in this respect, was the first and remains still the greatest master of representing character both as a stable soul and a wavering self. There is a substance that endures in Shakespeare's figures, and there is also a quicksilver rendition of the unsettling sparks. Racine and Tolstoy, Balzac and Dickens, follow in Shakespeare's wake by giving us some sense of pre-Oedipal sparks or drives, and considerably more sense of post-Oedipal character and personality, stabilizations or sublimations of the fetish-seeking drives. Critics like Leo Bersani and René Girard argue eloquently against our taking this mimesis as the only proper work of literature. I would suggest that strong fictions of the self, from the Bible through Samuel Beckett, necessarily participate in both modes, the sublimation of desire, and the persistence of a primordial desire. The mystery of Hamlet or of Lear is intimately invested in the tangled mixture of the two modes of representation.

Psychic mobility is proposed by Bersani as the ideal to which deconstructions of the literary self may yet guide us. The ideal has its pathos, but the realities of literary representation seem to me very different, perhaps destructively so. When a novelist like D. H. Lawrence sought to reduce his characters to Eros and the Death Drive, he still had to persuade us of his authority at mimesis by lavishing upon the figures of *The Rainbow* and *Women in Love* all of the vivid stigmata of normative personality. Birkin and Ursula may represent antithetical and uncanny drives, but they develop and change as characters pondering their own pronouncements and reactions to self and others. The cost of a non-Shakespearean representation is enormous. Pynchon, in *The Crying of Lot 49* and *Gravity's Rainbow,* evades the burden of the normative by resorting to something like Christopher Marlowe's art of caricature in *The Jew of Malta.* Marlowe's Barabas is a marvelous rhetorician, yet he is a cartoon alongside the troublingly equivocal Shylock. Pynchon's personages are deliberate cartoons also, as flat as comic strips. Marlowe's achievement, and Pynchon's, are beyond dispute, yet they are like the prelude and the postlude to Shakespearean reality. They do not wish to engage with our hunger for the empirical world and so they enter the problematic cosmos of literary fantasy.

No writer, not even Shakespeare or Proust, alters the available stock that we agree to call reality, but Shakespeare, more than any other, does show us how much of reality we could encounter if only we retained adequate desire. The strong literary representation of character is already an analysis of character, and is part of the healing work of a literary culture, which implicitly seeks to cure violence through a normative mimesis of ego, *as if it were stable,* whether in actuality it is or is not. I do not believe that this is a social quest taken on by literary culture, but rather that we confront here the aesthetic essence of what makes a culture *literary,* rather than metaphysical or ethical or religious. A culture becomes literary when its conceptual modes have failed it, which means when religion, philosophy, and science have begun to lose their authority. If they cannot heal violence, then literature attempts to do so, which may be only a turning inside out of the critical arguments of Girard and Bersani.

I conclude by offering a particular instance or special case as a paradigm for the healing enterprise that is at once the representation and the analysis of literary character. Let us call it the aesthetics of being outraged, or rather of successfully representing the state of being outraged. W. C. Fields was one modern master of such representation, and Nathanael West was another, as was Faulkner before him. Here also the greatest master remains Shakespeare, whose Macbeth, himself a bloody outrage, yet retains our imaginative sympathy precisely because he grows increasingly outraged as he experiences the equivocation of the fiend that lies like truth. The double-natured promises and the prophecies of the weird sisters finally induce in Macbeth an apocalyptic version of the stage actor's anxiety at missing cues, the horror of a phantasmagoric stage fright of missing one's time, of always reacting too late. Macbeth, a veritable monster of solipsistic inwardness but no intellectual, counters his dilemma by fresh murders, that prolong him in time yet provoke him only to a perpetually freshened sense of being outraged, as all his expectations become still worse confounded. We are moved by Macbeth, however estrangedly, because his terrible inwardness is a paradigm for our own solipsism, but also because none of us can resist a strong and successful representation of the human in a state of being outraged.

The ultimate outrage is the necessity of dying, an outrage concealed in a multitude of masks, including the tyrannical ambitions of Macbeth. I suspect that our outrage at being outraged is the most difficult of all our affects for us to represent to ourselves, which is why we are so inclined to imaginative sympathy for a character who strongly conveys that affect to us. The Shrike of West's *Miss Lonely-hearts* or Faulkner's Joe Christmas of *Light in August* are crucial modern instances, but such figures can be located in many other works, since the ability to represent this extreme emotion is one of the tests that strong writers are driven to set for themselves.

However a reader seeks to reduce literary character to a question of marks on a page, she will come at last to the impasse constituted by the thought of death, her death, and before that to all the stations of being outraged that memorialize her own drive towards death. In reading, she quests for evidences that are strong representations, whether of her desire or her despair. Such questings constitute the necessary basis for the analysis of literary character, an enterprise that always will survive every vagary of critical fashion.

EDITOR'S NOTE

This book brings together a representative selection of the best literary criticism that has been devoted to Ántonia, the heroine of Willa Cather's novel, *My Ántonia* (1918). I am grateful to S. T. Joshi for his skill and erudition in assisting me in editing this volume.

My introduction centers upon the poetics of loss intimately involved in the representation of Ántonia as a literary character. A selection of critical extracts follows, giving us a history of Ántonia's reception, from Randolph Bourne and H. L. Mencken through Robert E. Scholes and Ann Douglas, among others, and going on to such recent responses as those of Deborah G. Lambert and Linda Wagner-Martin.

Full-scale critical essays of the last thirty years commence here with John H. Randall III's rather extensive study of pastoral themes as exemplified by Ántonia's character. Richard Giannone emphasizes the role of music in portraying Ántonia, while William J. Stuckey disputes the agrarian interpretation, and finds instead a parable of art's triumph over life.

In Edward J. Piacentino's essay, Ántonia is seen as a triumph for the aesthetics of impressionism, after which Mary Kemper Sternshein gives us a vision of Ántonia as an exaltation of Nebraska as earth mother.

Patrick W. Shaw finds in Ántonia not the portrait of the author's nostalgia but rather a release from sexual dogma, granting Cather a fictive substitute for what societal repressions denied her. Feminist criticism, in its most recent phase, informs the three remaining essays, starting with Judith Fetterley's account of the representation of Jim Burden, and its relation to the dilemmas of a lesbian writer. Susan J. Rosowski also finds Ántonia to be at the center of a female world, one that repudiates male versions of mythic adventure. In this book's final essay, Hermione Lee delineates Ántonia as the inspiring force for Cather's imagination, a force that does not relieve that imagination from ending in "a deeply melancholy determinism."

INTRODUCTION

My Ántonia, the title of Willa Cather's most searching study both of her own longing and of our national nostalgias, remains our best entry into the analysis of Ántonia as a literary character. When Jim Burden calls his manuscript "My Ántonia," he highlights what it is that we mean when we remember a friend, and call her or him "my" followed by her or his given name. Burden loved and loves Ántonia, but was never her lover, and did not become her husband, indeed could not, for Burden is to be identified with Cather. We say "my" precisely where we have lost what we could never hope to have possessed, so that "my" in such a context is a metaphor or fiction, a verbal figure substituting for a desired but unlikely possession.

Ántonia is so moving and memorable a character because she brings together her author's image of erotic desire with our intense vision of a lost America, a land of pioneers who sought a better life than Europe afforded them. The Bohemian (Czech) girl Ántonia belongs to the visionary company of American fictive heroines that includes Hawthorne's Hester Prynne (*The Scarlet Letter*), James's Isabel Archer (*The Portrait of a Lady*), Faulkner's Caddy Compson (*The Sound and the Fury*), and Zora Neale Hurston's Janie Crawford (*Their Eyes Were Watching God*). Diverse as they are, all these are strong vitalists, women who carry the American version of the biblical Blessing, tragic or doom-eager as that carrying may become. Ántonia, despite her earlier experiental misfortunes, concludes in a happier destiny than any of the others, perhaps because she so authentically is loved by her creator, When Jim has his final vision of her, the perspective that dominates is not less than heroic:

> Ántonia had always been one to leave images in the mind that did not fade—that grew stronger with time. In my memory there was a succession of such pictures, fixed there like the old woodcuts of one's first primer: Ántonia kicking her bare legs against the sides of my pony when we came home in triumph with our snake; Ántonia in her black shawl and fur cap, as she stood by her father's grave in the snowstorm; Ántonia coming in with her work-team along the evening sky-line. She lent herself to immemorial human atti-

I

tudes which we recognize by instinct as universal and true. I had not been mistaken. She was a battered woman now, not a lovely girl; but she still had that something which fires the imagination, could still stop one's breath for a moment by a look or gesture that somehow revealed the meaning in common things. She had only to stand in the orchard, to put her hand on a little crab tree and look up at the apples, to make you feel the goodness of planting and tending and the harvesting at last. All the strong things of her heart came out in her body, that had been so tireless in serving generous emotions.

It was no wonder that her sons stood tall and straight. She was a rich mine of life, like the founders of early races.

A severe critic could remark that a fault of this vision is that it tells us more about Willa Cather than about Jim Burden, who narrates it. Even more severely, such a critic might note that this passage has elements of sentimentality, and is marked by dead metaphors: "something which fires the imagination," "stop one's breath for a moment," "strong things of her heart," "stood tall and straight," "a rich mine of life." Yet, for Cather, there can be no emotion in excess of Ántonia as object, and the worn diction is necessary for "immemorial human attitudes," for the "universal and true" in human relations. Cather takes deliberate risks whenever she directly presents Ántonia to us. How else is she to study the nostalgias? My Ántonia is an overtly Virgilian book, and its motto, from the Georgics, is at once elegiac and celebratory: "The best days are first to flee." For Cather, and for her readers, Ántonia is the emblem of lost first love, forever beyond reach, yet always justified by the novel's consoling final sentence: "Whatever we had missed, we possessed together the precious, the incommunicable past."

The past, whether Burden's or Cather's, may be incommunicable, as love is so often incommunicable, even by Willa Cather. What Cather is masterful at conveying is generosity as an aspect of love, and just that aspect is dominant in Ántonia's relationship with Jim. My own immediate memory whenever I think of My Ántonia is the lovely first encounter between Jim and Ántonia:

> She clapped her hands and murmured "Blue sky, blue eyes," as if it amused her. While we snuggled down there out of the wind, she learned a score of words. She was quick, and very eager. We were so deep in the grass that we could see nothing but the blue sky over us and the gold tree in front of us. It was wonderfully pleasant. After Ántonia had said the new words over and over, she wanted to give me a little chased silver ring she wore on her middle finger. When she coaxed and insisted, I repulsed her quite sternly. I didn't want her ring, and I felt there was something reckless and extravagant about her wishing to give it away to a boy she had never seen before.

As a privileged moment, this is worthy of the Turgenev of A Sportsman's Sketches. The teenage Ántonia already is what she will be always: loving, totally generous, free, at one with the earth. Overwhelmed, Jim is unable to respond fully, but this will remain for his lifetime the supreme epiphany, a shining-forth of a glory from the apparently mundane. And that glory is Ántonia's, indeed is Ántonia. Yet it is a radiance for Jim to behold, but not to experience. The subtlest revelation of Jim's (and Cather's) love for Ántonia comes in the dream-passage at the end of chapter XII, which suggests the erotic limitation imposed upon both Ántonia and Jim, so profound a taboo that even dreaming cannot undo it. After a single actual kiss from which Ántonia withdraws, in order to recognize that their fates are different, Jim finds that even in the world of wish-fulfillment, he never can possess Ántonia:

> Toward morning I used to have pleasant dreams: sometimes Tony and I were out in the country, sliding down straw-stacks as we used to do; climbing up the yellow mountains over and over and slipping down the smooth sides into soft piles of chaff.
>
> One dream I dreamed a great many times, and it was always the same. I was in a harvest-field full of shocks, and I was lying against one of them. Lena Lingard came across the stubble barefoot, in a short skirt, with a curved reaping-hook in her hand, and she was flushed like the dawn, with a kind of luminous rosiness all about her. She sat down beside me, turned to me with a soft sigh and said, "Now they are all gone, and I can kiss you as much as I like."
>
> I used to wish I could have this flattering dream about Ántonia, but I never did.

The reaping-hook, curved so as to lessen its role as male emblem, is held by Lena, whom Jim likes but does not love, while the erotic play with Ántonia participates in the "over and over" repetition, climbing and slipping down again, that hints at the desires of Cather herself. Jim's passivity in regard to Lena is clear enough, and perhaps he does not dream the same dream about Ántonia because he would be passive in that phantasmagoria as well. Ántonia would not be the memorable literary character she is, if she represented only Cather's true image of desire, as most certainly she does. But that desire is not for a person alone, however idealized. The reverberations of Ántonia's personality and ethical nature bring her into the arena of national myth, of our perpetual nostalgia for the pioneer spirit. Ántonia is finally a vivid image of a wholly natural woman, unspoiled by everything in the modern era that Cather despised and feared.

By concluding the novel with the vision of Ántonia as a natural mother, fulfilled in her children, Cather leaves herself, and us, with something of a gentle sadness. Our current conventions would have freed Cather from her reticences, but would they have enhanced her art? Certainly the question is open. Perhaps liberation would have been an aesthetic loss for Cather, though a human and psychological gain. A first-person narrator might have replaced the shadowy Jim, and cost us little as readers. But an Ántonia gained and known would not be "my" Ántonia, and that would be an authentic aesthetic sorrow.

—H. B.

CRITICAL EXTRACTS

RANDOLPH BOURNE

The story purports to be the memories of a successful man as he looks back over his boyhood on the Nebraska farm and in the little town. Of that boyhood Ántonia was the imaginative center, the little Bohemian immigrant, his playmate and wistful sweetheart. His vision is romantic, but no more romantic than anyone would be towards so free and warm and glorious a girl. He goes to the University, and it is only twenty years later that he hears the story of her pathetic love and desertion, and her marriage to a simple Bohemian farmer, strong and good like herself.

> She was a battered woman now, not a lovely girl; but she still had that something which fires the imagination, could still stop one's breath for a moment by a look or gesture that somehow revealed the meaning in common things. She had only to stand in the orchard, to put her hand on a little crab tree and look up at the apples, to make you feel the goodness of planting and tending and harvesting at last. All the strong things of her heart came out in her body, that had been so tireless in serving generous emotions.
>
> It was no wonder that her sons stood tall and straight. She was a rich mine of life, like the founders of early races.

My Ántonia has the indestructible fragrance of youth: the prairie girls and the dances; the softly alluring Lena, who so unaccountably fails to go wrong; the rich flowered prairie, with its drowsy heats and stinging colds. The book, in its different way, is as fine as the Irishman Corkery's *The Threshold of Quiet,* that other recent masterpiece of wistful youth. But this story lives with the hopefulness of the West. It is poignant and beautiful, but it is not sad. Miss Cather, I think, in this book has taken herself out of the rank of provincial writers and given us something we can fairly class with the modern literary art the world over that is earnestly and richly interpreting the spirit of youth. In her work the stiff moral molds are fortunately broken, and she writes what we can wholly understand.

—RANDOLPH BOURNE, "Morals and Art from the West,"
Dial, December 14, 1918, p. 557

H. L. MENCKEN

⟨*My Ántonia*⟩ is simple; it is honest; it is intelligent; it is moving. The means that appear in it are means perfectly adapted to its end. Its people are unquestionably real. Its background is brilliantly vivid. It has form, grace, good literary manners. In a word, it is a capital piece of writing, and it will be heard of long after the baroque balderdash now touted on the "book pages" is forgotten.

It goes without saying that all the machinery customary to that balderdash is charmingly absent. There is, in the ordinary sense, no plot. There is no hero. There is, save as a momentary flash, no love affair. There is no apparent hortatory purpose, no visible aim to improve the world. The whole enchantment is achieved by the simplest of all possible devices. One follows a poor Bohemian farm girl from her earliest teens to middle age, looking closely at her narrow world, mingling with her friends, observing the gradual widening of her experience, her point of view— and that is all. Intrinsically, the thing is sordid—the life is almost horrible, the horizon is leaden, the soul within is pitifully shrunken and dismayed. But what Miss Cather tries to reveal is the true romance that lies even there—the grim tragedy at the heart of all that dull, cow-like existence—the fineness that lies deeply buried beneath the peasant shell. Dreiser tried to do the same thing with both Carrie Meeber and Jennie Gerhardt, and his success was unmistakable. Miss Cather succeeds quite as certainly, but in an altogether different way. Dreiser's method was that of tremendous particularity—he built up his picture with an infinity of little strokes, many of them superficially meaningless. Miss Cather's method inclines more to suggestion and indirection. Here a glimpse, there a turn of phrase, and suddenly the thing stands out, suddenly it is as real as real can be—and withal moving, arresting, beautiful with a strange and charming beauty. . . . I commend the book to your attention, and the author no less. There is no other American author of her sex, now in view, whose future promises so much. . . .

—H. L. MENCKEN, "Mainly Fiction," *Smart Set* 58, No. 3 (March 1919): 141

HERBERT S. GORMAN

⟨. . .⟩ there is no particular rounded plot in *My Ántonia*. Here we have the story of a Bohemian girl, first of all, and her immigrant family secondarily set down penniless, confused and helpless in Nebraska. Ántonia is traced through the sympathetic eyes of the narrator, supposedly a man who grew up with her, from the time she first learns English as a child of 14 to that period of her life when her ten or eleven children cluster about her, and she can look back on her life discovering much that was good and other things that were not so good. There is a high naturalism in this narrative; an intense reality that pervades the book. Ántonia gradually unfolds before the reader until her life story may be taken as symbol of the life story of youth in Nebraska. Threading the book, almost as important as the tale, is the land. It influences character; it molds human beings. We cannot doubt in the last analysis that it is Nebraska that makes Ántonia what she is, gives her the superb poise and courage which is her portion, makes life hard but endurable.

—HERBERT S. GORMAN, "Willa Cather, Novelist of the Middle Western Farm," *New York Times Book Review*, June 24, 1923, p. 5

PERCY H. BOYNTON

Ántonia Shimerda is a Bohemian immigrant child of less than mediocre parentage, whose sole inheritance is a wholesome, hearty, clear-eyed courage. Brought up in the uses of adversity, she finds but one thing to which she can give a natural response; and that is, among the people of her own sort, "a kind of hearty joviality, a relish of life, not over-delicate, but very invigorating." This flourishes only among the folk who are held in despite by the respectables of the community. The dominant element are spiritually akin to the dominants of Spoon River and Gopher Prairie and Winesburg, Ohio, and to the selectmen of Friendship Village.

> The life that went on in them seemed to me made up of evasions and negations; shifts to save washing and cleaning, devices to propitiate the tongue of gossip. This guarded mode of existence was like living under a tyranny. People's speech, their voices, their very glances, became furtive and repressed. Every individual taste, every natural appetite, was bridled by caution. The people asleep in their houses, I thought, tried to live like the mice in their own kitchens; to make no noise, to leave no trace, to slip over the surface of things in the dark. The growing piles of ashes and cinders in the backyards were the only evidence that the wasteful, consuming process of life went on at all.

Ántonia has no spark of creative artistry; yet she feels the artist's desire to live a full, free life. She falls in love with a cheap seducer, and is abandoned on what she thinks is to be her honeymoon to become a mother without benefit of clergy. Later she marries a good, dull man, brings up a big family, and in the play of her native courage finds a very homely and very old-fashioned fulfilment of life. "That is happiness—to be dissolved in something complete and great." The greatness of Ántonia's achievement lies in the completeness of her dedication to her task—no less complete than that of Thea Kronborg. In Ántonia's contented domesticity Miss Cather offers a modern variation on an old theme. In the pages of Mrs. Stowe the latter stages of Ántonia's career would have been treated as steps of abnegation, the surrender to a sense of duty in a home on earth which would be rewarded by a mansion prepared on high. By most contemporary novelists it would be treated as a complete defeat, with no compensation either here or hereafter. But Miss Cather, with all her zest for studio life, has retained an imaginative regard for four walls and a hearthstone, and the vital experience of mothering a family.

—PERCY H. BOYNTON, "Willa Cather," *Some Contemporary Americans*
(Chicago: University of Chicago Press, 1924), pp. 168–70

ROSE C. FIELD

We spoke about *My Ántonia,* Miss Cather's story about the immigrant family of Czechs.

"Is *My Ántonia* a good book because it is the story of the soil?" we asked. She shook her head.

"No, no, decidedly no. There is no formula, there is no reason. It was a story of people I knew. I expressed a mood, the core of which was like a folk-song, a thing Grieg could have written. That it was powerfully tied to the soil had nothing to do with it. Ántonia was tied to the soil. But I might have written the tale of a Czech baker in Chicago and it would have been the same. It was nice to have her in the country, it was more simple to handle, but Chicago could have told the same story. It would have been smearier, joltier, noisier, less sugar and more sand, but still a story that had as its purpose the desire to express the quality of these people. No, the country has nothing to do with it, the city has nothing to do with it, nothing contributes consciously. The thing worth while is always unplanned. Any art that is a result of preconcerted plans is a dead baby."

—ROSE C. FIELD, " 'Restlessness Such as Ours Does Not Make for Beauty,' "
New York Times Book Review, December 21, 1924, p. 11

EDWARD WAGENKNECHT

Ántonia does not see the future of the land like Alexandra ⟨Bergson in *O Pioneers!*⟩: she is a part of it: she is sentient: she feels, she does not plan. But her feelings run deeper than Alexandra's and she has none of the Swedish girl's stolidness. She comes out of a family without the barest necessities of life. The mother and the older brother are petty, spiteful people—the narrowest and grubbiest sort of Czech. The father, a sensitive man of considerable cultivation, kills himself to escape conditions he is ill-fitted to endure. Ántonia herself is not idealized. When, after her father's death, she works in the fields like a man, she looses her "nice ways," as Jim's grandmother had said she would. "Ántonia ate noisily now . . . and she yawned often at the table and kept stretching her arms over her head, as if they ached." Later, when the Italian Vannis come to Black Hawk, she develops the dance craze and the things that go with it. Nothing really happens to Ántonia, in an objective

sense, save that she manages to get herself betrayed by a rascally railroad conductor and left with a baby to support. "She loved it from the first as dearly as if
she'd had a ring on her finger, and was never ashamed of it." As if this were not
audacious enough, Miss Cather then leaves Ántonia for twenty years, and re-
introduces her, the wife of a commonplace Bohemian, the mother of fourteen
children, "a battered woman" who has lost her teeth but never "the fire of life".
What would Sherwood Anderson have made of such a story! Miss Cather makes
it her most thrilling study in the fulfilment of a woman's life.

—EDWARD WAGENKNECHT, "Willa Cather," *Sewanee Review* 37, No. 2
(April–June 1929): 235

RENÉ RAPIN

With Ántonia we roam the boundless prairie, lost in the tall "shaggy red grass . . . ,
the color of wine stains"; we drift along the "dewy, heavy-odored cornfields";
perched "on the slanting roof of the chicken-house" we watch, on summer nights,
the lightning break "in great zigzags across the heavens," or "hear the felty beat of
the raindrops on the soft dust of the farmyard." We visit Ántonia in the Shimerdas'
hovel of a sod-house, Mr. Shimerda's dignified presence giving us a glimpse of an
older, mellower, soberer world, the mysterious, almost mythical world over the
seas. With Ántonia we call at Russian Peter and Pavel's, in open-mouth wonder
watch Russian Peter eating melons uncountable, the juice trickling from his greedy
mouth "down on to his curly beard." On winter nights, while drifts accumulate
outside and the world is a blur of spilling snow, snugly sitting round the old stove
in the Burdens' basement kitchen, with Ántonia we listen to wonderful stories—
stories of "gray wolves and bears in the Rockies, wildcats and panthers in the
Virginia mountains," and, best of all, the terrible, fascinating story of the bride
thrown over to the wolves by Russian Peter and Pavel.

The pages have the freshness, vitality and beauty of the country and the days
they recreate. Yet it is chiefly through Ántonia that they live, Ántonia, an eager,
passionate bit of womankind, strong as an ox and as stubborn, tenacious and
ambitious, generous and impulsive, a tall sturdy girl, a future mother of generations.

A peasant Thea, her deep-rooted virtues can only blossom out in the country,
on the big flat wind-swept tableland where there is space around her, room for her
to play unconstrained and free and write upon the horizon the great simple
gestures of man wringing his bread from the earth. In the town, where Parts II and
III of the book soon take her, Ántonia is under a cloud, we lose sight of her in the
crowd of chattering servant girls of which she is now part. For some two hundred
pages (Book II, *The Hired Girls,* Book III, *Lena Lingard,* Book IV, *The Pioneer
Woman's Story*) we see but little of her, until, towards the end of the book, we
meet her once more, the mother of almost a dozen children, "a battered woman
now," but intensely alive as ever.

A strong personality is Ántonia, a strong personality yet, like Thea Kronborg,
a very simple one, and so, for all her strength—strength of physique, strength of

character, strongly-defined idiosyncrasies—only in her own natural habitat can she hold our attention and capture our emotion. Willa Cather knew it. No sooner does she take Ántonia to the town, a small town in the prairie, than she tries to focus the reader's attention on Ántonia's friends, the other hired girls. The attempt is a vain one. We cannot forget Ántonia, and the book has become out of focus for the sake of two hundred dull pages concerning secondary characters whom we care little about. How could Willa Cather fail to see that with Ántonia's personality and Ántonia's conquest of the soil, her whole book stood and fell?

Her old enemy, sentimentality, her new friend, realism, here combined to blind her.

Sentimentality, Willa Cather had subdued without crushing it quite. But little apparent in *O Pioneers!*, in *The Song of the Lark* with Fred Ottenburg it raised its triumphant head again. But how did it creep into *My Ántonia?* Ántonia stood firm and sturdy, of the earth earthy, proof against the monster's touch. There was no weak spot in her. There was one in her creator. When Willa Cather, having written her first one hundred pages, looked upon her work and found it good, the tempter rose at her shoulder and whispered: "A brave, hardy creature this, but what about feminine charm?" Willa Cather resumed her work, and this is the picture she painted—Ántonia doing a man's work, breaking sod with the oxen, growing coarser every day:

> Her outgrown cotton dress switched about her calves, over the boot-tops. She kept her sleeves rolled up all day, and her arms and throat were burned as brown as a sailor's. Her neck came up strongly out of her shoulders, like the bole of a tree out of the turf.

- High time Ántonia remembered she is but fifteen, and a woman! And accordingly, thirty pages only further on, Ántonia dons a cook's apron at the Harlings in Black Hawk—a more feminine occupation that, the tempter ingratiatingly observes! And a pretty picture she makes, standing before a mixing-bowl in her tidy apron ... But where is the *real* Ántonia?

Perhaps I have exaggerated the part which affection for her heroine had in inducing Willa Cather to take Ántonia to the town. Yet who will say that sentimentality had no part in the sudden decision that took Ántonia from the plough? A sentimentality against which Willa Cather was all the less on her guard as it probably came to her dressed in the garb of that very realism, that same close adherence to her own experience which, in *O Pioneers!*, had saved her from both unreality and sentimentality. Realism, Willa Cather had not experienced yet, is a double-edged tool. A necessity in a novel which purports to represent a country and people which have played an important part in the writer's life, it should yet be kept a servant. Did Willa Cather sufficiently realize that realism and truth are not interchangeable terms? Patiently following Ántonia Shimerda's actual progress from care-free little girl to plodding farm-hand, from farm-hand to hired girl, and hired girl to wife and mother, Willa Cather neglected her artist's privilege, and duty, to excise, condense, select. The woman in her could care for Ántonia the hired girl as much as for Ántonia the farm girl; the artist should have seen that only the latter mattered, that the cook's apron hid where the farmer's masculine garb revealed the essential, the deeper Ántonia . . .

In *O Pioneers!*, and still more in *The Song of the Lark*, Willa Cather while controlling imagination by experience had kept experience subservient to passion, the latter book indeed deserving to be called, in Stuart Sherman's eloquent words, "Miss Cather's most intimate book—the book which she has most enriched with the poetry and wisdom and passion of her experience, and made spacious with the height and the depth of her desire." Where *The Song of the Lark* soared, *My Ántonia* kept close to the solid earth, which gave it its strength, preserved it from its predecessor's worst failures, yet left it, artistically, an inferior book, one that, however rich with experience, has not been made spacious with desire.

—RENÉ RAPIN, *Willa Cather* (New York: Robert M. McBride & Co., 1930), pp. 47–51

MAXWELL GEISMAR

In many respects, *My Ántonia* marks a gain in Cather's craft. Probably the accounts of the frontier land are even more graceful here; that childhood visit of Ántonia and Jim Burden to 'dog town' is a perfect little episode; while the story of Ántonia's Bohemian family, the Shimerdas, almost summarizes the story of all those 'strange uprooted people' who were among the first citizens of our western plains. But it is around Black Hawk, Nebraska, that *My Ántonia* centers, as Cather carries forward the chronicle of the frontier settlers to the framework of early western town life and the merchants and farmers, the commercial travelers, the eccentrics, and outcasts of what was almost a society of outcasts. Such portraits as Wick Cutter, the dissolute money-lender, or Lena Lingard, the Swedish farm girl; or scenes like those Saturday night operas in Black Hawk or the evenings at the Vannis's dancing pavilion; or frontier legends like that of Blind d'Arnault, the traveling Negro pianist who plays as though 'all the agreeable sensations possible to creatures of flesh and blood were heaped up in those black and white keys': these are among the most attractive passages in Miss Cather's early novels. She is shrewd too about 'the curious social situation' which arose in Black Hawk—that is, the class distinctions which developed between the merchants' daughters and the 'hired girls'—between native refinement and immigrant vitality—and the consequent effect of a whole new ethos of respectability upon the middle-class children. To dance 'Home, Sweet Home' with Lena Lingard, she says, was like coming in with the tide, while the bodies of the town girls never moved inside their clothes, and their muscles seemed to ask but one thing—not to be disturbed.

> The Black Hawk boys looked forward to marrying Black Hawk girls, and living in a brand-new little house with best chairs that must not be sat upon, and hand-painted china that must not be used. But sometimes a young fellow would look up from his ledger, or out through the grating of his father's bank, and let his eyes follow Lena Lingard, as she passed the window with her slow,

undulating walk, or Tiny Soderball, tripping by in her short skirt and striped stockings.

The country girls were considered a menace to the social order. Their beauty shone out too boldly against a conventional background. But anxious mothers need have felt no alarm. They mistook the mettle of their sons. The respect for respectability was stronger than any desire in Black Hawk youth.

And this guarded mode of existence, Cather's Jim Burden also thinks, was almost like living under a tyranny, where every individual taste, every natural appetite, was bridled by caution. These people tried to live like the mice in their own kitchens; 'to make no noise, to leave no trace, to slip over the surface of things in the dark.'

Yet the middle sections of *My Ántonia,* the sections on the hired girls and on Lena Lingard herself, represent a sort of climax in the novel's action. Cather's narrator is captivated alike by the physical charms of Lena Lingard and the moral stature of Ántonia Shimerda. (And there is that interesting split again between the ostensible heroine, Ántonia, the epitome of the frontier spirit, and Lena, who represents merely the frontier flesh, but who almost runs away with the show.) However, Jim Burden, the descendant of a Virginian family, can never actually make the break, and can never cross that social line which he sees so clearly and despises so heartily. Indeed, as he draws away from the western scene in later life, becomes legal counsel for a big railway, has a wife who plays patroness to the new poets and painters, and himself frequents London or Vienna, Jim Burden's memory of Ántonia becomes more precious. 'She lent herself to immemorial human attitudes which we recognize by instinct as universal and true. . . . She was a rich mine of life, like the founders of early races.' Very much like Scott Fitzgerald's western observer in *The Great Gatsby,* Willa Cather's narrator, when he decides to revisit the scene of his youth, has the sense of coming back home to himself. 'Whatever we had missed, we possessed together the precious, the incommunicable past.'

All the same, that closing scene of the novel in which we actually *see* Ántonia has some curious undertones. 'You really are a part of me,' Jim Burden tells her. 'I'd have liked to have you for a sweetheart, or a wife, or my mother or my sister— anything that a woman can be to a man.' 'Ain't it wonderful,' Ántonia answers, 'how much people can mean to each other?' Is it merely in the shadow of Burden's continental sophistication that Ántonia now seems so much cruder in sensibility and expression, as well as rather battered in appearance—as though she had reverted in some degree to the line of her peasant ancestors while Jim Burden has moved closer to his own more or less aristocratic forebears? The difference between them has never been quite so apparent as it is just when Jim Burden believes that the same road of 'Destiny' which has separated him from Ántonia has now brought them together again. . . .

—MAXWELL GEISMAR, "Willa Cather: Lady in the Wilderness,"
The Last of the Provincials: The American Novel 1915–1925
(Boston: Houghton Mifflin, 1947), pp. 163–66

ELIZABETH SHEPLEY SERGEANT

In the spring of 1916, I had the first inkling that Willa had a new story in mind. I never asked questions—she was the initiator of any communication about an unborn or unfinished work.

She had not been able to forget that, in these war days, the youth of Europe, its finest flower, was dying. Perhaps our American youth had also been designed for sacrifice—by now we feared so. But a growing vital work, with Willa, usually took precedence, even in her thoughts, over the life around her.

She had come in for tea at a small apartment facing south on a garden, in the East Sixties where I was living. As it was not far from Central Park, she arrived flushed and alert from one of her swift wintry walks. I think of her as always wearing red-brown fur in winter in those years; it made her hair shine, and she had the warmth, charm, assurance, and fullness of being that allied her, despite her individual direction, with *the* American woman in her forties. She said more than once to me that nobody under forty could ever really believe in either death or degeneration. She herself carried that physical nonchalance right on through her fifties.

While I boiled the kettle Willa sat down with Henry James's *Notes on Novelists* which lay on my writing table; turned to the passage where he says that the originator has one law and the reporter, however philosophic, another. "So that the two laws can with no sort of harmony and congruity make one household."

Willa was amused by James's elaborate, subtle phrases—a bit impatiently amused by now. But with this comment she fully agreed: she had not altogether banished the reporter in her last book. Now she aimed at a more frugal, parsimonious form and technique.

She then suddenly leaned over—and this is something I remembered clearly when *My Ántonia* came into my hands, at last, in 1918—and set an old Sicilian apothecary jar of mine, filled with orange-brown flowers of scented stock, in the middle of a bare, round, antique table.

"I want my new heroine to be like this—like a rare object in the middle of a table, which one may examine from all sides."

She moved the lamp so that light streamed brightly down on my Taormina jar, with its glazed orange and blue design.

"I want her to stand out—like this—like this—because she *is* the story."

Saying this her fervent, enthusiastic voice faltered and her eyes filled with tears.

Someone you knew in your childhood, I ventured.

She nodded, but did not say more.

So I sometimes wondered, later, whether she was thinking of Ántonia or Mrs. Forrester. Often she thought about her heroines for years before they appeared in a book.

—ELIZABETH SHEPLEY SERGEANT, *Willa Cather: A Memoir* (Philadelphia: J. B. Lippincott Co., 1953), pp. 138–40

EDWIN T. BOWDEN

For Willa Cather human strength and endurance on the frontier were in large part a matter of the strength of the family unit. And as the pioneer days disappear in her novel the family unity goes with them. The parallel to Bradford's description of the disappearance of the communal unity at Plymouth when the first frontier was conquered is striking; Governor Bradford and Willa Cather are making the same point. In *My Ántonia,* Jim Burden finds himself, almost to his surprise, trying to hoodwink his grandparents once he has settled down in the region. Many of the daughters of the farming families begin to move into town as hired girls, partly to make needed money for the family—family values are not so easily lost—and partly to escape the isolation and hard work of the farm. But many of the hired girls never go home again and slowly drift away from Nebraska entirely. They are no longer pioneers but simply young American girls. The town itself, in fact, is a mark of the disappearance of the early frontier—the Deerslayer hated the towns for just that reason—and it is fitting that the town of Black Hawk has importance only in the second half of *My Ántonia.* When the Burdens move into town, to be followed by the country girls, it is a sign of what is happening in the region. The high school, the ice cream parlor, Jelinek's saloon, the dances at the Vannis pavilion and the Fire-men's hall, all are a denial of the isolation of the frontier and the self-sufficiency of the family.

For all its huddling together and its social affairs, however, the town of Black Hawk is not so far from the isolation of the frontier as it might think. Jim Burden finds that he can be as lonesome in town as on the farm and that the national and social prejudices are as strong as ever. The immigrant farm girls are acceptable only as hired girls, and the boys of eastern American stock will marry only their own kind. Sylvester Lovett, the banker's son, may be infatuated with the sensual Lena Lingard, but he solves his problem by marrying an acceptable land-owning widow. The town in all its petty isolation is best summed up by Jim Burden during his discontented night prowls:

> They were flimsy shelters, most of them poorly built of light wood, with spindle porch-posts horribly mutilated by the turning lathe. Yet for all their frailness, how much jealousy and envy and unhappiness some of them man-aged to contain! The life that went on in them seemed to me made up of evasions and negations; shifts to save cooking, to save washing and cleaning, devices to propitiate the tongue of gossip. This guarded mode of existence was like living under a tyranny. People's speech, their voices, their very glances, became furtive and repressed. Every individual taste, every natural appetite, was bridled by caution.

The farming frontier, for all its own loneliness, has at least its heroic struggle with the land and the seasons, its family pitted together against nature and all adversity.

The background of Ántonia Shimerda, then, is one of middle-frontier isolation. But she herself, like Jim Burden the narrator, is not lonely or unhappy. Just as the

Deerslayer found self-fulfillment only in the isolation of the forest, and Huck Finn on the free-flowing river, so Ántonia finds self-fulfillment on the Nebraska prairie, although the fulfillment is of a quite different sort. Hers is neither the freedom of irresponsibility nor the romantic love of nature, the yearning for the primitive and unspoiled, the desire at heart for something distinct from the history and efforts of man, but rather love for the joining of man and nature into some greater whole than either can provide separately. The feeling is caught momentarily by Jim Burden on his arrival in Nebraska as he sits sunning himself in his grandmother's prairie garden:

> I was something that lay under the sun and felt it, like the pumpkins, and I did not want to be anything more. I was entirely happy. Perhaps we feel like that when we die and become a part of something entire, whether it is sun and air, or goodness and knowledge. At any rate, that is happiness, to be dissolved into something complete and great.

Coming early in the novel as it does, his feeling explains much of the mood of the novel and provides a preparation for what is to come and sympathy with the minds of the characters that Willa Cather likes.

Ántonia, paradoxically, is lonely only when she is caught up in the petty and artificial community life of the town: "'I'd always be miserable in a city. I'd die of lonesomeness. I like to be where I know every stack and tree, and where all the ground is friendly. I want to live and die here.'" On the prairie farm she expands to the limit of her being, and her inner horizon stretches toward the outer until the two join in one complete circle. Of course she is human and can have moments of loneliness: when her father dies she feels with him the isolation of her lot, and when she returns after being abandoned by her lover, feeling the momentary shame of her unborn child, she can only shrink within herself from the public gaze. But these moments pass and become in fact a part of her total feeling for life. She is no Coronado, whose memory is so carefully evoked, to die in the wilderness of a broken heart. And even in these moments of loneliness and depression she does not simply sit and suffer but throws herself with even greater vigor into the work of the farm. For work with the land is for her not simply a means of livelihood but a kind of immediate self-fulfillment. It is a means of joining her own being with that of nature and of drawing from each all of which it is capable, making of both on total being.

Jim Burden's final impression is one that catches up the essence of this organic unity:

> She had only to stand in the orchard, to put her hand on a little crab tree and look up at the apples, to make you feel the goodness of planting and tending and harvesting at last. All the strong things of her heart came out in her body, that had been so tireless in serving generous emotions.
>
> It was no wonder that her sons stood tall and straight. She was a rich mine of life, like the founders of early races.

As Jim sees, there is something vital about Ántonia that springs from the solitary land and returns to it again, making the land something more than just land. On the first arrival of the farming pioneers there had been nothing but grass and space: "There was nothing but land: not a country at all, but the material out of which countries are made." But years later, at the height of Ántonia's vitality, there are land and life and love—a family and a farm that defeat the isolation of the frontier and make human life and prairie nature one unified condition that can be called a country. The large family and the fruitful farm are the products of Ántonia, the "rich mine of life," but they are only outward and visible signs of an inward and even spiritual grace. For Ántonia is herself the spirit of the whole man and the prairie, the one unified being who can, not transcend the isolation and loneliness of the wilderness, but rather make of that isolation something fruitful and satisfying and complete.

For Willa Cather such a spirit is the real answer to the isolation of the American frontier. There are other answers, but none is so complete and so satisfying. The easiest, of course, if it is an answer at all, is simply to leave the farm as soon as possible. This is the answer of Lena Lingard, the literary foil to Ántonia in the novel, and for her at least it is not a contemptible answer either. By nature Lena does not belong on the frontier. With her sensual attraction and her pleasure-loving nature she is a girl of artificial civilization. It is fitting that she becomes a dressmaker, and a successful one, for the very luxury and artificiality of the craft is in keeping with her nature. The family to Lena is not a source of strength and vitality but rather a clog for her own development and a source of irritation and hindrance. Like Ántonia, she is not afraid of loneliness, but, unlike Ántonia, she wants a loneliness only of the sort that leaves her free and unhindered. When Jim Burden tells her that she will soon tire of the life in Lincoln and will want a family, she answers:

> "Not me. I like to be lonesome. When I went to work for Mrs. Thomas I was nineteen years old, and I had never slept a night in my life when there weren't three in the bed. I never had a minute to myself except when I was off with the cattle."

And Lena never does marry, despite her immediate attraction for men. She retains her inner isolation to the end, unwilling to merge it with the isolation of the land to become, by the paradox lived by Ántonia, "a part of something entire."

The Ántonias of the frontier, however, are rare. If they were not, the character would not be unique, as it is in this novel. Yet this Ántonia does represent something of the abiding human value of the isolation of the middle frontier, if only as a sort of ideal or potentiality. And Willa Cather, in other novels as well as this one, recognizes all too clearly that it is an ideal rapidly being lost: *O Pioneers!, The Song of the Lark, A Lost Lady, The Professor's House, Death Comes for the Archbishop, Shadows on the Rock,* all touch at least on the loss of a frontier ideal. But *My Ántonia* seems to place Willa Cather's sense of loss most clearly and most poignantly. In a somewhat fanciful sense, she herself is the most isolated and most lonely character of the novel. Jim Burden, the fictional narrator, after marrying a woman entirely unlike Ántonia comes back to Nebraska for a visit, and he says, "I had the sense of coming home to myself." In this mood he speaks for the entire novel. His recognition of the spiritual achievement of Ántonia, the deeper value of her character as it merges with that of the fruitful prairie, is a recognition of what he has himself missed, although he does not put the feeling in so many words. For he has refused the Nebraska life—although he has never rejected it—and feels the resulting loss. Rather ironically he has kept a slender tie by becoming legal counsel for one of the great Western railways. Without trying to draw any close parallel, the general analogy to the biography of Willa Cather herself is there by clear implication. Perhaps the general analogy would even help to explain the somewhat unsatisfactory character of Jim, who is a man but so often in the novel does not think or respond as a man would. Willa Cather has put so much of herself into him that she to some extent loses control of him as a fictional character.

Whatever the biographical analogy, the novel itself has a clear mood of lone-liness to convey to the reader. The words "lonely" and "loneliness" appear often in the novel, but the key word, occurring with enough frequency to make it a sort of verbal leitmotiv, is "homesick." Examples are ever present: "I knew it was home-sickness that had killed Mr. Shimerda"; "For the first time it occurred to me that I would be homesick for that river after I left it"; " 'It makes me homesick, Jimmy, this flower, this smell,' she said softly"; " 'It seems like my mother ain't been so homesick, ever since father's raised rye flour for her' " The word is right and proper, for this is a homesick novel. The pioneer families look back to the old country left behind and are homesick. Their children look back to the days of their childhood and are homesick. The novel itself looks back to the days of the middle frontier and is homesick. Only Ántonia resists this form of loneliness, for where she is she makes a home. But she in turn provides a source of homesickness, for she is the ideal of the frontier, a spirit to be looked back upon with longing from the present state of loneliness, a being complete in a world now incomplete.

My Ántonia is a novel about the past. Cooper had set *The Deerslayer* a century back in time. Twain had set *Huckleberry Finn* back nearly half a century, and Willa Cather sets the principal part of her novel back some thirty years or more. For all three, whatever their different views of human isolation and their different thematic answers to it, the frontier had disappeared and now belonged to a more heroic time in the past. Willa Cather's past has a particularly nostalgic tint, for it leads to the homesickness of the present. And the nostalgia in turn gives the past a suggestive value, leading, in one sense, to a softness of outline but, in another, to a vividness of impression that makes the moment or the object almost clearer and sharper than life itself. The momentary vision in the novel of the silhouette of a plow against the setting sun, a familiar example of the art of Willa Cather, stands as an example. It is almost too sharp, too perfect, yet it has a high suggestive value that captures the imagination. So, too, the events of Jim Burden's childhood—or Willa Cather's past—stand out in sharp and simplified outline, suggesting a time of heroic dimensions now gone. To this past the novel comes home again from a lonely and isolated present. "Some memories are realities, and are better than anything that can ever happen to one again." To those without the character of an Ántonia, the mature strength to see the self in relationship—almost moral relationship—to the surrounding world, isolation can be an element of time as well as of space, and loneliness is not restricted to the old frontier.

At this point the conclusion that *Huckleberry Finn* had suggested in the theme of isolation, the moral necessity for isolation to see itself in the perspective of the rest of humanity if it is to avoid the pain of loneliness, comes to its fulfillment. *My Ántonia* is thematically a long way from *The Deerslayer,* even if *Huckleberry Finn* is considered a step along that way. If isolation is not necessarily to be avoided, it is certainly not to be sought; and the most admirable is not the one who turns away from other humans and from ordinary life but the one who turns toward them for completeness of spirit. The answer that Bradford had urged for the question of isolation has proved the enduring one even though the literal frontier has disappeared in America. We still have our Huck Finns and our Ántonias—and for that matter our Natty Bumppos too—even though their backgrounds and their settings have gone. The frontier in America, and in its novel, has become a matter of mind or of view rather than a matter of place. But the problem of human isolation, made so vivid and immediate by the old frontier, remains a constant in American life on its new frontiers and continues to find its theme in the American novel.

—EDWIN T. BOWDEN, "The Frontier Isolation," *The Dungeon of the Heart: Human Isolation and the American Novel* (New York: Macmillan, 1961), pp. 46–54

ROBERT E. SCHOLES

R. W. B. Lewis in *The American Adam* has suggested that the "most fruitful" ideas circulating in nineteenth-century America were embodied in the image of "the authentic American as a figure of heroic innocence and vast potentialities, poised at the start of a new history." The currency of this image, according to Mr. Lewis, dates from the close of the War of 1812, and is prominent in the writings of both philosophers and journalists in pre–Civil War America. Mr. Lewis is relatively successful in demonstrating that men like Emerson, Thoreau, Holmes, Lowell and the elder Henry James were concerned with this vision of the new American man; but he is much less convincing when he attempts to show that their novelist contemporaries relied on this same notion in their works. He is put to such shifts as considering the *last* novel of Hawthorne and of Melville, rather than their *best* in his attempt to illustrate the ubiquity of the Adamic idea.

The great fruition in fiction of the theme of the heroic innocent in conflict with society actually occurred in the latter part of the nineteenth century and the early part of the twentieth. Whether this theme was really important in the works of Melville and Hawthorne, and whether novelists will find it stimulating or useful in the future are two questions beyond the scope of the present inquiry (though I suspect the answer to both should be negative). It is nevertheless interesting to note that the American Innocent was a major preoccupation of American novelists from James and Howells down to Willa Cather and F. Scott Fitzgerald. And it may be useful to examine exactly how one novelist, Willa Cather, made use of the Adamic myth in her fullest treatment of it: *My Ántonia.*

As Mr. Lewis distills it, the myth of Adam in America is that of an "individual emancipated from history, happily bereft of ancestry, untouched and undefiled by the usual inheritances of family and race; an individual standing alone, self-propelling, ready to confront whatever awaited him with the aid of his own unique and inherent resources." This Adamic person is "thrust into an actual world and an actual age," and, in the fully developed myth, undergoes a "fall": suffers "the necessary transforming shocks and sufferings, the experiments and errors . . . through which maturity and identity may be arrived at." Mr. Lewis is a bit mysterious about what he means by "identity," but self-knowledge or self-discovery are probably safe, if not totally accurate, substitutes.

The two central figures in *My Ántonia* are, in different senses, Innocents. Jim Burden, bereft of both his parents within a year, is removed from the warm and comfortable Virginia of his early days and thrust into the strange and frightening world of Nebraska. As he bumps along on the wagon ride to his new home, he feels that he has left even the spirits of his dead parents behind him:

> The wagon jolted on, carrying me I know not whither. I don't think I was homesick. If we never arrived anywhere, it did not matter. Between that earth and that sky I felt erased, blotted out. I did not say my prayers that night: here, I felt, what would be would be.

Ántonia Shimerda, though also a young, innocent creature in a raw country, is not bereft of the past as Jim Burden is. Ántonia's Bohemian ancestry is a part of her and exerts a decided influence on her present and future. We are reminded of this past constantly: by the Bohemian customs and culinary practices of the Shimerdas; by the observations of Otto Fuchs on the relationship of Austrians and Bohemians in the old country; and especially by the Catholic religion of the Bohemians, which is their strongest link with the past, and which serves to bind them together and to separate them from the Protestant society of their adopted land. But, most important, Ántonia herself cherishes her connection with the past. When Jim asks if she remembers the little town of her birth, she replies,

> "Jim . . . if I was put down there in the middle of the night, I could find my way all over that little town; and along the river where my grandmother lived. My feet remember all the little paths through the woods, and where the big roots stick out to trip you. I ain't never forgot my own country."

But despite the importance of the past for Ántonia, she and the other hired girls are figures of heroic and vital innocence, associated with nature and the soil. Like Lena Lingard, they all "waked fresh with the world every day" (p. 319). They are unused to the ways of society, and Ántonia, especially, is too trusting. Lena tells

Jim that Ántonia "won't hear a word against [Larry Donovan]. She's so sort of innocent" (p. 303). The struggle of the "hired girls" with society is one of the important themes of the novel. Jim Burden remarks that

> the country girls were considered a menace to the social order. Their beauty shone out too boldly against a conventional background. But anxious mothers need have felt no alarm. They mistook the mettle of their sons. The respect for respectability was stronger than any desire in Black Hawk youth.

This struggle of the country girls with the city is a very perplexing one, in which apparent victory and apparent defeat are both apt to prove evanescent in time. Lena Lingard and Tiny Soderball become successful, triumphing even in the metropolis of San Francisco, while Ántonia becomes the foolish victim of her love for a conniving railroad conductor. But Lena and Tiny succeed only in becoming more like the society from which they had been ostracized, while Ántonia, and the other country girls who stay on the land, ultimately change the structure of society itself. Jim Burden remarks,

> I always knew I should live long enough to see my country girls come into their own, and I have. Today the best that a harassed Black Hawk merchant can hope for is to sell provisions and farm machinery and automobiles to the rich farms where that first crop of stalwart Bohemian and Scandinavian girls are now the mistresses.

Jim Burden, like Lena and Tiny, has made his success in the city and on the city's terms. From the narrator of the introductory chapter we learn that Jim's personal life, his marriage, has not been a success though his legal work flourishes. Jim's failure to find happiness or satisfaction in his career and in the city, constitutes for him the "fall" into self-knowledge which is characteristic of the Adamic hero. It is Jim's recognition of his own fall that makes him superior to Lena and Tiny, and enables him to live vicariously through Ántonia and her children.

Ántonia's seduction is a more clear-cut "fall" than Jim's unhappiness, and her subsequent self-knowledge is more strikingly evidenced. When Jim meets Ántonia after she has had her illegitimate child, he notices "a new kind of strength in the gravity of her face." At this meeting she asks Jim whether he has learned to like big cities, adding that she would die of lonesomeness in such a place. "I like to be where I know every stack and tree, and where all the ground is friendly" (p. 363), she says; and after they part Jim feels "the old pull of the earth, the solemn magic that comes out of those fields at night-fall," and he wishes he could be a little boy again, and that his way would end there.

When Jim revisits Ántonia and her thriving family, she has in some ways relapsed toward the past. " 'I've forgot my English so,' " she says. " 'I don't often talk it any more. I tell the children I used to speak it real well.' She said they all spoke Bohemian at home. The little ones could not speak English at all—didn't learn it until they went to school." But her children, her involvement in life, makes her concerned for the future. She has lived "much and hard," reflects Jim as they meet, but "she was there, in the full vigor of her personality, battered but not diminished, looking at me, speaking to me in the husky, breathy voice I remembered so well." Jim, however, is not recognized by Ántonia at first, even though he has "kept so young." He is less battered, perhaps, but he is more diminished.

So it is that Ántonia, who is always conscious of the past, is nevertheless free of it, and capable of concern for the future. And her past is not merely that of a generation or so. Jim observes, "She lent herself to immemorial human attitudes which we recognize by instinct as universal and true.... It was no wonder that her sons stood tall and straight. She was a rich mine of life, like the founders of early races." Whereas Jim, who has no such connection with the past, who came to Nebraska without a family and rode on a wagon into a new life which he felt was beyond even the attention of God, is still bound by the recent past, by what has happened to him in his own youth, and he lives in both the present and the future only vicariously through the plans and lives of others. He reflects, "In the course of twenty crowded years one parts with many illusions. I did not wish to lose the early ones. Some memories are realities, and are better than anything that can happen to one again." Jim is haunted by the past, by the sense that, in the phrase of Virgil which is the novel's epigraph, *Optima dies ... prima fugit.* When he contemplates in the closing lines of his narrative the road on which he had entered his new life as a boy, he reconsiders his whole existence:

> I had the sense of coming home to myself, and of having found out what a little circle man's experience is. For Ántonia and for me, this had been the road of Destiny; had taken us to those early accidents of fortune which predetermined for us all that we can ever be. Now I understood that the same road was to bring us together again. Whatever we had missed, we possessed together the precious, the incommunicable past.

Ántonia's life is not tragic. She is neither defeated nor destroyed by life, not even diminished. Yet the distinguishing characteristic of this novel is its elegiac tone; the eternal note of sadness pervades especially the closing passages of the book. The direct cause of this element of sadness is the nostalgia of Jim Burden, through which the story of Ántonia filters down to the reader. But behind Jim Burden's nostalgia, and merged with it, is the nostalgia of Willa Cather herself.

There is a suggestion in this novel and in the earlier *O Pioneers!* that the younger brothers and the sisters of this splendid generation of pioneer women will not be their equals. Emil Bergson—the youth in *O Pioneers!* for whom his older sister Alexandra labors and plans—attends the university, escapes from the plough, only to ruin several lives through his adulterous love. And in *My Ántonia* there is the suggestion that the coming generations will be less heroic and more ordinary than the present breed. Jim Burden at one point muses on this problem, thinking of the hired girls in Black Hawk:

> Those girls had grown up in the first bitter-hard times, and had got little schooling themselves. But the younger brothers and sisters, for whom they

made such sacrifices and who have had "advantages," never seem to me, when I meet them now, half as interesting or as well educated. The older girls, who helped to break up the wild sod, learned so much from life, from poverty, from their mothers and grandmothers; they had all, like Ántonia, been early awakened and made observant by coming at a tender age from an old country to a new.

The circumstances which formed Ántonia will not be repeated; the future will be in the hands of a diminished race. It is the feeling which haunts Willa Cather's novel. Ántonia looks to the future of her children, but Jim Burden knows that the future will be at best a poor imitation of the past. Ántonia's life is a triumph of innocence and vitality over hardship and evil. But Willa Cather does not celebrate this triumph; rather, she intones an elegy over the dying myth of the heroic Innocent, over the days that are no more.

—ROBERT E. SCHOLES, "Hope and Memory in *My Ántonia,*" *Shenandoah* 14, No. 1
(Autumn 1962): 24–29

LOUIS AUCHINCLOSS

In 1916, on a trip back to Red Cloud, ⟨Cather⟩ drove out to a farm on the Divide to visit a Bohemian woman, Anna Pavelka, whom she had known and admired in her youth, and found her serene and happy, surrounded by many children. As E. K. Brown put it: "It seemed to her that this woman's story ran very close to the central stream of life in Red Cloud and on the Divide, that she stood for the triumph of what was vigorous, sound, and beautiful in a region where these qualities so often seemed to suffer repression or defeat." Even before her return to New York Willa Cather had started *My Ántonia* (1918).

The introduction to it, read in conjunction with the later preface to the reissue of *Alexander's Bridge,* presents a fascinating question to those who care how a novel is constructed. Jim Burden, who is to be the "I" of the story, tells another "I"—a character of undetermined sex who has grown up in the same Nebraska town with him—how he comes to write his memories of Ántonia. We learn from this prefatory "I" that Jim's wife is a snobbish society woman, a patroness of artists "of advanced ideas and mediocre ability," and that Jim, a successful railroad lawyer, lives largely apart from her, traveling back and forth across the great country which the rails of his road span. Success, however, has not destroyed his romantic disposition or his nostalgia for his Nebraskan boyhood which, both to him and to "I," is dominated by the memory of a Bohemian girl, Ántonia Shimerda. "More than any other person we remembered, this girl seemed to mean to us the country, the conditions, the whole adventure of our childhood." Jim later sends "I" the narrative that he has written, which is called *My Ántonia.* He insists that he has written it down as it has come to his mind and that "it hasn't any form."

Indeed, it seems not to have. Certainly without either the title of the novel or the introduction one would never on a first reading (at least until near the end) gather that it is primarily about Ántonia. The first part, "The Shimerdas," is much more concerned with Jim Burden's impressions of his grandparents' farm in Nebraska than with the Shimerdas, a poor Bohemian family in the neighborhood who are fighting a losing battle with a ragged farm for which they have paid too much. The narrative is interrupted by a bloodcurdling tale of a young bride and groom in Russia being thrown from a sled to halt pursuing wolves. It is a brilliant and horrifying little piece that has nothing to do with anything else in the novel. The part ends with the tragic suicide of old Mr. Shimerda, the defeated immigrant, in which Ántonia plays only a small part.

In the next part, "The Hired Girls," the Burdens and Jim move into the town of Black Hawk (as the Cathers moved to Red Cloud), and Ántonia leaves her family's farm to become a domestic servant at the Harlings', down the street. Here we begin to see her more clearly, particularly when she throws up her job rather than give up the weekly dances where Mrs. Harling feels that she meets bad company. "A girl like me has got to take her good times when she can." Then comes the episode of Mr. Cutter's attempted rape of Ántonia which tells us far more of him than of her. Mr. Cutter and his wife are a bizarre, Dickensian couple; he eventually murders her and kills himself, a provable few minutes later, to ensure that her next-of-kin will not share in his estate. The narrative then shifts altogether to Lena Lingard and Tiny Soderball, the hired girls who make good, one as a dressmaker and the other as a gold miner, and we learn only indirectly from the Widow Steavens that Ántonia has been seduced by Larry Donovan and abandoned with an illegitimate child. These most important events are seen fleetingly and at second hand. Not until the very end do we see Ántonia in the center of the stage when Jim Burden calls on her, many years later, to find her contentedly married to a poor but kindly farmer, Anton Cuzak, and surrounded by a big family of beautiful children, a far more fitting symbol of the fertile land than the old-maid Alexandra Bergson.

Jim Burden's statement that his narrative is without shape receives an echo in Willa Cather's preface to the reissue of *Alexander's Bridge*. After stating that a writer's best material is in himself, already molded, she proceeds thus: "If he tries to meddle with its vague outline, to twist it into some categorical shape, above all if he tries to adapt or modify its mood, he destroys its value. In working with this material he finds that he need have little to do with literary devices; he comes to depend more and more on something else—the thing by which our feet find the road home on a dark night, accounting of themselves for roots and stones which we had never noticed by day."

This passage comes very near to being her literary credo. It certainly shows how far she had come from Henry James. Yet the latter, who always recognized the first rate, even when its form was at variance with his theories, might have approved of *My Ántonia*. He shared, after all, its author's passionate admiration for Stevenson, whose loose, easily flowing nostalgic narratives are far closer to the Nebraska novels than *The Golden Bowl* or *The Wings of the Dove*.

One may speculate that Willa Cather wrote *My Ántonia* very much as Jim

Burden says *he* wrote it and that its shape, such as it is, is dictated by actual reminiscence. She freely admitted that Ántonia was closely modeled on Anna Pavelka, who had occupied in her childhood the same focal position that Ántonia had occupied in Burden's. Miss Cather was never much interested in what was or what was not a "novel." Fact, fancy, reminiscence, invention, what difference did it make? The mood, the unity, the finished product was all.

Elizabeth Sergeant describes a visit of Willa Cather to her apartment while she was still in the throes of putting her novel together: "She then suddenly leaned over—and this is something I remembered clearly when *My Ántonia* came into my hands, at last, in 1918—and set an old Sicilian apothecary jar of mine, filled with orange-brown flowers of scented stock, in the middle of a bare, round, antique table. 'I want my new heroine to be like this—like a rare object in the middle of a table, which one may examine from all sides.' "

Yet certainly Ántonia is not seen from all sides. One has only the dimmest conception of her relation with her seducer, and there is a great deal about her life as a hired girl that remains in the shadows. What is seen from all sides, being turned slowly for the reader like a statue on a revolving platform, is Jim Burden's (Willa Cather's) memory of Ántonia, and this becomes a thing complete in itself, so we are not disturbed by the missing pieces in Ántonia. It is not, therefore, so much a book about Ántonia as a book about someone's memory of Ántonia, in short, a book about nostalgia.

The relevance of all the details, including the terrible story of the wolves, is simply their relevance to Miss Cather. She selected, probably by a purely subjective test, the scenes and incidents that came to mind most vividly about her Nebraska childhood. The result, by whatever design, is triumphant. The finished work is bathed in the serene, golden mood of recaptured time. The "precious, the incommunicable past" *has* been communicated. It has become almost synonymous with the flat, endless Nebraska plains and rough, shaggy, tall red grass over which, as it seemed to the young Jim Burden, one could walk to the very edge of the earth. "The light air about me told me that the world ended here: only the ground and sun and sky were left, and if one went a little farther there would be only sun and sky, and one would float off into them, like the tawny hawks which sailed over our heads making slow shadows on the grass."

Ántonia, with her love, her patience, her philosophic acceptance of betrayal, her honesty and simplicity, contains the soul of the land and its pioneer farmers. "She had only to stand in the orchard, to put her hand on a little crab tree and look up at the apples, to make you feel the goodness of planting and tending and harvesting at last. . . . She was a rich mine of life, like the founders of early races." She is more than a figure remembered; she is the very process of remembering. Willa Cather was to equal this accomplishment in the future; she was never to surpass it.

—LOUIS AUCHINCLOSS, "Willa Cather," *Pioneers and Caretakers: A Study of 9 American Women Writers* (Minneapolis: University of Minnesota Press, 1965), pp. 102–6

ANTHONY CHANNELL HILFER

E. K. Brown suggests that "what is excellent in *My Ántonia* does not depend on a masculine narrator. It inheres in the material itself and in appreciation of it, which might have been just as sensitive, just as various, if Willa Cather had presented her story omnisciently." Willa Cather, however, needed a narrator precisely because the excellencies of *My Ántonia* do not inhere in the material itself. Ántonia, the focus of the novel's values, is not unbelievable but neither is she very interesting. Her characterization never justifies the emotional weight Cather brings to bear upon her. Thus someone must be in the book to tell the reader how important Ántonia is; the evaluator must be a character so the reader can at least believe that the *character* feels the emotion although the reader himself is unable to. Jim Burden accounts for the presence of the emotion in the book although he cannot transfer it. The very title of the novel shows the necessity of Jim Burden. *His* Ántonia.

Ántonia does not justify the weight of emotion Miss Cather puts upon her, but she and the other immigrant girls in their vitality and freedom do serve as an effective foil to the narrowness and sterility of the self-complacent Anglo-Saxon citizens of Black Hawk, Nebraska. The real energy of Miss Cather's novel is in her rejection of the official culture of the town. True, the town is no Bricksville, Arkansas, but rather "a clean well-planted little prairie town." There is a curious social situation in this town. The young men of the town are all attracted to the immigrant girls who come into town to work as maids, working to help their fathers out of debt and to send the younger children in the family to school. "Those girls have grown up in the first bitter-hard times, and had got little schooling themselves. But the younger brothers and sisters, for whom they made such sacrifices and who have had advantages, never seem to me, when I meet them now, half as interesting or as well educated. The girls, who helped to break up the wild sod, learned so much from life, from poverty, from their mothers and grandmothers; they had all, like Ántonia, been early awakened and made observant by coming at a tender age from an old country to a new." The immigrant girls are interesting for two reasons: they make a fresh individual response to their new country, and they retain vestiges of old world culture. In their individual response to the new world, they come closer to having an organic relation to it than the older, more conventionalized English settlers. Their freedom is compared with the narrowness and lack of vigor of the town girls:

> Physically they were almost a race apart, and out-of-door work had given them a vigor which, when they got over their first shyness on coming to town, developed into a positive carriage and freedom of movement, and made them conspicuous among Black Hawk women.
>
> That was before the day of High-School athletics. . . . There was not a tennis-court in the town; physical exercise was thought rather inelegant for the daughters of well-to-do families. Some of the High-School girls were jolly and pretty, but they stayed indoors in winter because of the cold, and in summer

because of the heat. When one danced with them, their bodies never moved inside their clothes; their muscles seemed to ask but one thing—not to be disturbed....

The daughters of Black Hawk merchants had a confident, uninquiring, belief that they were "refined," and that the country girls, who "worked out," were not.

The townspeople feel innately superior to the immigrants through mere pride of race: "If I told my schoolmates that Lena Lingard's grandfather was a clergyman, and much respected in Norway, they looked at me blankly. What did it matter? All foreigners were ignorant people who couldn't speak English. There was not a man in Black Hawk, who had the intelligence or cultivation, much less the personal distinction, of Ántonia's father. Yet people saw no difference between her and the three Marys; they were all Bohemians, all 'hired girls.' " It is this feeling of superiority that prevents intermarriage between the immigrants and the English-speaking people:

The Black Hawk boys looked forward to marrying Black Hawk girls, and living in a brand-new little house with best chairs that must not be sat upon, and hand-painted china that must not be used. But sometimes a young fellow would look up from his ledger, or out through the grating of his father's bank, and let his eyes follow Lena Lingard, as she passed the window with her slow, undulating walk....

The country girls were considered a menace to the social order. Their beauty shone out too boldly against a conventional background. But anxious mothers need have felt no alarm. They mistook the mettle of their sons. The respect for respectability was stronger than any desire in Black Hawk youth.

Later the vigorous dancing of the Bohemian girls at the Firemen's Hall is compared with the utter deadliness of the typical town life, a deadliness Willa Cather sums up in a descriptive passage:

On starlight nights I used to pace up and down those long cold streets, scowling at the little, sleeping houses on either side, with their storm windows and covered back porches.... The life that went on in them seemed to me made up of evasions and negations; shifts to save cooking, to save washing, and cleaning, devices to propitiate the tongue of gossip. This guarded mode of existence was like living under a tyranny. People's speech, their voices, their very glances, became repressed. Every individual taste, every natural appetite, was bridled by caution. The people asleep in those houses, I thought, tried to live like the mice in their own kitchens; to make no noise, to leave no trace, to slip over the surface of things in the dark. The growing piles of ashes and cinders in the backyards were the only evidence that the wasteful, consuming process of life went on at all.

It is this kind of life that is the background for Ántonia's spontaneity. The contrast of immigrant vigor with native sterility and conformity is a trick that Willa

Cather uses as well as H. L. Mencken. She had a great deal of feeling for the immigrants, desiring to celebrate those who had conquered and to mourn those who had been broken in the new world. The village rebels were apt to look kindly on almost any variation from the native American type of middle-class Protestant English or Scotch-Irish ancestry. Thus in *Spoon River Anthology,* Masters, no Catholic, praised the Catholic priest in Spoon River, speaking *in propria persona* rather than through an epitaph. In Willa Cather's novels, immigrants always are more in touch with both life and art than the native born. In *The Song of the Lark,* Miss Cather had concentrated on the immigrant's spontaneous response to art; in *My Ántonia,* she concentrated on the immigrant's spontaneous response to life.

—ANTHONY CHANNELL HILFER, "Willa Cather: The Home Place, Stultification and Inspiration," *The Revolt from the Village 1915–1930* (Chapel Hill: University of North Carolina Press, 1969), pp. 94–98

ANN DOUGLAS

In *My Ántonia,* Cather's answer to the question, "Who encompasses, who embodies America?" clearly lies in the figure of Ántonia Shimerda herself. The Bohemian woman is finally not a character but a figure held up for our adoration. The book in structure and feeling resembles a medieval triptych of a saint's life: a central portrait backed and adorned by smaller scenes illustrating various aspects of her trials, temptations, and virtues. A representative of the active life Ántonia is nevertheless searched by the story, by Jim Burden's memory, for her contemplative value. She is finally not a person but a place; she gathers us in, she welcomes us home. One of the few native-born Americans in the book, Jim, a Jamesian character in several ways, is among its few expatriates. Ántonia, who has forgotten her English and raised her family to speak Bohemian, belongs.

At the end of *My Ántonia,* a debt has been paid, rites of possession have been performed. Jim has told Ántonia's story, Ántonia has reclaimed Jim, the land has taken Ántonia: Cather has repossessed her continent. She has not anatomized her country's society as George Eliot did so unsurpassably in *Middlemarch;* she has not conveyed the sensibility of its culture, as Virginia Woolf did so unerringly in *Mrs. Dalloway;* she has hardly dissected its disease as Harriet Beecher Stowe did so passionately in *Uncle Tom's Cabin;* she certainly has not recorded the voices issuing from its torture chambers as Sylvia Plath did so uncannily in *Ariel.* She has done much less—and much more.

—ANN DOUGLAS, " 'Willa Cather's Heroines Tend to Be Survivors,' " *University: A Princeton Quarterly* No. 61 (Summer 1974): 8

PHILIP GERBER

Superficially the story of Ántonia Shimerda seems cut from a quite different piece of cloth than its predecessors. A Bohemian girl, she is trapped in the worst possible conditions on the Nebraska Divide: indentured to a town family, uneducated, bereft of special talents, so trusting as to be easy prey to a glib scoundrel. Yet, maintaining a steellike equanimity, she becomes a farmer's wife, mother to a houseful of happy children. Hers is the rarest of Cather's lives—a joyous one.

For Ántonia, no iron bridges span obedient rivers, no spread of prairie transforms into pasture and cornfield, and no audiences pay homage to a perfect aria. The professional career underlying previous stories is entirely removed, allowing Cather to show "just the other side of the rug, the pattern that is supposed not to count in a story." Celebration of professional fulfillment broadens to a struggle for personal identity. Ántonia's instinct plunges her always into life's mainstream, disregarding money, position, possessions, or career. To live merely for the rich experience of living itself is the "career" she labors at with as much diligence as Kronborg ever practiced her scales. One thinks of Thoreau withdrawing to Walden purposely to confront life, drive it into a corner, and derive its essential quality—all to determine whether it be mean or fine and finally to be able to say that he had lived. So armed with a fierce necessity to breath and act Ántonia rises relatively unscathed from ordeals that might ruin a lesser spirit. Lacking any "talent," she possesses the gift of a warm heart, a buoyant sense of humor, and an infinite capacity for enthusiasm.

This pursuit of life—not to achieve any lofty aim but merely to go with the tides, to exist fully, passionately—was foreign to Cather's nature. But the more she came to understand the toll exacted by a career, the more attractive seemed the life given over wholly to immediate experiences, and the more she came to admire—almost to envy—those equipped to approach their lives in this seemingly easy fashion. Cather could never truly comprehend such persons, the Ántonias of the world. The Thea Kronborgs, the Alexandra Bergsons she knew intimately, for they were so nearly surrogates for herself. In contrast, Ántonia Shimerda required not analysis but worship. She was to be marveled at, something like a Sequoia that stands forever in contradiction of all one's experience.

Thus Cather needed to contemplate her heroine from a safe distance in order to protect herself (as author) from an involvement so intimate that it might reveal her inability to project the girl's personality firsthand. When Cather was writing *The Song of the Lark,* her delight at and fascination with the creative process had allowed her to crawl temporarily inside the skin of another individual. But this was not possible with Ántonia; she and the Bohemian girl had too little in common. Cather's solution was to tell the story through the viewpoint of a relatively detached narrator. It was a relatively common device, much used by Henry James, that Cather's knowledge of painters and their methods would seem to have suggested. Elizabeth Sergeant remembers a discussion of artistic form and technique that occurred in the spring of 1916, when Willa Cather was beginning *My Ántonia.* Cather learned forward suddenly, took a Sicilian apothecary jar filled with orange-brown flowers, and placed it alone on an antique table. For a moment she might have been a painter setting up a still-life arrangement. "I want my new heroine to be like this," she said, "like a rare object in the middle of a table, which one may examine from all sides. I want her to stand out—like this—because she *is* the story."

The narrator whom Cather selected, Jim Burden, allows for Ántonia to be examined in this manner and the various "sides" from which she is seen correspond to the different ages at which Jim knows (of) her—as a child, as an adolescent, as a maiden in full bloom, and finally as a mature woman. Because Jim Burden himself grows older as the story progresses and because his experiences alter him as Ántonia's experiences alter her, each successive view or "side" from which she is observed is more complex and more interesting. At the same time, the adoption of Jim's point-of-view not only explains but actually mandates the episodic structure of the novel. In the introductory chapter Jim is shown as he emphasizes the personal nature of his memoir: "He . . . wrote on the pinkish face of the portfolio the word, 'Ántonia.' He frowned at this a moment, then prefixed another word, making it 'My Ántonia.' That seemed to satisfy him." The most effective way for Jim to create the really strong impressions that will make the manuscript-Ántonia *his* and not another's is to see or hear of her at widely scattered but fairly regular intervals—above all at moments of significance in her life. This, of course, is the manner in which the novel proceeds.

Even though Sarah Orne Jewett had warned Cather about the risks involved in using a masculine viewpoint in fiction, Cather felt that in this case nothing but a male narrator would suffice, hazardous as the experiment might be and artificial as it might appear if she failed. Her decision to use Jim Burden was not happenstance but, on the contrary, carefully reasoned out. Ántonia was to be created from a group of real-life models, and since the most interesting things about these women had been told to Cather by men, she felt that logically Ántonia's story should be presented through the memory of a man. Because the novel was to be a story of feeling, rather than a flurry of plot and action, Jim Burden would tell it in the first person; thus would the emotions involved be best expressed. To establish the nostalgic mood that would color the novel, Cather borrowed from Russian and French literature the device by which an author (unnamed, but clearly Cather herself meets the narrator (Jim Burden) on a transcontinental train: the pair reminisce about a person (the Bohemian girl) they both knew as children, an experience that triggers the narrator's written account—the remainder of the book.

Cather's introduction was calculated to serve a further purpose: that of establishing about Jim Burden certain important facts that affect the story he tells. A mature man of the world, he is able now to evaluate Ántonia's worth more fully than he could at an earlier, less experienced age. Because he is childless and unhappy in his marriage, he tends to look backward rather than forward; therefore, his dwelling with such concentration and sympathy upon his early, happy years— and the Bohemian girl who influenced them—is made more plausible. Finally, Cather felt that the struggle she had gone through in order to ghostwrite S. S. McClure's autobiography, and the resounding success she had made of it, had equipped her to handle a masculine viewpoint convincingly. She felt she had been able to "become" Mr. McClure because she knew him so thoroughly; she was positive that in *My Ántonia* she could achieve the same success with Jim Burden because (although she declined to name a specific individual) she intended to base her narrator on a man she knew fully as well as she knew McClure.

In its elementals Ántonia's story tallies with the novels preceding it: a young person's struggle, obstacles to be surmounted, contrasts sharpening the central actor's achievement. But the world of art aside, Ántonia surpasses previous Cather protagonists in maintaining an integrated personality. It is for her to avoid Thea's dry preoccupation, Alexandra's sense of confinement, and Bartley Alexander's dread that middle age will be a dark cloud blotting the sun from his universe. One need not search outside the novel for comparisons, however, for a contrast with the conventional success story is built into the fabric of *My Ántonia* itself. Jim Burden, in his forties, is a member of an important New York legal firm, is instrumental in the progress of a great railway, and is married to a handsome woman of social prominence. But the reader knows him to be far from fulfilled; his childlessness and marital estrangement dampen his spirits, and his greatest thrill seems to derive from opportunities to sponsor others' dreams, now that his own are over. By contrast, Ántonia in her middle years shines "in the full vigour of her personality, battered but not diminished." She is at the close of the novel fully as life loving as she was when, an immigrant girl of fourteen and bright as a new dollar, she rode the Burlington into the Nebraska plains.

Her secret is enthusiasm—to retain a child's delight in existence. Her effervescence contrasts with the aridity of lives around her. The tone is set when in the opening pages of the novel, Jim Burden thinks of Ántonia and her difference from his "unimpressionable" wife, so "temperamentally incapable of enthusiasm." Set down on the raw Divide, where Ántonia's great desire to learn alerts her to every aspect of the wild land, she contrasts with her own depressive father, who is Cather's last fictional rendering of the Sadilek suicide that never loosed its grip on her imagination. In Black Hawk, town girls are but pale tintypes beside the living, breathing vigor of the immigrant girls, of whom Ántonia is the prime representative. Eventually, those daughters of merchants and tradesmen—trapped in their mystique of "refinement," corseted literally and figuratively by the demands of convention and reared with blind trust in their natural superiority—provide too simple a contrast; and the phenomenon of Ántonia must be presented within her own small circle. For she is not wholly typical; Tiny Soderball, to cite one instance, who becomes the greatest worldly success among the immigrant group, dwindles into "a thin, hard-faced woman, very well dressed, very reserved in manner . . . like someone in whom the faculty of becoming interested is worn out." Ántonia is cut from sturdier goods; she wears well, showing her quality even when threadbare.

In her struggle to tame life, Ántonia gropes; fumbling repeatedly, she runs a zigzag path but makes relentless progress. If ever there were a true-born victim of circumstance, it should be she: a stranger, unacclimated to frontier life, unable to speak the lingua franca, socially outcast, with a defeated dreamer for a father, a harridan for a mother, a sullen lout for a brother. But Ántonia transcends every disadvantage and does so without soiling herself. Every day she runs barefoot to the Burden home to pick up a few English phrases. No corner of the plains is exempt from her inquiring eye. She is no scholar, of course, for there is no time for school: "I ain't got time to learn," she tells Jim; "I can work like mans now. My mother can't say no more how Ambrosch do all and nobody to help him. I can work as much as him. School is all right for little boys. I help make this land one good farm."

Lacking the resources of an Alexandra, she cannot erect a farming empire; instead, yielding to inevitable conditions, she goes to town as hired girl to the Harlings, where she is exposed to new ways and put in touch for the first time with civilized refinements. She throws herself into those aspects of social life open to Bohemian girls, but she keeps her individuality intact by refusing to drop the new friends made in the "dancing school" tent, even when refusal to conform threatens to cost her the household post on which she exists. When at last Ántonia is betrayed in the only way she could be, self-blinded to the hypocrisy of the railroader who seduces her, this betrayal and the child she bears leave her self-esteem unscarred. Eventually, with the man meant to be the "instrument of her special mission," she mothers her large family, giving herself without reservation to the renewal of life. Those close to Ántonia see her life as ideal. To Cather she is cause for celebration; she justifies the human race.

To what extent the story of Ántonia Shimerda fits into the characteristic pattern of "artist's youth" is a question answered by Cather herself, and in the simplest manner. Of the painter, writer, sculptor, singer there is no question; but in the new dimension Cather includes as artists "the German housewife who sets before her family on Thanksgiving Day a perfectly roasted goose" and "the farmer who goes out in the morning to harness his team, and pauses to admire the sunrise." Ántonia's function is to epitomize this group: "One of the people who interested me most as a child was the Bohemian hired girl of one of our neighbors, who was so good to me. She was one of the truest artists I ever knew in the keenness and sensitiveness of her enjoyment, in her love of people and in her willingness to take pains." After celebrating the ultimate professional achievement— a portrait of success exceeding Thea Kronborg's is inconceivable—Cather caps her theme of youthful struggle with the saga of this hired girl's personal triumph. The entire story is a paean, and no Cather heroine evokes such admiration as this Bohemian girl who is so warmly eulogized as the novel ends:

> She lent herself to immemorial human attitudes which we recognize by instinct as universal and true. . . . She was a battered woman now, not a lovely girl; but she still had that something which fires the imagination, could still stop one's breath for a moment by a look or gesture that somehow revealed the meaning in common things. She had only to stand in the orchard, to put her hand on a little crab tree and look up at the apples, to make you feel the goodness of planting and tending and harvesting at last. All the strong things of her heart came out in her body, that had been so tireless in serving generous emotions.
>
> It was no wonder that her sons stood tall and straight. She was a rich mine of life, like the founders of early races.

—PHILIP GERBER, "Rich Mine of Life: *My Ántonia*," *Willa Cather*
(Boston: Twayne, 1975), pp. 87–92

CLARA B. COOPER

"Androgyny," from the Greek "andro" (male) and "gyne" (female), defines a condition under which the rigidly defined characteristics and bias of male/female are liberated from the limitations of the "appropriate." The conventional view of "masculine" implies, among other qualities, competitiveness, imperturbability and vigour; while the predominant "feminine" attributes equate with gentleness, submission and frailty. These "official" conceptions are a legacy from the Victorian middle-class social status of respectability, and yet Coleridge's vision affirmed that great minds tend to be androgynous. Androgyny postulates a reconciliation between the sexes by permitting a broad range of experiences in which women can be competitive and aggressive, while men do not lose their masculinity by exhibiting intuitive and tender feelings. An easily identifiable androgynous person in Western literature is Dionysius in Euripides' *Bacchae*. Thomas Rosenmeyer defines Dionysius' role as the epitome of "universal vitality," which explains why the descriptive comments of those who encounter him in the drama are contradictory, for "a god cannot be defined." Similarly, in Eastern literature the impressions of Krishna as seen by the many *gopis* (milkmaids) do not coincide. The gods are all things to all persons, for the god-head is neither man nor woman, but more a coalescence of man-in-woman/woman-in-man.

In *My Ántonia,* Willa Cather, whose mind was androgynous, discloses a "feminine" sensitivity in describing the sunflower-bordered wagon tracks and the foreign old women on the farms who represent the older world across the sea, while in her personal life she is revealed as a "masculine," tough-minded ambitious young woman from the provinces, with an ardour to match her determination to succeed in a man's world—magazine writing and editing. In her novels, especially in *My Ántonia,* Willa Cather's androgyny is evidenced by her refusal to categorize her characters into conventional sexual divisions. She creates a woman-in-man narrator, Jim Burden, whose delicacy of thought and tenderness of heart stand out in sharp contrast to the other, less sensitive, characters. While the Bohemian immigrants are loud and grasping, Jim with an understanding heart realizes that they are new to the land and hence frightened about any loss, however small it might be. He therefore makes allowances for their rough, rude and greedy attitudes. Jim also possesses the masculine drives of dependability and self-reliance. He offers Ántonia and her younger sister Yulka a ride in his new, horse-drawn sleigh, but when it gets cold, Jim can be depended upon to give the younger girl his long scarf to keep her from becoming half-frozen. Like Shakespeare, in his portrayals of Rosalind and Portia, Willa Cather was aware that "masculine and feminine qualities in proper balance, are essential to the expression of humanity." (Carolyn G. Heilbrun, *Toward a Recognition of Androgyny*). The man-in-woman heroine, Ántonia Shimerda, displays a "masculine" pattern of self-expression; she is hardy and pugnacious, necessary qualities for conquest of the untamed land. Yet her feminine impulse leads to her seduction by a pseudo "train-crew aristocrat." Throughout the novel, Jim and

Ántonia coil and recoil upon their dispositions, until each attains a resilient self-hood.

The novel opens on the Divide, when Jim Burden, a young boy, arrives to live with his grandfather. Jim's age, experiences and personal history closely parallel Willa Cather's own and the selection of a male viewpoint was due to the "strong masculine element rooted deep in her personality" (James Woodress, *Willa Cather: Her Life and Art*). Like Willa Cather, Jim also comes to Nebraska from Virginia at a very young age. Both are romantics at heart and have a vaguely spiritual nature. In both, the windblown seas of Nebraska grass create the sensation of being absorbed into something great and good. The Shimerdas are neighbours and their daughter, Ántonia, four years older than Jim, becomes his friend and playmate. Jim follows the "masculine" pattern by killing a very large rattler while Ántonia in the proper "feminine" fashion stands by awestruck. When Jim's reaction to his instinctive but foolhardy act leaves him limp and weak, Ántonia's "feminine" wiles of expressed appreciation and admiration soon have the young lad proud and exulting, as though he were a dragon-slayer.

But the pattern shifts when Ántonia and Jim are in their adolescence. From a "feminine" passivity, Ántonia takes on a "masculine" aggressiveness. She becomes a farmhand and even her appearance undergoes a change. She becomes "rough," proud of her strength, sunburned and "sweaty." Jim remains active-passive till the end. While successful in the world—he becomes a legal counsel for one of the great Western railways—his personal life is a disappointment. His wife is energetic, handsome, but "temperamentally incapable of enthusiasm"; yet Jim in his passivity, harbours no grievance, even though his marital happiness has submerged like Atlantis. Though Camus says that it is not easy to return to Ithaca, unlike Odysseus Jim makes the journey with ease to his "other mind" which is woman. Tiresias-like, Jim's "feminine" sensitive narration of the story is set against his "masculine" discerning love for the vast Nebraskan land, "not a country at all, but the material out of which countries are made."

Towards the end of the novel there is another deviation in Ántonia's psyche. This time Ántonia has become all woman, although an unwed, deserted mother, who yet moves through this experience of betrayal of wholeness. Her greatness gradually assumes mythic proportions; a new strength and gravity is discernible in her face and she seems unashamed of her illegitimate daughter. She is as proud as if she had "a ring on her finger." Ántonia now represents the mother-figure infused with a "masculine" strength, for though she is "battered" she is in no way "diminished." As she does not wholly believe herself to have sinned, so in an inexplicable way she had not sinned at all. The inner glow has not faded, nor has she lost the fire of life. She is sustained by her sense of her destiny, which is to be a strong, rich "mine of life."

Willa Cather was able to imaginatively recreate in art the androgynous ideal which she herself possessed. Though Jim Burden reveals a "romantic disposition," like Emity Brontë's in *Wuthering Heights,* Willa Cather's androgynous vision in *My Ántonia* portrays a great love that is not romance—instead it is an androgynous realization of "what a little circle man's experience is." Finally, Ántonia, like Willa Cather, and like the Heavenly Venus of new-Platonism, Dionysius of Greek mythology or Krishna of the philosophy of India, becomes the completely androgynous ideal.

—CLARA B. COOPER, "The Central Androgynous Characters in *My Ántonia*," *Indian Journal of American Studies* 9, No. 2 (July 1979): 65–67

C. HUGH HOLMAN

My Ántonia is an account of the childhood, adolescence, and young adulthood of Ántonia Shimerda Cuzak, as viewed from the vantage point of twenty years after by Jim Burden, who grew up with her. Jim is the grandson of a well-established Nebraska family, and he has all the advantages which wealth and position can offer one on the Nebraska plains. Ántonia is the daughter of a poor Bohemian immigrant family. At the time of the narration of the story Jim's life has moved from countryside to the small town of Black Hawk, from there to the University of Nebraska, from there to Harvard, and now he is living in New York City as the attorney for one of the great western railroads. In all this movement from the early history of the nation, represented through the first farming settlements, back eastward through the stages of history to the nation on the verge of the First World War, Jim has had success, but his marriage is without children and unhappy; his life is somehow empty; and when he looks back upon the path which he has followed, he is haunted by the attraction of an earlier, simpler life closely associated with the soil, a life represented by Ántonia. The novel is his account of what *his* Ántonia has meant to him. Although Willa Cather in an interview said that Jim "was to remain a detached observer, appreciative but inactive, rather than take a part in [Ántonia's] life," the novel is, as many critics have pointed out, a double story in which Jim Burden is far too important to be merely the narrator of someone else's life. The more closely we look at the novel, the more important and central Jim's role appears, for Ántonia tends to become, as David Daiches has noted, "an objectification of the observer's emotions . . . her growth, development, and final adjustment is a vast symbolic progress interesting less for what it is [*sic*] than for what it can be made to mean. . . . Throughout the book the narrator's sensibility takes control. Jim is much more than a narrative device; he becomes a fundamental element in the theme, which is essentially that described in the epigram on the title page, "*Optima dies . . . prima fugit*," the best day flies first. He is the medium for expressing this recognition of the nostalgic sense that, as the obligations of civilization and history increasingly impress their weight upon the individual, they carry him further and further away from the good, simple, and pastoral life of which Ántonia remains a hardy representation.

Perhaps the most famous metaphor in the novel is the one which occurs at the end of chapter 14 of Book II, in which Jim and the hired girls, on a picnic see a plough that "magnified across the distance by the horizontal light [of the setting sun behind] . . . stood out against the sun, was exactly contained within the circle of the disk; the handles, the tongue, the share—black against the molten red. There it was, heroic in size, a picture writing on the sun." This symbolic representation of the heroic days of the West before the coming of everything that Jim's later life is to represent, most of the critics have praised for its beauty and its promise of optimistic strength. They have failed to read the paragraph which follows it: "Even when we whispered about it, our vision disappeared; the ball dropped and dropped until the red tip went beneath the earth. The fields below us were dark, the sky was growing pale, and that forgotten plough had sunk back to its own littleness somewhere on the prairie." This awareness of darkness approaching, of the diminished possibilities of the simple and primitive, of the cost which the severe struggle will exact is firmly impressed upon Jim Burden, primarily through his long and affectionate regard for the hard life of Ántonia. At the end of Book I, when Ántonia is talking with Jim at his grandfather's home, she says, " 'If I live here, like you, that is different. Things will be easy for you. But they will be hard for us.' " And indeed so they proved to be.

John H. Randall III is only partially right when he says, "The use of a double protagonist has certain advantages: it allows one character to be an actor and the other a spectator; one can be youth which performs and accomplishes unthinkingly, the other middle age which can interpret the significance of action in others but itself has lost the capacity to act." More is at stake in *My Ántonia* than the contrast between the active and the contemplative life. Ántonia represents the strength, the freedom, and the fecundity—in the final book she is virtually an Earth Mother—which opened the frontier and built the West, and with courage and enormous vitality survived scorching summers and the grimness of winter. Jim represents that diminished quality which follows upon the early triumph of vigor and action. The emotion which this book consistently evokes is that of nostalgic longing, of the backward look toward the lovely and lost past. At the conclusion Jim, a somewhat cynical and successful man, looks back to say, "I had the sense of coming home to myself, and of having found out what a little circle man's experience is." This attitude is quite comparable to that of Miles Coverdale, though Coverdale came to distrust the pastoral element in life and Burden has to come to distrust the to-him-necessary urban element. But the emotion which floods the book is not this distrust but a sense of the beauty of what is lost: "Whatever we had missed, we possessed together the precious, the incommunicable past."

—C. HUGH HOLMAN, "The *Bildungsroman*, American Style,"
Windows on the World: Essays on American Social Fiction
(Knoxville: University of Tennessee Press, 1979), pp. 183–85

PAUL A. OLSON

The book in which Cather is most explicitly epic in her treatment is *My Ántonia*. Her earlier book, *O Pioneers!*, gives us the metamorphic mode: Marie and Emil killed under the mulberry tree, Alexandra early sending roots into the prairie ground like some old Baucis without a Philemon, Crazy Ivar in his fervor mediating between the world of prairie and the world of human culture like some Dionysius of the land. Proceeding in almost the sequence of the nineteenth-century Latin curricula, from Ovid to Virgil, Cather invents in *My Ántonia* a "georgic epic," as Fielding had invented a "comic epic in prose." Her epic has a woman as hero and fields for monster-filled waters. Cather creates or develops the sense that what is happening is Virgilian and epic by creating Jim Burden as her spectator-narrator, a classicist before whose inner eyes the events of Virgil's history pale as he looks on his own remembrance of things past; he also in his reflection defines, by indirection, Cather's sense of the relationship of her craft to her sense of place. Her model is Gaston Cleric, classicist at the University of Nebraska, for whom the texts of antique poetry were never mere texts but meant to imagine a life:

> He could bring the drama of antique life before one out of the shadows—white figures against blue backgrounds. I shall never forget his face as it looked one night when he told me about the solitary day he spent among the sea temples at Paestum: the soft wind blowing through the roofless columns, the birds flying low over the flowering marsh grasses. . . .

As Jim Burden meditates on the meaning of classical life and of the *Aeneid* as "mother to me and nurse in poetry," a second set of pictures (the reverse of the second *Aeneid* picture which appears in Tom Outland's imagination) arises behind the text of the *Aeneid:*

> While I was in the very act of yearning toward the new forms that Cleric brought up before me, my mind plunged away from me, and I suddenly found myself thinking of the places and people of my own infinitesimal past. They stood out strengthened and simplified now, like the image of the plough against the sun. They were all I had for an answer to the new appeal. I begrudged the room that Jake and Otto and Russian Peter took up in my memory, which I wanted to crowd with other things. But whenever my consciousness was quickened, all those early friends were quickened within it, and in some strange way they accompanied me through all my new experiences. They were so much alive in me that I scarcely stopped to wonder whether they were alive anywhere else, or how.

The heroic forms which fill Jim Burden's imagination are a "strengthened and amplified" "Jake and Otto and Russian Peter"; these are, unlike the dead Trojan races of the mesa civilization, the avatars of a new epoch in a new world.

Later in the book, Ántonia is described as "a rich mine of life, like the founders of early races," i.e., like the epic heroes. She is apotheosized in Jim Burden's memory in "immemorial human attitudes" that one recognizes as "universal and true":

> Ántonia had always been one to leave images in the mind that did not fade—that grew stronger with time. In my memory there was a succession of such pictures, fixed there like the old woodcuts of one's first primer: Ántonia kicking her bare legs against the sides of my pony when we came home in

triumph with our snake; Ántonia in her black shawl and fur cap, as she stood by her father's grave in the snowstorm; Ántonia coming in with her work-team along the evening sky-line.

This is, of course, half of the epic purpose in Virgil—to memorialize the universal and true *as the heroic* in the particular form in which history offers it to human memory. The other half of it is to show how Destiny has led the hero to take hold of its design and to carve out a pattern of life laid out before by transcendent powers in order to rescue an old or create a new civilization.

Thus, the conclusion of the book comes as the fulfillment of Jim Burden's perception that what he is dealing with in his imagination is material that somehow deserves to stand by Virgil: "For Ántonia and for me, this had been the road of Destiny; had taken us to those early accidents of fortune which predetermined for us all that we can ever be. Now I understood that the same road was to bring us together again. Whatever we had missed, we possessed together the precious, the incommunicable past." Burden constructs this meditation on destiny as he looks at the road over which he and Ántonia have come when as children they first arrived on the frontier, as his memory recapitulates it with such vividness that he can touch its feelings—can by contemplating it "come home to himself" and know "what a little circle man's experience is." In the communion of shared memory, Ántonia and Burden stand as persons whose "roads will bring them together again"; yet, in the distinctiveness of their fortune's accidents they were "predetermined" to separate—some would say opposite—destinies.

These opposite and yet crossed destinies are those of the lover of the *patria* and its hymner; though the creator, Jim Burden, is represented as a disappointed legal counsel for one of the "great western railways," the legal portfolio which, in the fiction, he is represented as having presented to Miss Cather is not that of a failed lawyer, but that of one of those who can say without diffidence, "*Primus ego in patriam mecum* ... deducam Musas" [for I shall be the first, if I live, to bring the Muse into my country (*patria*)]: "Cleric had explained to us that 'patria' here meant, not a nation or even a province, but the little rural neighbourhood on the Mincio where the poet was born. This was not a boast, but a hope, at once bold and devoutly humble, that he might bring the Muse (but lately come to Italy from the cloudy Grecian mountains), not to the capital, the *palatia Romana,* but to his own little 'country'; to his father's fields ..."

Cleric then goes on to speculate that Virgil in dying remembered this passage, and "decreed that the great canvas [of the *Aeneid*], crowded with figures of gods and men, should be burned rather than survive him unperfected." The dying poet then turned his mind to his "perfect utterance," the *Georgics,* "where the pen was fitted to the matter as the plough is to the furrow." As he gave up his life, he is said to "have said to himself, with the thankfulness of a good man, 'I was the first to bring the Muse into my country,'" i.e., his *patria.* For Cather and Jim Burden, the Muse must come to Nebraska. Indeed, in a few pages, Burden understands his Muse—as he sees Lena Lingard in the lamplight. He thinks of her, as in a dream, "coming across the harvest-field in her short skirt," beneath her the Virgilian motto, "*Optima dies ... prima fugit"*; with her also the memory of the Danish laundry girls and the three Bohemian Marys. Suddenly he understands what the Muse is: "It came over me, as it had never done before, the relationship between girls like those and the poetry of Virgil. If there were no girls like them in the world, there would be no poetry." Thus if Ántonia is the *Aeneas* of his georgic world, Burden is its Virgil.

The world of *My Ántonia* is also, subtly, an epic world where a "New Rome" can be built. To return to the "road" contemplated at the end of the book: the road is first experienced as like a pathless sea—no road could be made out, only undulating land over the edge of the world, beyond the gods and prayer. Later this same country is described recurrently as sealike and as covered with red grass "the colour of wine-stains, or of certain seaweeds." We are once again with Homer's wine-dark sea. Once one has the sense that a Homeric or Virgilian comparison is invited, one can quite easily develop the analogies, half-analogies, and ironic contrasts between the world which possesses Jim's imagination and the *Aeneid;* Shimerda's suicide, remembering the old civilization, and Dido's as the representative of the civilization which will pass away, are parallel as are Shimerda's funeral and in an ironic way the burial of Palinurus. The monsters of the prairie—the serpent which looks like the serpent of Eden and is barely killed, the wolves whose hungry howls parallel those of Russia and haunt the anarchist Russian Pavel's imagination like some great recapitulation of the anarchist Cyclops' hunger for men—all of these are real horrors on the sea of grass. Black Hawk is like a barren Carthage. The Wick Cutter episode, based as it is on Pluto's rape of Proserpina and his carrying her off to the underworld, parallels the dark side of the underworld visit in Virgil; the young group's journey to the "blond pastures" to contemplate the past and future of the *patria* plays off against a similar action in Virgil's Elysian fields. When Aeneas sees the weapon which will create Rome's future, he sees sword and shield with scenes of the Roman future on it and his breastplate of hard bronze "massive and ruddy coloured like to some lowing cloud/when it catches fire from the rays of the sun and glows afar" (8.613–43). Ántonia and her band see the emblem of their future also alight with the setting sun:

> Presently we saw a curious thing: There were no clouds, the sun was going down in a limpid, gold-washed sky. Just as the lower edge of the red disk rested on the high fields against the horizon, a great black figure suddenly appeared on the face of the sun. We sprang to our feet, straining our eyes toward it. In a moment we realized what it was. On some upland farm, a plough had been left standing in the field.

The sun has become a heroic shield and against it the emblem of the country's future—the plow. All of this done delicately—a nuance here and here; never mere equations between the books.

But the end of the epic is to show an old civilization ended and a new one founded. After the hero has completed his journey and acquired the strength he needs in his battles with phantasmagoria, his final test is generally a great battle fought for a great marriage—Odysseus for Penelope, Aeneas for Lavinia—from which union the new nation will spring. There is no great battle in *My Ántonia*, only Ántonia's battle to save the farm and herself after being abandoned by Donovan, her Circe. Ántonia is like a "founder of early races," but her marriage is as much to the soil and the garden as to her husband, and she is not presented simply as a mother to a race. The journey, the conquest of plains monsters—both the physical ones and the antisocial ones (Cutter, Donovan, Krajiek, Russian Pavel), the descent into Black Hawk's dark world and its surrounding Elysian fields, the tests of spirit and courage are not designed to bring Ántonia to the formation of such a society as the *Aeneid* envisages—a Roman city whose laws will endure forever. Her journey ends in a garden, a family garden, as the more perfect work which the *Georgics* propose. Her place is the *patria*—the little rural neighborhood—the emblem of the good society to the Virgil of the *Georgics* who wished to prevent the further urbanization of Rome and to restore the yeomanry to a well-tended countryside. Why Virgil turned to the urban imperial idealism of the *Aeneid* is not clear; clearly, Burden (and, I think, Cather) regard the technique and content of the former work as superior to that of the *Aeneid*. Cather makes her "epic" celebrate its values. In the ending of *My Ántonia*, she celebrates the ethnic cultures which were being trodden under in World War I, the rural life which urbanization was destroying. She celebrates the cultivation of fields, of trees and vines, and of cattle in terms quite as eloquent as those of Virgil. All she leaves out are the bees and Orpheus's descent to recover the bees, a motif covered for her purposes in Ántonia's descent. The victorious garden at the end has an almost visionary perfection.

   My Ántonia has in it that rooted life, ethnic Czech and georgic in tenor, before which that faith in rootlessness, chauvinism, urbanization, and technology which marked World War I America fades into triviality. Ántonia can no longer handle a gun. She is a citizen of that garden whose serpent is killed—where a putting of the hand on the crab-apple tree can "make you feel the goodness of planting and tending and harvesting at last." She is fully a woman, and she embodies the Mother Earth beneath her feet. Interestingly, Cather also breaks the epic pattern and locates heroic achievement in the under classes: in a Czech woman—this during the period of the most intense anti-"central-European ethnic" prejudice which our country has known. That she sees the heroic as deriving from explicit private or mystical religious experience I doubt; there is, however, if I read the book aright, a strain of Czech freethinkerlike embodied pantheism represented in Ántonia's response to the earth and to those around her. Cather is too subtle to make explicit what is the spirit which moves her hero. Thus in all three areas—the displacement of epic pattern, the displacement of the ruling class, and the use of nonordinary religious experiences as a source of the heroic—Cather resembles our other two writers. She differs only in her level of achievement, which is extraordinary indeed.

—PAUL A. OLSON, "The Epic and Great Plains Literature: Rølvaag, Cather, and Neihardt," *Prairie Schooner* 55, Nos. 1/2 (Spring–Summer 1981): 278–84

MICHAEL PETERMAN

Ántonia, the Bohemian immigrant girl, is of course Cather's symbol for the vitality of the Nebraska prairie. "[She] seemed to mean to us the country, the conditions, the whole adventure of our childhood," writes Cather's narrator in the "Introduction." For Wallace Stegner, Ántonia "all but *is* the land." In the novel's full perspective, she emerges both as the symbol of the land's fertility and as priestess to its power. Her virtual disappearance from the "Lena Lingard" section is thus not the structural flaw several critics have suggested; to be in Lincoln or any city for very long would constitute a violation of Ántonia's symbolic role in the novel. During this time while Jim and Lena experience the attractions of the city, Ántonia returns to the prairie, undergoing a sort of transcendence there and becoming the "rich mine of life." Jim celebrates at the novel's end. Not only does she bear and raise her children but she plays her selfless part in transforming the rough, wild Nebraska prairie into the garden the Cuzak farm becomes. The trees Ántonia first planted here are emblematic; she tells Jim, "they were on my mind like children." At the same time Ántonia's "disappearance" is consistent with Jim's exposure to the urban possibilities of Lincoln and the uncommitted sexuality of Lena. If he struggles initially to maintain a romantic innocence concerning sexual matters, he comes through experience to realize that Ántonia by nature escapes unproductive and merely indulgent attitudes to sex. Larry Donovan can only make her pregnant; he cannot misdirect her energy.

The Ántonia who emerges in the novel's final section is thus fully transformed—she is strong, healthy, good, successful, seemingly ageless. In cadences and images that recall certain of Robert Frost's poems, Jim eulogizes his Ántonia's quiet achievement:

> She lent herself to immemorial human attitudes which we recognize by instinct as universal and true. I had not been mistaken. She was a battered woman now, not a lovely girl; but she still had that something which fires the imagination, could still stop one's breath for a moment by a look or gesture that somehow revealed the meaning in common things. She had only to stand in the orchard, to put her hand on a little crab tree and look up at the apples, to make you feel the goodness of planting and tending and harvesting at last. All the strong things of her heart came out in her body, that had been so tireless in serving generous emotions.

Thus she embodies the humanizing power of the land that earlier fascinated Cather in *The Song of the Lark:* "It was hard to tell about it, for it had nothing to do with words; it was like the light of the desert at noon, or the smell of the sagebrush after rain; intangible but powerful. [Thea] had the sense of going back to a friendly soil, whose friendship was somehow going to strengthen her; a naïve, generous country that gave one its joyous force, its large-hearted, childlike power to love, just as it gave one its coarse, brilliant flowers."

—MICHAEL PETERMAN, " 'The Good Game': The Charm of Willa Cather's
My Ántonia and W. O. Mitchell's *Who Has Seen the Wind,*"
Mosaic 14, No. 2 (Spring 1981): 98–99

MICHAEL A. KLUG

In *My Ántonia,* Cather transformed her quarrel with herself into a great work about American schizophrenia. The terms of the conflict are set up early in the novel in the description of the prairie. The new land is the promise of freedom from the past, a fresh chance for man to live in harmony with himself and nature. But it also means death, the death of the individual or unique self. Jim Burden is awestruck by his first passing glimpse of the prairie. He has found the open country without human or natural boundaries, "no fences, no creeks or trees, no hills or fields." The past with all its restrictions is wiped out. The authority of parents and even of God seems part of that world he has left behind. There is only the land, waiting to take him in. But surrendering to that wide embrace of earth and sky, Jim already senses that a part of him must be "erased, blotted out." A day or so later when Jim first ventures out into the prairie, he finds the same invitation and the same threat. He touches the pulse of the world, alive in "the fresh, easy-blowing morning wind, and in the earth itself." Here at the edge of creation, he can float off and join the hawks in the sky. His great moment comes when he lies down in his grandmother's garden and is released into the world of nature that hums around him: "I kept as still as I could. Nothing happened. I did not expect anything to happen. I was something that lay under the sun and felt it, like the pumpkins, and I did not want to be anything more. I was entirely happy. Perhaps we feel like that when we die and become a part of something entire, whether it is sun and air, or goodness and knowledge. At any rate, that is happiness; to be dissolved into something complete and great." To be dissolved in nature brings total happiness, the happiness of the anonymous and unconscious world, and for the moment Jim wants nothing more. But he cannot hold on to this innocent joy without surrendering that part of himself that can live only in striving and opposition and that must establish boundaries against the rest of the world. If he were to live solely in nature, he would also have to be buried in it. The two faces of nature appear in the conflicting images of the prairie that recur through the novel. The prairie releases Jim and Ántonia onto the "roads to freedom," but it just as surely drives life underground—the first half of the novel is filled with images of buried existence. Even the owls are forced into a "subterranean habit," and Jim and Ántonia sense that "winged things who would live a life like that must be rather degraded creatures." Mr. Shimerda represents the sacrifice that the prairie demands. He has an artist's soul and is at home in the world of human creation—the world of ideas and the imagination. When he leaves that world he is in exile. The land drains his spirit; he moves across its immensity "as if he had no purpose" or is driven into refuge in Krajiek's cave. In the end his music dries up, and he destroys himself rather than go on without it.

The inevitable conflict between the individual and nature is the basis of the tension that draws Jim and Ántonia together and at the same time separates them. Jim is another of Cather's romantic idealists. He seeks a separate fate, and he leaves the home place so that he can "make something" of himself. At university he finds that the doorway that opens on "the world of ideas" closes upon the world of

nature, family and friends. But Jim is not as pure a pilgrim of the ideal self as Thea
Kronborg or Godfrey St. Peter. He cannot cut his ties with the prairie and its life;
it keeps returning with the memory of what he has lost and must somehow
recover. At the center of his memory is Ántonia, who lives by the counter urge.
When her father dies, she loses her immediate contact with the life of the mind
and imagination and the chance to pursue a destiny that is separate from the
land. Once she embraces her fate, she becomes a part of the familiar, unconscious world, where she knows "every stack and tree, and where all the ground
is friendly."

Neither Jim nor Ántonia makes the "right choice." In this novel, Cather shows
that the individual and the collective fate are both insufficient in themselves. Ántonia
is at home in nature and her family, but she pays a price. She loses all those things
her father lived for and cherished, and she is well aware of her loss: "My father, he
went much to school. He know a great deal; how to make fine cloth like what you
not got here. He play horn and violin, and he read so many books that the priests
in Bohemie come to talk to him." She can share only vicariously in the life of the
mind through her love for Jim. She wants Jim to have a different fate from her own
and so she insists that he go to school and "learn fine thoughts" and tries to protect
him from being trapped into domestic life. She sees, just as Jim does, that he is to
fulfill the life of her father. Jim is a modest narrator and does not have much to say
about his accomplishments, but it is clear that he becomes an important man. In an
incomplete way, he does make something of himself. But if Jim's life is a success, it
is also a disappointment because he has lost his immediate contact with nature and
with the human family.

The polarity of Jim and Ántonia supplies the dramatic force of the most
powerful scene in the novel. At the end of Book Four, Jim comes to visit Ántonia,
who has returned to the farm to make a home for her fatherless daughter. Jim and
Ántonia have been separated for two years and will not see each other again for
twenty more. They meet in the fields as Ántonia is shocking wheat and move
towards Mr. Shimerda's grave as the "fittest place to talk to each other." Here,
where the dreamer sleeps in the wild prairie, they set their courses for life. Jim is
to go into the great world to pursue his hopes. Ántonia is to stay behind with her
child and the land. Jim cannot remain with Ántonia without betraying his dream of
a separate fate. Ántonia cannot go with Jim without betraying her love for her child
and her land. To keep faith with their deepest commitments they must lose each
other. In this separation we see the irreparable division in Cather and in American
life—the impossibility of reconciling the demands of personal ambition and the
claims of love. Each is incomplete and fragmented. Only in the memory can they
be whole and one. They vow to be true to each other in memory, and for a
moment they are joined together against the long years of separation. As they walk
across the fields, they see in nature the sign of their equilibrium: "The sun dropped
and lay like a great golden globe in the low west. While it hung there, the moon
rose in the east, as big as a cartwheel, pale silver and streaked with rose colour, thin
as a bubble or a ghost-moon. For five, perhaps ten minutes, the two luminaries

confronted each other across the level land, resting on opposite edges of the world." In this "singular light" the world comes into focus. Jim feels "the old pull of the earth"; Ántonia possesses the spirit that moves Jim and her father.

In the twenty years that follow, Jim and Ántonia live out their fates. When Jim returns home he finds that Ántonia is the mother of a whole tribe of sons and daughters and is the heart of a large and successful farm. The final picture of Ántonia is Cather's strongest case for life within the sphere of common things. Ántonia has grown older, but she still has all her old "fire of life." She is obviously content with the familiar round of children and land. But her life denies something that Cather could never forget—the spirit's hunger to be free of the commonplace and to pursue a special fate. Ántonia does not complain or indicate any dissatisfaction, but Jim senses where such a life falls short when he is with her sons and begins to feel "the loneliness of the farm-boy at evening, when the chores seem everlastingly the same, and the world so far away" and again when he is alone with Ántonia's husband. Cuzak, like Jim and Mr. Shimerda, hungers for the cosmopolitan life—for cities, theaters, music. He has become "the instrument of Ántonia's special mission" and confesses that at times life on the farm has nearly driven him "crazy with lonesomeness." If life on the land is incomplete, the life that Jim finds in the great world is even more so. He is childless. Like Lena Lingard and Tiny Soderball he has spent his creative energy in making a self and has none left over for sons and daughters. Jim returns home, but he can never fully be at home. He can only borrow Ántonia's family, just as she can only borrow his personal achievement.

—MICHAEL A. KLUG, "Willa Cather: Between Red Cloud and Byzantium,"
Canadian Review of American Studies 12, No. 3 (Winter 1981): 293–96

DEBORAH G. LAMBERT

In childhood, Ántonia is established as the novel's center of energy and vitality. As a girl she is "bright as a new dollar" with skin "a glow of rich, dark colour" and hair that is "curly and wild-looking." She is always in motion: holding out a hand to Jim as she runs up a hill, chattering in Czech and broken English, asking rapid questions, struggling to become at home in a new environment. Wanting to learn everything, Ántonia also has "opinions about everything." Never indolent like Lena Lingard, or passive like her sister Yulka, or stolid like the Bohemian girls, Ántonia is "breathless and excited," generous, interested, and affectionate. By the end of her childhood, however, intimations of her future social roles appear.

When Ántonia reaches puberty, Cather carefully establishes her subordinate status in relation to three males, and these relationships make an interesting comparison with Alexandra's and Thea's. First, Ántonia's brutal brother, Ambrosch, is established as the head of the house and the "important person in the family." Then Jim records his need to relegate Ántonia to secondary status and receive deference, since "I was a boy and she was a girl," and in the farcical, pseudo-sexual snake-killing episode, he believes he accomplishes his goal. In fact, he and Ántonia enact a nearly parodic ritual of male and female behavior: in his fear, he turns on her with anger; she cries and apologizes for her screams, despite the fact that they may have saved his life; and she ultimately placates him with flattery. Forced to leave school, she soon relinquishes all personal goals in favor of serving others. No longer resentful or competitive, she is "fairly panting with eagerness to please" young Charley Harling, the son of her employers: "She loved to put up lunches for him when he went hunting, to mend his ball-gloves and sew buttons on his shooting coat, baked the kind of nut-cake he liked, and fed his setter dog when he was away on trips with his father." Cather's protagonist has been reduced to secondary status, as Alexandra and Thea were not: having challenged our expectations in earlier works, Cather retreats in this novel to the depiction of stereotypical patterns.

The second book of My Ántonia, with its insinuative title "The Hired Girls," dramatizes the emergence of Ántonia's intense sexuality and its catastrophic effects on her world. Now a beautiful adolescent woman, Ántonia is "lovely to see, with her eyes shining and her lips always a little parted when she danced. That constant dark colour in her cheeks never changed." Like flies the men begin to circle around her—the iceman, the delivery boys, the young farmers from the divide; and her employer, Mr. Harling, a demanding, intimidating, patriarch insists that she give up the dances where she attracts so much attention. When she refuses, he banishes her from his family. Next becoming the object of her new employer's lust, Ántonia loses Jim's affection and, by the end of the summer, has embarked on a disastrous affair with the railroad conductor, Donovan. Ántonia's sexuality is so powerful, in Cather's portrayal, that it destroys her oldest and best friendships and thrusts her entirely out of the social world of the novel.

Jim's intense anger at Ántonia once again reveals his fear, this time a fear of her sexuality that is almost horror. When Cutter attempts to rape her, Jim, the actual victim of the assault, returns battered to his grandmother's house. He then blames Ántonia and her sexuality for Cutter's lust, and recoils from her: "I heard Ántonia sobbing outside my door, but I asked grandmother to send her away. I felt I never wanted to see her again. I hated her almost as much as I hated Cutter. She had let me in for all this disgustingness." This eruption of sexuality marks the climax, almost the end, of the friendship between Ántonia and Jim, and after this, Ántonia is virtually banished from the novel.

At this point, Cather, evidently retreating from the sexual issue, broadens the novel's thematic focus. Jim and Ántonia do not meet again for two years, and all of Book III is devoted to Jim's frivolous, romanticized affair with Lena Lingard, with which he and the reader are diverted. Moreover, the events of Ántonia's life—her affair with Donovan, her pregnancy, her return home, the birth of her daughter— are kept at great narrative distance. Two years after the fact, a neighbor describes these events to Jim as she has seen them, or read about them in letters. Yet, as though banishing Ántonia and distracting Jim were not sufficient, her sexuality is diminished and then, finally, destroyed. After a punitive pregnancy and the requisite abandonment by her lover, she never again appears in sexual bloom. The metaphoric comparisons that surround her become sexually neutral, at best. In one example her neck is compared to "the bole of a tree," and her beauty is cloaked: "After the winter began she wore a man's long overcoat and boots and a man's felt hat with a wide brim." Her father's clothes, like Mr. Harling's ultimatum, seem well designed to keep Ántonia's sexuality under wraps.

After a two-year separation, during which Ántonia returns to her brother's farm, bears her child, and takes up her life of field work, Jim and Ántonia meet briefly. Dream-like and remote, their meeting is replete with nostalgia not readily accounted for by events; as Jim says, "We met like people in the old song, in silence, if not in tears" (p. 319). Inappropriately, though in a speech of great feeling, Ántonia compares her feeling for Jim to her memory of her father, who is lost to her for reasons that the text does provide:

"... you are going away from us for good.... But that don't mean I'll lose you. Look at my papa here, he's been dead all these years, and yet he is more real to me than almost anybody else. He never goes out of my life."

Jim's response expresses similar nostalgia and an amorphous yearning:

"... since I've been away, I think of you more often than of anyone else in this part of the world. I'd have liked to have you for a sweetheart, or a wife, or my mother, or my grandmother, or my sister—anything that a woman can be to a man.... You really are a part of me."

The seductive note of sentiment may blind us as readers to the fact that Jim might offer to marry Ántonia and instead abandons her to a life of hardship on her brother's farm with an empty, and ultimately broken promise to return soon. Cather forcibly separates Jim and Ántonia because of no logic given in the text; we have to assume that her own emotional dilemma affected the narrative and to look for the reasons within Cather herself.

Following this encounter is a twenty-year hiatus: when Jim and Ántonia finally meet again, the tensions that have lain behind the novel are resolved. Ántonia, now devoid of sexual appeal, no longer presents any threat. In addition, she has been reduced to a figure of the greatest conventionality: she has become the stereotypical earth mother. Bearing no resemblance to Cather's early female heroes, she is honored by Jim and celebrated by Cather as the mother of sons. By the novel's conclusion, Cather has capitulated to a version of that syndrome in which the unusual, achieving woman recommends to other women as their privilege and destiny that which she herself avoided. While recognizing the conflict that issues in such self-betrayal, one also notes the irony of Cather's glorification of Ántonia.

Autonomy and unconventional destiny are available only to the subordinate characters, Lena Lingard and Tiny Soderball, two of the hired girls. Lena, having seen too much of marriage, child-bearing and poverty, has established a successful dress-making business and, despite her sensuous beauty, refrained from marriage. Her companion, Tiny, made her fortune in the Klondike before settling down in San Francisco. They lived in a mutually beneficial, supportive relationship: "Tiny audits

Lena's accounts occasionally and invests her money for her; and Lena, apparently, takes care that Tiny doesn't grow too miserly," Jim tells us. Both Lena and Tiny are independent and unconventional; Lena particularly understands and values the single self. In a revealing detail, she instructs her brother to buy handkerchiefs for their mother with an embroidered "B" for her given name, "Berthe," rather than with an "M" for mother. Lena, who describes marriage as "being under somebody's thumb," says, "It will please her for you to think about her name. Nobody ever calls her by it now." Although relegated to subordinate roles, these women are initially presented favorably; but, by the end of the novel, Cather simultaneously praises Ántonia's role as mother and demeans the value of their independent lives.

In her concluding gesture, Cather offers a final obeisance to convention. Her description of Lena and Tiny undercuts their achievement and portrays them as stereotypical "old maids" who have paid for their refusal of their "natural" function. Thus, Tiny has become a "thin, hard-faced woman, very well dressed, very reserved" and something of a miser: she says "frankly that nothing interested her much now but making money." Moreover Tiny has suffered the "mutilation" of her "pretty little feet"—the price of her unnatural success in the Klondike. Though a little more subtly, Lena is similarly disfigured, physically distorted by her emotional abberation. Jim presents her as crude and overblown in a final snapshot: "A comely woman, a trifle too plump, in a hat a trifle too large . . . " So it is, too, with their friendship, Jim's barren account stresses unpleasantness about clothes and money and implies that an edge of bitterness has appeared. So much for female independence and success; so much for bonds between women. Cather, through Jim's account of them, has denigrated Tiny and Lena and their considerable achievement. In betraying these characters, versions of herself, Cather reveals the extent of her self-division.

Equally revealing is the transformation of Ántonia in the concluding segment. Now forty-four, she is the mother of eleven children, a grandmother without her former beauty. So changed is she that Jim at first fails to recognize her. She is "grizzled," "flat-chested," "toothless," and "battered," consumed by her life of childbearing and field work. The archetypal mother, Ántonia now signifies nourishment, protection, fertility, growth, and abundance: energy in service to the patriarchy, producing not "Ántonia's children" but "Cuzak's boys" (despite the fact that five of the children mentioned—Nina, Yulka, Martha, Anna, and Lucie—are girls). Like Cather's chapter title, Jim recognizes only the male children in his fantasy of eternal boyhood adventure, forgetting that in an earlier, less conventional and more androgynous world, his companion had been a girl—Ántonia herself.

Now Ántonia is glorified as a mythic source of life. Not only the progenitor of a large, vigorous family, she is also the source of the fertility and energy that have transformed the barren Nebraska prairie into a rich and fruitful garden. From her fruit cellar cavern pour forth into the light ten tumbling children—and the earth's abundance as well. In the images of this conclusion, she, no longer a woman, becomes Nature, a cornucopia, a "mine of life." Representing for Jim "immemorial human attitudes" which "fire the imagination," she becomes an idea and disappears

under a symbolic weight, leaving for his friends and companions her highly individ-
ualized male children.

The conclusion of *My Ántonia* has usually been read as a triumph of the
pioneer woman: Ántonia has achieved victory over her own hard early life and
over the forces of Nature which made an immense struggle of farm life in Nebraska. But in fact, as we have seen, Cather and her narrator celebrate one of our
most familiar stereotypes, one that distorts and reduces the lives of women. The
image of the earth mother, with its implicit denial of Ántonia's individual identity,
mystifies motherhood and nurturing while falsely promising fulfillment. Here Cather
has found the means to glorify and dispose of Ántonia simultaneously, and she has
done so in a way that is consonant with our stereotypical views and with her own
psychological exigencies. The image of Ántonia that Cather gives us at the novel's
conclusion is one that satisfies our national longings as well: coming to us from an
age which gave us Mother's Day, it is hardly surprising that *My Ántonia* has lived on
as a celebration of the pioneer woman's triumph and as a paean to the fecundity
of the American woman and American land.

Cather's career illustrates the strain that women writers have endured and to
which many besides Cather have succumbed. In order to create independent and
heroic women, women who are like herself, the woman writer must avoid male
identification, the likelihood of which is enhanced by being a writer who is unmarried, childless, and a lesbian. In the case of *My Ántonia*, Cather had to contend not
only with the anxiety of creating a strong woman character, but also with the fear
of a homosexual attraction to Annie/Ántonia. The novel's defensive narrative structure, the absence of thematic and structural unity that readers have noted, these
are the results of such anxieties. Yet, because it has been difficult for readers to
recognize the betrayal of female independence and female sexuality in fiction—
their absence is customary—it has also been difficult to penetrate the ambiguities
of *My Ántonia*, a crucial novel in Cather's long writing career.

—DEBORAH G. LAMBERT, "The Defeat of a Hero: Autonomy and Sexuality in
My Ántonia," *American Literature* 53, No. 4 (January 1982): 685–90

JOHN J. MURPHY

In *My Ántonia*, Cather's Virginian, Jim Burden, expresses an affinity with Nature
similar to ⟨Owen⟩ Wister's ⟨in *The Virginian*⟩. When he sits in his grandmother's
sheltered garden, the earth feels warm under him, and as he crumbles it through
his fingers, "I was something that lay under the sun and felt it, like the pumpkins, and
I did not want to be anything more. . . . [T]hat is happiness; to be dissolved into
something complete and great." This Nature philosophy, Virginia origins, and the
fact that he moves to the West are about all he shares with Wister's hero. Jim is
too passive and too inexperienced for a heroic role, which is not Cather's intention
for him. Assuming instead a role similar to that of the tenderfoot narrator, he will
focus on a heroic character very different from Wister's. The circumstances of the

opening of *My Ántonia* are curious variations on the opening of *The Virginian*. Each begins on a train, and the narrator first meets at a railway station the special character who will symbolize his West. Cather's intentional altering of typical Western formulae is obvious. Jim is reading a life of Jesse James when informed by the conductor of the Bohemian family in the car ahead but is too shy to visit them and returns to his Wild West biography. At the Black Hawk station he sees Ántonia huddled with her family but is quickly diverted by his grandfather's hired man, Otto Fuchs, a typical citizen of the Wild West, who "might have stepped out of the pages of 'Jesse James.' He wore a sombrero hat, with a wide leather band and a bright buckle, and the ends of his mustache were twisted up stiffly, like little horns. He looked lively and ferocious, I thought, and as if he had a history." It is not Fuchs, however, but the humble immigrant girl who will become the "central figure" that will "mean . . . the country, the conditions" of Jim's Western experience.

In the penultimate chapter Jim recalls Ántonia in "a succession of . . . pictures, fixed [in his memory] like the old woodcuts of one's first primer: Ántonia kicking her bare legs against the sides of my pony when he came home . . . with our snake; Ántonia in her black shawl and fur cap, as she stood by her father's grave; Ántonia coming in with her work-team along the evening skyline." To these might be added: Ántonia in the cheerful Harling kitchen; Ántonia in a copied velveteen dress dancing at Firemen's Hall; Ántonia in a man's overcoat, pregnant, driving her steers homeward in the snow; finally, Ántonia, battered and brown, surrounded by the children tumbled from the dark fruit cave into the sunlight. Such pictures trace her development as a symbol of the West. We meet her earlier than we do Wister's hero and take our last look when she is about forty-four.

During her childhood phase Ántonia is distinguished among the Shimerdas as the favorite of her father, who provides the family with aristocratic quality. However, the Shimerdas are generally degraded. Swindled by their countryman Krajiek, who lives off them like a rattlesnake among prairie dogs, they inhabit a cave (Ántonia and her little sister Yulka are forced to sleep in a hole in the earth wall), depend on handouts and even come to expect them. Mrs. Shimerda's crude resentfulness and her son Ambrosch's sullenness are aggravated by hard times and cold and give the family a poor reputation. Mr. Shimerda remains sadly refined, however, taking whatever solace he can in daughter Ántonia's potential, appealing to Jim to teach her English. Like her father, who tries to explain that they were not beggars in the old country, Ántonia is embarrassed by her mother's alternating moods of scorn and subservience.

During the few months her father survives in Nebraska, she is free to discover with Jim the country she will one day symbolize. They share the golden foliage of autumn and spectacular sunsets, and sled through snow-covered fields. Ántonia makes distinctions between the Old World and America, and provides cultural dimension through European references. This happy sharing of the land by the two children, despite the recurring reminders of Shimerda disasters, contributes the novel's most delightful pages. The highlight of these days is the snake episode, in which Ántonia, the heroic character, instigates the situation, must be rescued by Jim, the narrator, and then through her enthusiasm romanticizes the event. Childhood ends abruptly for Ántonia when her father takes his life. We see her in the icy snow, dressed in handouts and hugging her sister Yulka, while the neighbors nail down the coffin lid.

The second phase of the hero is largely one of brutalization, but it is also the beginning of her involvement with the soil. Her brother Ambrosch, ambitious to improve the farm and make money, replaces her father as the force in her life, and Ántonia soon grows boastful like her mother, refuses Jim's reading lessons, and decides against school: "I ain't got time to learn," she tells Jim. "I can work like mans now. . . . I help make this land one good farm." She also dismisses housekeeping and domestic niceties: "Oh, better I like to work out-of-doors than in a house! . . . I not care that your grandmother say it make me like a man." Shimerda arrogance during this phase leads to a falling out with the Burdens. Previously embarrassed by her mother's crude behavior, Ántonia now follows the old lady's example, taunting "in a spiteful, crowing voice" when she meets Jim and Jake on the road after the horse collar incident. Boastful of her muscles, careless in her habits, sloppy at table, she disgusts Jim because she has become coarsely masculine: "Whenever I saw her come up the furrow, shouting at her beasts, sunburned, sweaty, her dress open at the neck and her throat and neck dust-plastered, I used to think of the tone in which poor Mr. Shimerda, who could say so little, yet managed to say so much when he exclaimed, 'My Ántonia.'"

Much of her bravado and fidelity to Ambrosch amounts to a survival effort, and Jim initially fails to detect the sacrifice involved in her neglect of the finer things she still associates with her father. At times she reveals a desire for what she gives up: "Sometime you will tell me all those nice things you learn at the school," she asks at one point, "won't you, Jimmy?" That the girl must be brutalized by the conditions of the country her family has come to for opportunities is, of course, an irony; it becomes poignant as well when, after all her boasting, she reveals to Jim her attraction to the refined life at the Burdens': "'I like your grandmother, and all things here,' she sighed." But she immediately defends cooperating with Ambrosch: "If I live here, like you, that is different. Things will be easy for you. But they will be hard for us."

Cather's hero needs rescue, not in a mock adventure from a rattlesnake but from brutalizing labor in the fields. Grandmother Burden and Mrs. Harling convince Ambrosch to allow her to take a job with the Harlings in Black Hawk, and thus begins her domestic refinement. Although the Black Hawk experience will lead to disgrace, Ántonia can appreciate its benefits in retrospect: "I'd never have known anything about cooking or housekeeping if I hadn't [come to town]. I learned nice ways at the Harlings', and I've been able to bring my children up so much better. . . . If it hadn't been for what Mrs. Harling taught me, I expect I'd have brought them up like wild rabbits." She achieves some self-sufficiency at this point, due to Mrs. Harling's insistence that an allowance be kept from the wages sent home to Ambrosch, and she rewards the efforts made in her behalf, excelling in housekeeping and baking and demonstrating the unusual maternal instincts that will eventually define her mission. She is in every way a perfect partner for Mrs. Harling. Strong, independent, and original, they share fondness for children, animals, and gardening. "They liked to prepare rich, hearty foods and to see people eat it; to make up soft white beds and to see youngsters asleep in them." In the picture we have of her at this point she is surrounded by children in the Harling kitchen baking cookies and telling stories.

As a foil to Ántonia and this picture of domestic happiness, Cather introduces Lena Lingard, a hired girl companion who has rejected marriage and motherhood for a career in dressmaking. Lena is disruptively sexual and causes Ántonia to grow dissatisfied with the restrictions of life at the Harlings'. From the start, Lena makes an issue of independence and freedom. When Ántonia hesitates to accept an invitation to her room because, she says, Mrs. Harling "don't like to have me run much," Lena's response shows pluck: "You can do what you please when you go out, can't you?" After Ántonia is "discovered" by the young bloods of Black Hawk and noisy backyard rendezvous ensue, she informs the disapproving Harlings that "A girl like me has got to take her good times when she can. . . . I guess I want to have my fling, like the other girls" (p. 208). She leaves the Harlings to work for the Cutters, who pay more and have no children.

Ántonia now becomes one of several hired girls considered dangerous to the social order maintained by Pennsylvanians, Virginians, and other established settlers. The immigrant girls are ambitious to improve themselves but forced into menial positions because they are too deficient in English to teach school and are presumed inferior: "All foreigners were ignorant people who couldn't speak English," and all hired girls are simply servants whose "beauty shone out too boldly against a conventional background." With Lena's help Ántonia acquires a cheap, stylish wardrobe and becomes the outstanding member of this "free and easy" set, parading in feathered bonnets and high heels before the local high school boys. Jim reflects that these girls "were growing prettier every day, but . . . I used to think with pride that Ántonia, like Snow-White . . . was still 'fairest of them all.'" Ántonia is pursued, first by the iceman, the delivery boys and young farmers, then by the sons of established Americans, including Jim, whose efforts are awkward and ridiculous, evoking from her responses which reveal her own conservatism. She is careful to protect him from the hired girls and expects him to do better: "You are going away to school and make something of yourself," she insists. "I'm just awful proud of you. You won't go and get mixed up with the Swedes, will you?"

Ántonia's lifestyle during this phase is no more genuine than the mannish one assumed after her father's death. Her natural innocence and refined femininity become clear when she congratulates Jim on his commencement oration and, at the picnic, when she tells him the circumstances of her parents' marriage. Her friend Anna Hansen suggests the compromise she and many of these girls have made in America: "It must make you very happy, Jim, to have fine thoughts . . . and words to put them in. I always wanted to go to school, you know." Despite her worldly-wise facade, Ántonia is vulnerable to the dangers of Black Hawk. The evil money-lender Wick Cutter tries to rape her, and she is exploited by Larry Donovan, a railroad conductor and notorious womanizer. We see her at this time in her inexpensive velveteen dress copied from Mrs. Gardener's original velvet, dancing and obviously infatuated with Donovan at Firemen's Hall.

Ántonia's darkest period, her most difficult test of character, is subsequent to her abandonment by Donovan. She later reveals to Jim that her tendency to doglike infatuation and her inability to believe harm of anybody she loves contributed to her trouble. Her trusting, open temperament becomes her weakness; as Lena comments during the Donovan affair, "She's so sort of innocent." Jim's and the reader's distance from the events of Ántonia's disgrace enables Cather to transform it into a heroic test. When Jim returns to Nebraska after two years of study at Harvard, he hears the story from Widow Steavens, who got the details from Ántonia herself. Donovan had promised marriage, arranged for Ántonia to come to Denver, got her pregnant, and jilted her. She returned to the farm, worked in the fields as she had after her father's death, and seemed "so crushed and quiet that nobody seemed to want to humble her" (p. 314). She confided her thoughts of death to Mrs. Steavens, and her feeling that she was "not going to live very long ..."

The climax of this dark period is the birth of the baby one cold night after a day full of chores. The simplicity of the telling is evocative, almost biblical, transforming disgrace into a heroic event: "She got her cattle home, turned them into the corral, and went into the house, into her room behind the kitchen, and shut the door. There, without calling to anybody, without a groan, she lay down on the bed and bore her child." Ántonia now revealed her independent spirit in her dedication to her baby, and publicized her pride in it by having a crayon enlargement displayed in a gaudy frame at the Black Hawk photographer's. A new sense of purpose replaced her thoughts of death: "[E]verybody's put into this world for something," she later tells Jim, "and I know what I've got to do. I'm going to see that my little girl has a better chance than ever I had. I'm going to take care of that girl, Jim." There is little indication at this time of the magnitude of her maternal destiny. Although Mrs. Steavens recognizes that Ántonia "is a natural-born mother," she laments, " 'I wish she could marry and raise a family, but I don't know as there's much chance now.' "

Twenty years later when he visits Ántonia, Jim explains the unique quality of her mission. Although flat-chested and without teeth, she possesses "something which fires the imagination, could still stop one's breath for a moment by a look or gesture that somehow revealed the meaning in common things. She had only to stand in the orchard, to put her hand on a little crab tree and look up at the apples to make you feel the goodness of planting and tending and harvesting at last." Although she resembles the Queen of Italy in her sensitivity toward all of life, her apotheosis does not depend upon accomplishments associated with worldly prestige. References to Tiny Soderball's fortunes and Lena's glamor are foils to scenes of Ántonia on her farm: at the dinner table, with "two long rows of restless heads in the lamplight, and so many eyes fastened excitedly upon her as she sat at the head of the table, filling the plates and starting the dishes on their way"; at the fruit cave, when her children "came running up the steps together, big and little, tow heads and gold heads and brown, and flashing little naked legs; a veritable explosion of life out of the dark cave into the sunlight."

Nor does her apotheosis derive from the dominant culture. Her rescue has not been by an established American but by a fellow Bohemian immigrant, Anton Cuzak, a cousin of the Black Hawk saloonkeeper. This "crumpled little man, with . . . one shoulder higher than the other," works the soil beside her as a yoke mate more than romantic partner. Ántonia has reverted from the Americanzation of her Black Hawk years and has difficulty speaking English because her family speaks Bohemian at home: "The little ones could not speak English at all—didn't learn it until they went to school." Pictures of Prague once sent by Jim are the prized decoration in the parlor. Old World identification and the obvious struggle to provide for so many children ("You wouldn't believe, Jim, what it takes to feed them all!") become conditions of her enthronement in the orchard like a maternal goddess, "a rich mine of life, like the founders of early races."

—JOHN J. MURPHY, "The Virginian and Ántonia Shimerda: Different Sides of the Western Coin," *Women and Western American Literature,* ed. Helen Winter Stauffer and Susan J. Rosowski (Troy, NY: Whitston, 1982), pp. 167–74

SHARON O'BRIEN

In writing *My Ántonia* (1918), considered by many critics her finest novel, Cather drew once more on the past for inspiration, this time transforming her childhood memories of the Bohemian farm girl Annie Sadilek into artistic expression. In Ántonia Shimerda, Cather offers a different version of the creative woman. Like Alexandra and Thea, she is linked with the land and its generative power, but Ántonia does not self-consciously shape or transform its energies into art. Like Cather's farm wife whose Thanksgiving meals rivaled novels and operas, Ántonia is linked with the un-self-conscious, ongoing creative processes of life. Connected with fertility and nurturance, she tends her children and her garden with equal care. When Jim Burden returns to her farmhouse after a twenty-year absence, he sees the miracle of birth she suggests re-enacted before his eyes. After leaving the fruit cave with Ántonia, he looks back to see her children "running up the steps together, big and little, tow heads and gold heads and brown, and flashing little naked legs; a veritable explosion of life out of the dark cave into the sunlight." The use of the womb/cave image implies her difference from Thea. In *The Song of the Lark,* the cave was the retreat from which the daughter was reborn as autonomous artist; here it reflects the mother's powerful fertility. Jim's meditation on Ántonia's transcendent meaning further suggests her alliance with the life force: "She had only to stand in the orchard, to put her hand on a little crab tree and look up at the apples, to make you feel the goodness of planting and tending and harvesting at last" (p. 353). By the end of the novel, Ántonia is an archetypal figure, the Earth Mother who nourishes all life. "She was a rich mine of life," Jim reflects, "like the founders of early races."

Jim's romantic vision of Ántonia as the mother of sons who stood "tall and straight" makes any simplistic feminist reading of the novel suspect. Ántonia is strong and admirable and she endures (despite missing teeth and weathered skin), but like Faulkner's Dilsey or Lena Grove, she is not a complex human being but a mythic figure viewed through male eyes. Jim's construct (the book is *My Ántonia*), she is not an autonomous subject but another version of woman as Other. But Cather, unlike Faulkner, is not promoting a romanticized male myth about women; whereas Faulkner creates Lena, Jim creates the mythic Ántonia. The reader has seen her realistically described in the early chapters and so is aware of how Jim transforms her in the final pages of the novel. In the unusual introduction where Cather introduces Jim Burden to the reader as the actual author of the novel, she stresses that *My Ántonia* is *his* version of Ántonia when she has him change the title from *Ántonia* to *My Ántonia,* the addition suggesting both possession and subjectivity.

Critical debate has centered on whether Jim's deification of Ántonia is positive or not, and hence on whether he is a reliable narrator. Although most critics trust Jim's perceptions and see the novel as a celebration of Ántonia and the American frontier, in a provocative, ground-breaking article Blanche Gelfant argued that Jim's perceptions are untrustworthy. Beset by sexual fears, she contends, he eulogizes the asexual mother Ántonia and shuns the sensual Lena, celebrating childhood and the past because he is afraid to grow up. Thus his romanticizing of Ántonia stems from his own inadequacies. "He can love only that which time had made safe and irrefragable—his memories," and thus Jim "succumbs to immobilizing regressive needs." Gelfant's article illuminates patterns in the novel unnoticed by other critics that reveal the fear of sex and passion we have seen in "The Elopement of Alan Poole" and *O Pioneers!:* Pavel and Peter's terrible story of the bride fed to the wolves; Jim's fight with the phallic snake whose "loathsome, fluid motion" makes him sick; Jim's disturbing dream of the seductive Lena with a threatening reaping-hook in her hand; Wick Cutter's attempted rape of Jim in Ántonia's bed. In contrast to "Elopement" and "The Burglar's Christmas," here Cather splits the erotic and the maternal sides of the mother between Lena and Ántonia, and Jim is drawn irresistibly toward Ántonia and the safety of a passionless relationship mediated by distance and memory.

The question of whether he "succumbs to immobilizing regressive needs" is complex, and the answer to it depends on an analysis of the relationship between author and narrator, which unfortunately is also extremely complex. Does Jim speak for Cather? Or is there ironic distance between author and narrator? The answer to both questions is yes. At times Jim is Cather's mask and spokesman, whereas at others she is ironically detached from him. This wavering distance between author and narrator makes settled interpretation difficult and probably accounts for the novel's conflicting readings; it's hard to locate Cather's point of view in this text. In the introduction Cather seems to make her separation from Jim Burden definitive by insisting that he, not she, wrote the narrative the reader is going to encounter. This unusual device, which Cather employs nowhere else, suggests that she wished to stress their separation. Her choice of a male narrator might at first seem further evidence of her wish to create a distinction between author and character, but this differentiation lessens when we note that many of the incidents of Jim's early years parallel hers. In addition, as we have seen, Cather frequently chooses male characters as masks, and since the Black Hawk years of Jim's acquaintance with Ántonia cover his adolescence, the period when Cather masqueraded as William, the sex difference between author and narrator does not seem that significant. Cather's paradoxical detachment from Jim and fusion with him continues throughout the text. At times she undercuts his perceptions; for example, the reader sees the irony when Jim first declares his superiority to the cowardly Black Hawk boys who fear the sensuous hired girls, and then flees from Lena Lingard to the celibate scholarly world ruled by the aptly named Gaston Cleric. But in the novel's conclusion Cather does not seem to question Jim's transformation of Ántonia into a "rich mine of life" nor challenge his view that in returning to Ántonia and childhood he is "coming home to [him]self." Does this mean that Cather is being both sexist and regressive here, viewing her heroine through the filter of a limiting female stereotype and celebrating the joys of returning to childhood? It does not seem to me that she is unthinkingly perpetuating and sanctioning limiting male views of women. First of all, Jim Burden is more the author's mask than a fully imagined male character, so in the novel's conclusion we are presented with a *woman's* construction of another woman's meaning, with Cather again resorting to camouflage when revealing her deepest preoccupations. In addition, although the Earth Mother can be a limiting stereotype, the image of woman as possessing mythic powers of fertility and nurturance could be interpreted as Cather's re-claiming and reworking of a male-perpetuated stereotype which she uses to enhance rather than limit woman's dignity and stature.

The question of whether we should call this a regressive fantasy remains. Gelfant argues that "retrospection, a superbly creative act for Cather, becomes for Jim a negative gesture." In this view, Cather is driven by the same urges as her narrator—to return to the past and retrieve the child's relationship with the mother—but she writes a novel from these urges, whereas the narrator is passive and empty, a "wasteland" figure. Certainly Cather's satisfying of regressive urges in the creative process was a positive way of dealing with such impulses, but I would argue that Jim does the same. Finally he is not regressive in the sense that William was in "The Burglar's Christmas"; Jim, as Cather's fiction has it, does not merely narrate a story. He *writes the novel*. He thus is Cather's alter ego, the author compelled to create by the conflicts he cannot fully resolve in life, moved like Willa Cather to write by his yearning for a lost maternal figure, Ántonia Shimerda/Annie Sadilek.

—SHARON O'BRIEN, "Mothers, Daughters, and the 'Art Necessity':
Willa Cather and the Creative Process," *American Novelists Revisited:
Essays in Feminist Criticism,* ed. Fritz Fleischmann (Boston:
G. K. Hall, 1982), pp. 284–87

JAMIE AMBROSE

No single work (with the possible exception of 'Old Mrs. Harris') contains so many clearly traceable elements of Willa Cather's life as does *My Ántonia*. Red Cloud appears again, this time as Black Hawk. William and Caroline Cather are present as Josiah and Emmaline Burden. The entire Miner family play the parts of the Harlings; Herbert Bates serves as the model for Gaston Cleric. Even secondary characters, such as Blind d'Arnault, the Negro pianist, or Wick Cutter, the degenerate moneylender, have their origins in people from Cather's past. The author herself is thinly disguised as James Quayle Burden, better known as Jim, and the description of his personality written into the introduction could easily be used as a definition of Willa Cather.

Jim Burden possessed a 'naturally romantic and ardent disposition', which, the author decided, 'made him seem very funny as a boy'—a reference to her own youthful eccentricities perhaps? It is precisely that ardent quality, however, that has been the secret of his success. 'He loves with a personal passion the great country through which his railway runs and branches', we are told, and even though he is now a mature middle-aged man, Jim is still able 'to lose himself in those big Western dreams'. He could be Willa Cather's twin, right down to his changeable blue eyes.

The most revealing phrase comes when the anonymous author makes a deal with Jim. It is agreed that they should each write down their impressions of Ántonia, a Bohemian girl they knew on the Divide, and the heroine of the novel. 'Of course', Jim replies ponderously, 'I should have to do it in a direct way, and say a good deal about myself. It's through myself that I knew and felt her. . . .'

And here we are left with an enigma. Willa Cather was to say in an interview that most of what she knew about Annie Sadilek, Ántonia's real-life counterpart, had come from the impressions of young men who knew her; Woodress adds that she wrote as much to Will Owen Jones, maintaining that, due to her experience of ghosting for S. S. McClure, she felt competent to write as from a first-person male character. Yet so many of Jim Burden's experiences are clearly her own, and the narration *is* direct, does reveal much about herself; one wonders whether Cather didn't use this male character as a shield for her private life—not necessarily in lesbian terms, but because prying eyes annoyed her in any case. The true extent to which Jim Burden is autobiographical will always be subject to speculation; there is no such problem, however, with Ántonia herself, the heroine of the novel.

Ántonia Shimerda, the Bohemian immigrant girl around whom the story revolves, was based upon a real-life friend of the Cather family, Annie Sadilek, whom Cather always tried to visit during her trips back to Red Cloud. Three years after *My Ántonia* was published, Willa Cather would declare that Annie was 'one of the truest artists I ever knew in the keenness and sensitiveness of her enjoyment, in her love of people and in her willingness to take pains'. In short, Annie was a natural artist, an unconscious embodiment of both land and woman, as strong and beautiful an image in herself as the famous plough against the sun. If Thea Kronborg emerged as vital because she had been endowed with Cather's own passion, how much more alive does Ántonia seem—she had, after all, been modelled upon a living being whom the author loved deeply. Because the story was one of feeling, Cather chose to construct it in the first person. The result of that emotional depth has frequently been called the finest of Cather's novels.

In telling the story, the author discarded the excessive detail she had used in *The Song of the Lark* (between Fremstad's magnetism and her own emotional/ mnemonic outpourings, Cather had been unable to resist the urge to tell everything). With the character of Annie Sadilek, she returned to the process of simplification and began to act upon the principles of writing which were eventually set down in 'The Novel Démeublé', her essay on the 'unfurnished' novel. 'The higher processes of art', she declared, 'are all processes of simplification. The novelist must learn to write, and then he must unlearn it. . . .' And to be sure, *My Ántonia* is beautiful in and because of its simplicity.

Five sections trace the life of Ántonia Shimerda through the eyes of Jim Burden: as a child enduring the harsh life of the Divide; as a hired girl at the Miners' in Black Hawk; as the young woman Jim leaves behind when he goes away to college (away from him, Ántonia goes on to her fate of pregnancy and abandonment by an unscrupulous railroadman); finally, some twenty years later, Jim returns to the Divide to find that Ántonia has come into her own at last. In direct contrast to his own unhappy union, she is married and radiant, the wife of a good-hearted, unambitious Bohemian (Anton Cuzak) and the mother of a swarm of beautiful children. The children are her crowning glory; all will grow up unashamed of their native tongue, and all will adhere to the old-fashioned values and manners that were so dear to Willa Cather's heart. They are Ántonia's legacy: hope for the future, carrying within themselves the traditions of the past.

Though haggard and worn by the end of the novel, Ántonia is none the less Cather's greatest triumphant persona, the embodiment of all that is good in life and love, a natural Madonna of the Plains, a shining symbol of the art of life. Years before, when Jim was about to leave for college, he, Ántonia, and two other 'hired girls' (the term grated upon Isabelle's Eastern sensibilities) had gone on a farewell picnic beside the river on the edge of town. As the sun began to set, they witnessed the following scene—surely one of the most-quoted passages of American literature:

> Just as the lower edge of the red disk rested on the high fields against the horizon, a great black figure suddenly appeared. . . . In a moment we realized what it was. On some upland farm, a plough had been left standing in the field. The sun was sinking just behind it. Magnified across the distance by the horizontal light, it stood out against the sun, was exactly contained within the circle of the disk; the handles, the tongue, the share—black against the molten red. There it was, heroic in size, a picture writing on the sun.

The greatness of the image lasts only for an instant; then it fails, absorbed once again into the vastness of the prairie. Although the vision may be taken to stand for a number of things—the enduring quality of man and the country, for example—the impression is most like Ántonia herself.

After seeing her as a triumphal figure in the midst of her family, Jim thinks that Ántonia had always been a woman to leave 'images in the mind that did not fade—that grew stronger with time'. His musing searches for the secret of her inner beauty: 'She still had that something which fires the imagination, could still stop one's breath for a moment by a look or gesture that somehow revealed a meaning in common things. . . . She was a rich mine of life, like the founders of early races.'

Alexandra Bergson comes to terms with the land, using her love and under-standing strength to create a life out of the soil. Thea Kronborg reconciles herself to the passion of music. Both possess a singlemindedness of purpose, great love, and great imagination, and both achieve success at a price. While sharing their traits of love and strength, Ántonia Shimerda brings with her a subtle difference. She does not strive consciously towards an ideal; she simply lives and loves, loves everything: land, people, life itself. She reveals an ideal by her own existence, and though she, too, has suffered hardship—a father's suicide, a slavedriving brother, a lover's desertion—hers is the most complete triumph.

In one respect, Ántonia may almost be viewed as a synthesis of Alexandra and Thea. Alexandra is an extension of nature; Thea, an extension of the beauty of the creative impulse. Both join together in Ántonia who, with the strength of one and the sensitivity of the other, becomes a nearly perfect whole. There are, however, several characteristics which the three heroines have in common. All come from foreign stock; two of the three are immigrants and retain the use of their mother tongue and, while Thea was born in the New World, it is her Old-World Swed-ishness that sets her apart—one could never classify her as belonging to the 'Americans'. All are strong women, survivors, yet they manage to retain a high degree of sensitivity in a harsh environment; and all, of course, have come through hardship to triumph.

When the novels are viewed as a whole, they are suggestively autobiographi-cal, indicating that Cather had been reliving her own past, coming to terms with it through writing her books. In the first, the land is the overpowering image, just as it was to Willa the child. Next, art comes to the fore and, through Thea, one can see Cather's own awakening to creative talent, and the subsequent struggles to-wards success; while the *Lark* was being written, she was experiencing her own 'debut' with *O Pioneers!*—much like Thea's arrival at the Met. Finally, these two lives are combined in Ántonia. By writing herself so vividly into the novel, Cather had come to terms with her own origins once and for all, discovering the great depth of her love not only for the land but also for the arts and for the intrinsic beauty of life and its natural, human and eternal manifestations in the beauty of 'common things'. She had come to realise that there was just as much 'art' contained in a large, loving Bohemian family in Nebraska as there was in the voice of a Wagnerian prima donna; Cather had caught up with herself, with her own present. It is no coincidence that Jim Burden's narrative ends with an account of his 'revisi-tation' to Ántonia after a long absence. A few years previously Cather herself had

had just such an encounter with Annie Sadilek, now Pavelka. With *My Ántonia* she had finally arrived at the present. The only part of her own early life as yet unreconciled was her Virginian heritage, and that would take almost a lifetime to achieve.

—JAMIE AMBROSE, *Willa Cather: Writing at the Frontier*
(Oxford: Berg, 1988), pp. 95–99

SUSIE THOMAS

My Ántonia, then, may be read as a *Georgic* with epic overtones. But it differs from Virgil in one important respect in that its emphasis is female. Epic, and even pastoral, is largely a male affair, but Cather focused her attention on the pioneer women. Although the narrator is male he is not in himself of paramount importance. He exists — as a sympathetic involved narrator, informed with a Virgilian perspective in order, largely, to evoke them. And the fact that she chose a male narrator was simply one of convenience; she said at the time that she had no intention of 'writing like a man' but clearly she could not have used a female narrator to describe the hired girls without introducing irrelevant complications.

Ántonia, of course, is the most compelling of Cather's 'jeunes filles en fleur' but she is only one of a group. Indeed there is a kind of female network in the novel with the connections between families, and the relations between the generations, being maintained largely by the women. When Jim arrives in Nebraska, for example, it is his grandmother with whom he establishes a relationship; his grandfather remaining always a distantly impressive figure, benignly patriarchal. Mrs. Burden is domestic, capable, humorous and frank: 'a strong woman, of unusual endurance'. It is she who visits the Shimerdas, takes the provisions, and when Ántonia later comes to town, Mrs. Burden finds her a job with Mrs. Harling. The young Bohemian and the middle-aged Norwegian suit each other very well: 'There was a basic harmony between Ántonia and her mistress. They had strong, independent natures, both of them . . . They loved children and animals and music, and rough play and digging in the earth.' They are powerful figures who dominate without being dogmatic.

Frances Harling is a pioneer woman in a different way. She is in partnership with her father and the two of them 'discuss grain-cars and cattle, like two men.' She knows all the farming families in the area and feels an almost maternal concern for them; her interest 'was more than a business interest. She carried them all in her mind as if they were characters in a book or a play'. She often steps in to save them from the unscrupulous money lender, Wick Cutter. The important role played by women in the life of the community is underlined when Ántonia falls into social disgrace; only the Widow Steavens befriends her and it is she who tells Jim, Ántonia's story.

The immigrant girls relate to the older women in a social scheme which is both Virgilian and matriarchal: '[They] learned so much from life, from poverty, from their mothers and grandmothers; they had all, like Ántonia, been early awakened and made observant by coming at a tender age from an old country to a new.' The girls feel particularly the older women's sense of exile. Tiny Soderball hopes her mother will not feel so 'homesick' since they began growing rye; Anna takes home canned fish for her rambling grandmother who ' "thinks she's at home in Norway" '; Lena works so that her mother can move out of the sod house, knowing that ' "the men will never do it" '.

Respectable Black Hawk looks down on them as ignorant foreigners who are in service but it is because the girls work and remain loyal to their families that their farms do better than their neighbours'. Jim's partisan narration trumpets their success:

> I always knew I should live long enough to see my country girls come into their own, and I have. To-day the best that a harassed Black Hawk merchant can hope for is to sell provisions and farm machinery and automobiles to the rich farms where the first crop of stalwart Bohemian and Scandinavian girls are now the mistresses.

Part of Black Hawk's fear stems from the hired girls' looser 'morality'. Tiny Soderball, working at the hotel, flirts with the travelling salesmen; Lena has a series of lovers; while the three Bohemian Marys 'were the heroines of a cycle of scandalous stories' and are considered 'as dangerous as high explosives'. The young men of the town would rather dance with the fresh-smelling Danish girls who work in the laundry than with their frigid classmates but though the girls, as Ántonia says, are out to get their good times while they can, they are not interested in catching husbands. We do not hear each of their destinies but Tiny remains unmarried, making a fortune in the Klondike; Lena too remains single, prospering as a dressmaker, while Ántonia marries from among her own people.

Lena's aversion is not to men but to marriage, providing an interesting contrast with Ántonia. Lena has a very attractive character: practical and sensuous — a waltz with Lena was like coming in with the tide — and somehow perpetually innocent. Even as a smartly dressed townswoman she still seems like the cowgirl with white legs who unwittingly drove Ole Benson mad with desire. She is determined to become independent and to help her family but she has no intention of marrying: 'She remembered home as a place where there were always too many children, a cross man and work piling up around a sick woman' (291). In the end she lives comfortably, takes lovers when she chooses, and turns down all suitors for her hand: ' "It's all being under somebody's thumb" '.

The hired girls' various destinies are all presented as equally valid. Whether they become farmers, prospectors or business women they are all pioneers. Cather neither judges nor prescribes: Lena's childlessness is not sterile, Ántonia's poverty is not failure. Ántonia is the most engaging and sympathetic of all Cather's creations. She is vividly brought to life through a series of scenes filtered through Jim's cherishing memory. She first appears as the pretty little Bohemian girl, unable to speak a word of English, and the object of her father's adoration. After his death she is set to work by her brother. She ploughs the fields and does heavy chores:

'the farm-hands around the country joked in a nasty way about it'. She brags about her strength and eats noisily 'like a man'. Sunburned and sweaty, clad in her dead father's boots, in the fields all day, Mrs. Shimerda fears that she'll lose all her nice ways" '. ' "She is determined that her family will prosper in the New World despite their poor start and is defensive at the least suggestion of being patronised. When Jim, for example, quotes his grandfather's weather forecast, Ántonia rudely remarks ' "He not Jesus" '.

She is seen next in more propitious circumstances, working for the Harlings in Black Hawk. Here she sews, bakes, sings, tells stories and plays with the children. She is both in service and part of the family, without conflict, until the arrival of the dancing tent. After this she thinks of nothing but clothes and having her ' "fling" '; she moves to the Cutter's house so that she will have more free time. Wick Cutter's attempted rape (Jim has been planted in Ántonia's bed to foil him) is as hilarious as anything in Mark Twain but it has sinister overtones for, despite her strength and intelligence, Ántonia's sexuality necessarily makes her vulnerable. Her seduction by the worthless Larry Donovan is not narrated directly. 'Poor Ántonia's' disgrace occurs while Jim is away. The events are narrated by the Widow Steavens with an almost Biblical resonance: ' "She got her cattle home, turned them into the corral, and went into the house, into her room behind the kitchen, and shut the door. There, without calling to anybody, without a groan, she lay down on the bed and bore her child." ' Ántonia refuses to become pathetic or to be ashamed of her child, deliberately having her baby's photograph on display in the photographer's window in Black Hawk.

Her final manifestation is as the pioneer mother, married to Ánton Cuzak and presiding over her prodigious family. Jim delays visiting her, fearing that she will have become 'aged and broken'. The male disillusion on discovering that the beautiful girl next door has turned into a dull middle-aged housewife, which crops up with predictable regularity in fiction, is exposed here for all its sentimentality. It is one of the novel's crowning glories that though Ántonia is changed—practically toothless, even—she is still radiant: 'Ántonia came in and stood before me; a stalwart, brown woman, flat-chested, her curly brown hair a little grizzled. . . . She was there, in the full vigour of her personality, battered but not diminished'. With her children teeming around her on the bright, sunny farm, Ántonia has been described as an incarnation of Venus Genetrix.[9] But only Cather could create an earth mother with such an inconspicuous bust line.

Ántonia's household is a Bohemian one: Jim is offered coffee and *kolaches*, pictures of Prague hang on the parlour walls, the children cannot even speak English until they go to school. John J. Murphy in his essay 'The Virginian and Ántonia Shimerda' notes this, and relates it to the fact that Ántonia is seduced by an American and 'rescued by one of her own, Ánton Cuzak'. He refers to this as an '[understandable] cultural reversion' and seems to feel that it requires some kind of apology or explanation: 'She inhabits an immigrant West opposed in many ways to the dominant culture, and identifies with the differences which have limited her.' Cather, however, would certainly not have regarded the Old World heritage as a limiting factor—quite the reverse—for the novel is about the transplanting of European culture in American soil and repeatedly affirms Old World values. Moreover, the prospect of a 'dominant culture' is exactly what Cather objected to, fearing that it would amount to little more than bland conformity and standardisation. As I tried to show earlier, part of her intention in *My Ántonia* was precisely to show that there was an alternative to the prevailing 'white', male, Protestant mythology of the West.

Cather's ideal was an intermingling of Old and New; a rich, regional variety. When Jim, for example, makes a picture book for Yulka that snowy Christmas, he uses coloured pictures from cards he had 'brought from [his] "old country"', Virginia. What depressed Cather was the thought that the past—whether colonial or immigrant—could be lost, discarded in the race to get ahead, and that the distinctive customs of each area—born of the marriage of native geography and European settlement—could be obliterated in a vast sameness stretching from one end of America to the other. The 'conservatism' of her later years was really this: despair that the descendants of the Old World immigrants would trade in their household gods for automobiles.

Ántonia's life is, as Murphy suggests, limited: she could not go to school or marry one of Black Hawk's respectable citizens but she has an identity of her own, a language, beliefs and values. More importantly, she hands these on to her children who grow up both with an awareness of their national origins and full able to take advantage of the opportunities in America. Ántonia on the farm, then, is not in retreat from Black Hawk. She inherits from her father and bequeaths to her own children the Virgilian love of old customs, rituals and beliefs; the continuity of the Old World in the New.

The transplanting of European culture to America is given a literal embodiment in a motif which occurs frequently in Cather's work: her immigrants are invariably to be found planting trees, protecting them from frost and watering them during the long hot summers. One can think of the Kohlers in *The Song of the Lark*, the Shabatas in *O Pioneers!*, or old Appelhof in *The Professor's House* and for all of them planting and tending has a Virgilian significance, both for its natural value (remembering the treatise on the propagation of trees in the *Georgics*) and as an act of reverence; a reminder of the distant homeland. It seems fitting that one of the final images of Ántonia should be in a garden and that it should be connected with her Virgilian 'mission' as the founder of a new civilisation:

> She had only to stand in the orchard, to put her hand on a little crab tree and look up at the apples, to make you feel the goodness of planting and tending and harvesting at last. . . .
>
> It was no wonder that her sons stood tall and straight. She was a rich mine of life, like the founders of early races.

—SUSIE THOMAS, "The Golden Girl of the West: My Ántonia,"
Willa Cather (London: Macmillan, 1990), pp. 92–98

LINDA WAGNER-MARTIN

Cather's *My Ántonia* made her craft, and her ability to disguise what her story implied, even clearer. Using the obtuse and romantic Jim Burden as narrator, Cather created a fiction that both revealed and obscured its protagonist. If a reader were to rely on Jim's recounting, he or she would never understand the power and sacrifice of Ántonia's life because Burden himself does not understand the story. (His self-satisfied postscript to her story, in which he and her husband and children become friends, leaves Ántonia out entirely, beyond picturing her as some earth mother in residence.) Cather's experimentation with point of view—the remarkable device of having the Widow Steavens provide the most wrenching story, of Ántonia's betrayal—marks this as a classic modernist text.

F. Scott Fitzgerald learned a great deal from *My Ántonia*—and from Cather's *A Lost Lady*, in which the story is again told through the eyes of a male character rather than from the perspective of the woman protagonist—when he created Nick Carraway to narrate *The Great Gatsby*. The double novel, the story of two characters inextricably interwoven, was a useful form, but in the case of Cather's using it to allow a male character to tell a woman's story, it was probably misleading. Her structure allowed her narrative to remain socially conservative (the male narrator's views represented mainstream opinion, judging and lamenting the woman's choices). Cather as author was then able to cast doubt on the premise that a male narrator could tell a woman's story accurately.

For instance, Jim sees the country roads—along which migrants, including Ántonia, labor unendingly—as "roads to freedom," bordered with sunflowers. The reader knows that Jim has never worked in that countryside. The child of a middle-class family, destined to be educated and sent away from the prairie, he has shared none of the immigrant families' experiences. Ironically, during their childhood, Ántonia was the storyteller, not Jim. As he recalled, "We all liked Tony's stories. Her voice had a peculiarly engaging quality; it was deep, a little husky, and one always heard the breath vibrating behind it. Everything she said seemed to come right out of her heart." The stories Ántonia tells are so realistic as to be macabre. They are about the grotesques of the farm life, far from the happy-ending placebos that Jim chooses to recount. The discrepancy between what Ántonia tells when they are growing up, and what Jim fashions in his maturity, warns the reader that the latter's accounts are not trustworthy. Nostalgia has colored his memories.

In both *My Ántonia* and *A Lost Lady*, the narrator is not only male; he is a young male who, supposedly, matures as the story develops. First, the romantic adolescent is responsible for the narration; then the adult male whose life has been reasonably pleasant. Each tells the account of a complex woman. The result of this narrative control is that the reader mistrusts all information that comes by way of this narrator. The novel becomes a fragmented assortment of pieces of text, and the reader's work is to put those pieces together reasonably. For all its smooth delivery of event, both of Cather's novels are as intricately structured as any modernist fiction.

Cather's language is also misleadingly effortless in its polish and choice of diction. Because the narrators are educated boys and men, living with well-educated families and heading themselves for polite social lives, their word choice is appropriate. Occasionally the reader hears the real words of Ántonia and Marian Forrester, but those episodes serve only to point up the differences between the women as they are "recollected" by the narrators and the characters as they existed in their own language and being. For instance, when Marian comes to the law office to use the telephone after Frank Ellinger has married, Niel would have used different language and a different set of circumstances to remember that episode. As it is, he cuts the telephone lines with scissors before Marian can tell Frank off completely—saying he does not want the telephone operator to know the story. Her emphatic dialogue leaves no question as to her anger that her lover has married ("Play safe! When have you ever played anything else? You know, Frank, the truth is that you're a coward; a great, hulking coward. Do you hear me? I want you to hear"). In response to this powerful scene, Niel says only, "For once he had been quick enough; he had saved her."[9] Cutting telephone lines does not save the angry woman at all, and her collapse shows the agony of rage she suffers. The emotional lives of both Ántonia and Marian are so far removed from the understanding of their narrators that Cather barely escapes being cynical. As My Ántonia ends, for example, Jim Burden is filled with self-congratulatory good feeling: he has returned, and he has befriended Ántonia and her family and her husband, Cuzak. He thinks with pleasure on the rest of his life in that role of friend: "My mind was full of pleasant things; trips I meant to take with the Cuzak boys, in the Bad Lands and up on the Stinking Water. There were enough Cuzaks to play with for a long while yet. Even after the boys grew up, there would always be Cuzak himself!" The irony of Jim's coming to find Ántonia and ending up with a ready-made family of young boys who adore him, or another male comrade he can feel superior to, points again to the unsettling kind of characterization Cather allows in the text. Ántonia was never anything other than a male appendage—someone's daughter, someone's sister, someone's servant girl, someone's mother and wife. In the highest praise Jim is possible of giving, he says to her, "I think of you more often than of anyone else in this part of the world. I'd have liked to have you for a sweetheart, or a wife, or my mother or my sister—*anything that a woman can be to a man*" (emphasis added).

—LINDA WAGNER-MARTIN, *The Modern American Novel 1914–1945: A Critical History* (Boston: Twayne, 1990), pp. 16–18

CRITICAL ESSAYS
John H. Randall III
THE WORLD OF NATURE

Themes of *My Ántonia*

My Ántonia is the most famous of Willa Cather's prairie novels and is generally considered to be her best. It contains the fullest celebration ever to come from her pen of country life as opposed to the life of the cities, for the book is one long paean of praise to the joys of rural living and shows her a passionate advocate of the virtues of a settled agricultural existence. In *My Ántonia* the rural-urban conflict hardly seems to exist. The characters pass from farm to town or city and back again without feeling any incompatibility between value systems; instead they manage to extract the maximum of joy from each. But it is always the country to which they return; Ántonia permanently after a brief sojourn in Black Hawk (Red Cloud) and Denver, and the narrator Jim Burden periodically whenever he can get away from his job in a large Eastern city. Native born or immigrant, all the good characters in the book sooner or later yield to the spell of the land, and there is no doubt in the author's mind as to whether country or city is the real America.

My Ántonia thus clarifies certain values which *O Pioneers!* had left up in the air. It is as if Willa Cather had finally made up her mind that her true allegiance was to the soil. The earlier book had shown that life on the farm yielded satisfactions which were deep but narrow; certain things essential to civilized existence just were not to be found there. In the later work all that anyone could ever hope for is pictured as being found on a farm. Ántonia has managed to make her husband happy for twenty-six years in one of the loneliest regions in the world, even though he was a city man and occasionally had spells of homesickness for the theaters and lighted cafés of the Old World.

But more important than this, the two books show different stages in the

From *The Landscape and the Looking Glass: Willa Cather's Search for Value* (Boston: Houghton Mifflin, 1960), pp. 105–8, 119–22, 127–30, 138–49.

development of civilization. In *O Pioneers!* the greatest interest centers on the actual taming of the earth, the breaking of the virgin soil; only incidentally is it concerned with the attempt to found a family. The love of Emil and Marie is snuffed out and so cannot take root, and the proposed marriage of Carl and Alexandra is postponed until after the book's ending. In *My Ántonia,* on the other hand, there is much less emphasis on pioneering. What interested Willa Cather here is the quality of life on the plains, and for once in her career she focuses squarely on and affirms human relations. Much of the book deals with the attempts of the internal narrator and his heroine to come to grips with their emotional involvement with people. This finally results in Ántonia's establishing a domestic household as a going concern and the narrator's failing to do so. Ántonia's great achievement and the chief subject of the book is the founding of a family.

Ántonia and Jim: The Contrasting Life Cycles

My Ántonia has an interesting and rather peculiar introduction or prologue. In it Willa Cather pretends to have met Jim Burden, the fictitious narrator of the tale, on a train and has them agree that each one of them shall set down on paper his impressions of Ántonia, a mutual friend of their childhood. After months go by they meet again to find that Jim is the only one who has written anything; the rest of the book purports to be his manuscript. Thereafter Willa Cather herself drops out of the story as a separate character. The book that follows really consists of the parallel stories of Ántonia and Jim. The narrator points this out to us while explaining what he has written. "I simply wrote down what of herself and myself and other people Ántonia's name recalls to me. I suppose it hasn't any form. It hasn't any title either."[1] Then he clinches the fact that this is to be the story of a relationship rather than of an individual by changing the wording on the front of the manuscript from "Ántonia" to "My Ántonia."[2]

My Ántonia is usually called a novel with a single protagonist—the heroine— and the narrator has been considered relatively unimportant.[3] I would like to suggest a different interpretation, because the role played by Jim Burden seems to me far too important to be merely that of a first-person onlooker who is relating someone else's story. He enters into the action too much, for one thing. In the early part of the book the Burden family is continually trudging over to their neighbors the Shimerdas to see if they can help them out. Later on there is a long section in which Jim attends the University of Nebraska and flirts with Lena Lingard; here Ántonia scarcely even appears. Even in the parts of the book where Ántonia and Jim appear together, Jim's reactions to events are at least as important as hers. If Willa Cather wanted her heroine to hold the undisputed center of the stage, she should have focused less attention on her narrator. As it is, the center of interest shifts back and forth between Jim and Ántonia, and the result is best understood as the story of parallel lives.

In her later novels Willa Cather often has a double protagonist such as this, one of whom resembles herself and the other someone who is not herself but whom she admires. One of these usually stands for the contemplative life, the other for the life of action. The use of a double protagonist has certain advantages: it allows one character to be an actor and the other a spectator; one can be youth which performs and accomplishes unthinkingly, the other middle age which can interpret the significance of action in others but itself has lost the capacity to act. In *My Ántonia* this double protagonist consists of Jim Burden and Ántonia, who, true to the best traditions of the romantic movement, stand for head and heart, respectively. It is as if Ántonia actually lives life, while Jim merely records it, or at best lives vicariously through her. When he is with her, Jim is a complete personality and reaches his highest development as a human being, but his personal life falls apart when he leaves her, however successful he may be in his professional role. Later in the book when he returns to visit Nebraska after a twenty years' absence, he finds out just how far Ántonia has forged ahead of him during that time. He is generous enough to rejoice in her good fortune, but it merely underlines his own lack of progress, and even regression, during that same interval. The more she tells him about her successful present, the more his mind wanders back to thoughts of their childhood together. Together he and the friend of his youth make a complete personality, but it is Janus-faced, one of them looking forward and the other back. Ántonia has the whole future for her domain; Jim Burden has only the past.

The principle on which this parallel story is constructed is that of development by contrasts. For in spite of early childhood experiences shared together, the lives of the two protagonists are radically unlike. Ántonia comes to Nebraska as an immigrant and in addition to other hardships of the plains has to face a language barrier; Jim Burden comes from Virginia and faces no such problem. Ántonia comes from a family wracked by internal dissensions, and her father is so unhappy that he commits suicide, largely because her mother is not a homemaker; Jim's family is a well-knit group in which order and happiness are maintained by a pair of extremely competent homemakers, his grandparents. The Shimerdas suffer from poverty for a great many years; the Burdens never have to meet this particular difficulty. As a result Jim can leave home and receive a university education, while Ántonia cannot even afford to take time off from the farm to attend grade school and learn English properly. Finally Jim leaves Nebraska for good to make his home in a large Eastern city where he enters into an unhappy and childless marriage; Ántonia stays on in Black Hawk and after a single unsuccessful effort succeeds not only in marrying but in founding a dynasty, having eleven children by the time Jim comes back to visit her twenty years later.

Although the two lives run parallel and are given almost equally extensive treatment, no doubt is left in the reader's mind that Ántonia is the one who has achieved the real success. Willa Cather loads the story in Ántonia's favor, not only by emphasizing Jim's obvious admiration for her, but by making all the significant action take place in Nebraska; Jim Burden's marriage and Eastern career are mentioned merely in passing. Accordingly, the early years on the plains are heavily stressed. This is not surprising, since the two main characters see relatively little of each other after childhood. But it does contribute mightily to the mood of nostalgia which is so strong an ingredient in Jim Burden's personality and which swells toward the end of the book into a hymn of praise for the past which Willa Cather aptly sums up in a line quoted from Vergil: "*Optima dies . . . prima fugit*" (*Georgics*, III, 66–67).

Death in Winter and the Hardness of Life

One of the strong points of *My Ántonia* as compared with Willa Cather's other novels is that in it she comes closer than she usually does to facing the problem of evil and suffering in life. This frankness in recognizing the reality of problems which are ultimately insoluble gives the book an emotional depth which one looks for in vain in much of her work. If by evil we mean anything impairing the happiness or welfare of a person or depriving him of good, there is a good deal of evil in *My Ántonia*. Briefly, the varieties Willa Cather describes can be summed up under three headings: natural or external nonhuman evil, man-made evil inflicted by other people, and evil which is self-inflicted.

Natural evil is the simplest of the three and in a sense is no problem at all. One meets it on the frontier or elsewhere by pitting oneself against the forces of nature, and one either succeeds or fails. Sometimes one proves oneself a man by overcoming natural forces, as does the youthful Jim when he kills the great rattlesnake which attacks him in prairie-dog town. Sometimes it is the forces of nature which triumph over man.

Man-made evil inflicted by other persons is more complicated and cannot be summed up so easily. I have described how the Bohemian Krajiek exploited his fellow countrymen the Shimerdas. Another example is Wick Cutter, the Black Hawk money lender, whom Willa Cather treats as a comic character in spite of the ferocious reputation she gives him. He fastens like a bloodsucker upon the poverty-stricken farmers of the neighborhood, and Grandfather Burden has had to rescue more than one poor devil from his clutches. He has an interestingly unhappy relation with his wife which can be summed up by her remark to him when, in exhibiting some of her chinaware to a caller, he accidentally drops a piece: "Mr. Cutter, you have broken all the commandments—spare the finger-bowls!"[4] As they grow older they quarrel continually over the disposal of his estate should she survive him; he is afraid that it will all go to her "people," whom he hates. He finally solves the problem melodramatically by murdering her and then shooting himself an hour later, after firing a shot out the window to insure the presence of witnesses to testify to the fact that he had survived his wife and that therefore any will she might have made would be invalid. Willa Cather's comic treatment of Wick Cutter tends to preclude any real consideration of the moral implications of his acts, since he is turned into a character in a grand farce. As a comic figure of evil he lacks reality and seems to have no relation to the world as we know it; evidently Willa Cather does not intend to have him taken too seriously.

A more telling example of man-made evil inflicted by others can be found in Ántonia's pregnancy. She falls in love with a railroad conductor named Larry

Donovan, a "train-crew aristocrat" who fancies himself a ladies' man; he lures her to Denver with promises of marriage and then deserts her, leaving her with a child on the way. Unlike the love passages in *O Pioneers!* this is not presented directly to the reader. Instead of being narrated by Jim Burden, it is told to him by another person, the Widow Steavens, since the episode has occurred after Jim has left the University of Nebraska for Harvard. The Widow Steavens is a pioneer, an older woman of the same generation and stature as Jim's grandparents, and so her comments on the tale carry a moral authority which they would not if they had issued from the lips of a younger person. In her mouth the story of Ántonia's seduction assumes overtones that are almost tragic: the bad prosper, the good come to misfortune through their very virtues, and no one knows why:

> "Jimmy, I sat right down on that bank beside her and made lament. I cried like a young thing. I couldn't help it. I was just about heart-broke.... My Ántonia, that had so much good in her, had come home disgraced. And that Lena Lingard, that was always a bad one, say what you will, had turned out so well, and was coming home here every summer in her silks and her satins, and doing so much for her mother. I give credit where credit is due, but you know well enough, Jim Burden, there is a great difference in the principles of those two girls. And here it was the good one that had come to grief!"[5]

For all her heartbrokenness the Widow Steavens does not turn against Ántonia as Jim does; with the ferocity of youth he cannot forgive her for becoming an object of pity. The Widow Steavens, on the other hand, is able to accept the fact that there is a tragic incomprehensibility in the fates meted out to human beings; she can admit that Ántonia has made a mistake and still believe in her. This makes her superior to Jim, whose immediate reaction to Ántonia is one of rejection as soon as the image he has of her is broken. Jim is a typical Willa Cather character in this; he makes a hard-and-fast rule about people and things and prefers to see the world in terms of black and white.

But Ántonia does not remain an object of pity for long. Like Hester Prynne, she gains from suffering a new kind of strength, and finally is accepted even by the community:

> "Folks respected her industry and tried to treat her as if nothing had happened. They talked, to be sure; but not like they would if she'd put on airs. She was so crushed and quiet that nobody seemed to want to humble her."[6]

Her bitter experience has given her more self-knowledge than Marie Shabata ever had a chance to learn; she now knows the dangers as well as the delights of unbridled spontaneity and of absolute commitment to the objects of one's affection. As she tells Jim when he comes back to visit her twenty years after, "The trouble with me was, Jim, I never could believe harm of anybody I loved."[7]

One would expect the birth of Ántonia's illegitimate child to form the climax of the book, but no. The whole episode is only thirty pages long and is related to Jim Burden by a third person, the Widow Steavens. In other words, the reader is not once removed from the action but twice removed from it. This in itself is the most significant thing about the whole event. It shows a trait highly characteristic of Willa Cather's fiction—that in it she did not really want to present directly any sort of serious human conflict. The really emotional situations, the scenes in which it was necessary to face up to the hard facts about human nature and passions, she avoided if she could. Of *My Ántonia* she said:

> There was material in that book for a lurid melodrama. But I decided that in writing it, I would dwell very lightly on those things that a novelist would ordinarily emphasize, and make up my story of the little, every-day happenings and occurrences that form the greatest part of everyone's life and happiness.[8]

If this was her attitude one may ask why she bothered including the story of the birth of the baby at all. For she was not bound to follow in every detail the life of the person upon which the character of Ántonia was based. The fact that she chose both to include the episode and to treat it in the precise way that she did indicates that she was bent on devaluing some of the devastating conflicts that occur in life, particularly those relating to sex. And if this is so she is being dishonest and evasive, and her representation of the human scene suffers from distortion in consequence.

Country vs. Town: The Superiority of the Countryside

The middle portion of the book, which is largely the story of Jim's school and college days, deals with a problem which we have seen was left unsolved at the end of *O Pioneers!* and which is unresolved in Willa Cather's work as a whole. It is the problem of the relative advantages between country and town. Although the book ends with a glorification of the life of the country, it turns out to be a qualified glorification. Ántonia may become an earth-goddess, but she gets many of her good qualities from her father, who was a town dweller. Thus Willa Cather's idea of the good country life really turns out to be that of one in which urban and rural traits which she considers desirable are combined.

My Ántonia's middle section opens with the removal of the Burdens from farm to town. Just as in the book's first part the edge is taken off the strangeness of Jim's arrival in the West by a description of the cozy life led by Jim's grandparents, so the town is rendered more friendly to him by the description of another family whom he admires, the Harlings. These nextdoor neighbors are as much paragons of town life as the Burdens were of life in the country. The father and eldest daughter are in business—a calling which the later Willa Cather comes to detest; yet she has nothing but approval for them. The father is quite authoritarian: when he is at home no one is allowed to make any noise, and he insists on having all his wife's attention to the exclusion even of his children. He is much more authoritarian than the bearded patriarch who was his country counterpart, for Mr. Harling is not shown as having a saving sense of humor; but, far from resenting this, Jim seems to find it interesting and rather grand. There is no doubt that Willa Cather enjoyed the portrayal of authoritarian personalities. The oldest daughter, Frances Harling, is her father's business associate and takes care of his transactions for him while he is away on trips. Jim admires her, too, and finds her quite as satisfactory a human being as if she were a man.

Into this ménage Willa Cather introduces Ántonia, who, tiring of the rough life she knows on the farm, comes into town to "go into service," thus hoping to earn money for the folks back home and at the same time see a little more of life than had hitherto come her way. Through the agency of the Burden family she goes to work for the Harlings. She immediately becomes popular with her employers, and they carry on the process of education which had been begun by her father but which would never have gotten very far if it had been left in the tender hands of the grabby Mrs. Shimerda and the sullen Ambrosch. Jim, too, finds himself drawn to the brightly lighted Harling home, from which seem to emanate all the most desirable things in civilization:

> Frances taught us to dance that winter, and she said, from the first lesson, that Ántonia would make the best dancer among us. On Saturday nights, Mrs. Harling used to play the old operas for us—"Martha," "Norma," "Rigoletto,"—telling us the story while she played. Every Saturday night was like a party. The parlour, the back parlour, and the dining-room were warm and brightly lighted, with comfortable chairs and sofas, and gay pictures on the walls. One always felt at ease there. Ántonia brought her sewing and sat with us—she was already beginning to make pretty clothes for herself. After the long winter evenings on the prairie, with Ambrosch's sullen silences and her mother's complaints, the Harlings' house seemed, as she said, "like Heaven" to her.[9]

Part of the reason Mrs. Harling is able to educate Ántonia is that, town-bred or not, she is essentially the same kind of person that Ántonia is. Both have a deep instinctive response to life:

> There was a basic harmony between Ántonia and her mistress. They had strong, independent natures, both of them. They knew what they liked, and were not always trying to imitate other people. They loved children and animals and music, and rough play and digging in the earth. They liked to prepare rich, hearty food and to see people eat it; to make up soft white beds and to see youngsters asleep in them. They ridiculed conceited people and were quick to help unfortunate ones. Deep down in each of them there was a kind of hearth joviality, a relish of life, not over-delicate, but very invigorating. I never tried to define it, but I was distinctly conscious of it. I could not imagine Ántonia's living for a week in any other house in Black Hawk than the Harlings'.[10]

In spite of her great fondness for her employers, Ántonia finally leaves them. One night a young man who has escorted Ántonia home from a dance tries to kiss her, and when she protests—because he is going to be married the following

Monday— he uses strong-arm tactics and she slaps him. The autocratic Mr. Harling
has heard all this and puts his foot down: she will have to stay away from Saturday
night dances or else find a new place. Ántonia utterly refuses: nothing is going to
make her give up her good times, and so she and the Harlings part.

Ántonia's revolt against the Harlings is only one extension of the rebellion she
had already begun against her own family. It is a rebellion in favor of the good things
of life; years of drudgery on a remote farm with only an unpleasant mother and
brother for company had begotten in her a fierce desire to enjoy life's sweets. To
us the rebellion seems mild, since it consists chiefly of having a good time and going
out with young men to dances, although it culminates in her being "fooled" by Larry
Donovan's promise of marriage and having a baby by him after he had abandoned
her. The significance of her rebellion is that it shows Ántonia's asserting her independence from her family as well as from the Harlings. This is a vitally important
step for Willa Cather's early heroines, since they seem to feel that without completely rejecting parental authority they cannot be individuals in their own right.

My Ántonia is unique in Willa Cather's early writing in that in it she for once
represents a happy marriage and a family at its best; that is, she is able to feel more
attraction for the family than revulsion against it. Later on, Ántonia, this noncon-
formist and rebel against the family, lives to marry and found a family of her own;
having experienced many sides of life, she now knows a good deal of what life is
about, and is all the better a mother for it. To achieve this effect, Willa Cather has
manipulated the plot so that Ambrosch and Mrs. Shimerda are as unattractive as
possible; thus a revolt from them is a revolt toward life itself. Ántonia must rebel
against a bad family before she can set up a good family. Thus she is able both to
be a rugged individualist and later on to enjoy the advantages of group membership
too.

The Fruition of the Soil: The Garden of the World

If one of the main themes of My Ántonia is the superiority of the countryside
and the excellence of rural life, the chief image that Willa Cather uses to express
that excellence is one we have already come across in discussing O Pioneers!: that
of the garden of the world. It is in fact the basic metaphor of the whole book;
everything in the novel leads up to the final section in which Ántonia has become
the mistress of a large and fertile farm.

The garden image is present in the minds of both Willa Cather and some of
her characters. Not the least of Grandfather Burden's insights is his ability to
understand the larger meaning of the enterprise in which he and his neighbors are
engaged. To the hundreds of thousands of toiling individuals who settled the West
it must have seemed that each of them was seeking solely to improve his own lot,
but according to the thinking of the time they were actually fulfilling a much larger
destiny. The settlement of America was considered to be a part of a divine plan.
When the great basin of the Mississippi Valley was completely populated, it was to
become not only an earthly paradise of the inhabitants, who would thus live in a

latter-day Garden of Eden, but also the whole earth's granary; by means of its immense fertility it would feed the people of Europe and Asia as well. Willa Cather had hinted at this in *O Pioneers!;* in *My Ántonia* she makes it quite explicit:

> July came on with that breathless, brilliant heat which makes the plains of Kansas and Nebraska the best corn country in the world. It seemed as if we could hear the corn growing in the night; under the stars one caught a faint crackling in the dewy, heavy-odoured cornfields where the feathered stalks stood so juicy and green. If all the great plain from the Missouri to the Rocky Mountains had been under glass, and the heat regulated by a thermometer, it could not have been better for the yellow tassels that were ripening and fertilizing the silk day by day. The cornfields were far apart in those times, with miles of wild grazing land between. It took a clear, meditative eye like my grandfather's to foresee that they would enlarge and multiply until they would be, not the Shimerdas' cornfields, or Mr. Bushy's, but the world's cornfields; that their yield would be one of the great economic facts, like the wheat crop of Russia, which underlie all the activities of men, in peace or war.[11]

This is one way in which Willa Cather adjusts Nebraska to the macrocosm and gives local happenings a cosmic importance.

But it is not merely the garden that Willa Cather is celebrating in *My Ántonia;* it is a garden with people living in it, and the people form one of those tightly knit Willa Cather families. The ultimate achievement of Willa Cather's heroine in *My Ántonia* is the setting up of a family. The whole drive of her nature is toward this; we could have guessed it from the description of the basic likeness between Ántonia and her town employer, Mrs. Harling:

> They loved children and animals and music, and rough play and digging in the earth. They liked to prepare rich, hearty food and to see people eat it; to make up soft white beds and to see youngsters asleep in them.[12]

Ántonia makes two attempts at marriage and the founding of a family: the first is unsuccessful but the second succeeds. The unsuccessful attempt with Larry Donovan has already been discussed. Ántonia's second attempt comes to a better fruition. Jim Burden does not witness the events leading up to it, since after graduation from college he has moved east permanently, but he does hear that another Bohemian has married her, that they are poor, and that they have a large family. He does not come back to visit his home town for nearly twenty years, and when he does he is afraid to visit Ántonia. "In the course of twenty crowded years one parts with many illusions," he says. "I did not wish to lose the early ones. Some memories are realities, and are better then anything that can ever happen to one again."[13] In such brief passages as this he lets the reader know that he has become disappointed in life, that he has been beaten in the things that really count. But his dread turns out to be needless, for Ántonia when he sees her is not a disappointment to him; she has become old and battered, but her vitality is undiminished. She is surrounded by a large happy brood of eleven children, all of whom either come tumbling around him in curiosity to see the man their mother has talked so much about, or else are attractively shy. Ántonia's fecundity is a sign of vitality and success, and the nicest compliment she can pay to some friends of their youth, the three Bohemian Marys, is that they are now married and have large families of their own. The lack of offspring, on the other hand, she regards as a sign of failure. Significantly enough, when she hears that Jim Burden has no children she becomes embarrassed, and tries to shift the conversation to a more neutral subject.

The relation between the various members of this large and happy family are of intense interest to Jim, who feels that he himself has failed at human relations. He observes that there is a kind of physical harmony between them, and that they are not afraid to touch each other.[14] They take great pride in each other, and particularly in their wonderful mother.[15] He describes the attitude of husband and wife toward each other as being "easy friendliness touched with humor."[16] Father Cuzak in particular seems to express his affection for his family by finding them highly amusing: "He thought they were nice, and he thought they were funny, evidently."[17] It is clear that love is the tie that binds them all together, and that they are very happy in one another's affection. And yet there is some slight suggestion of tension between Cuzak, the city-bred man, and Ántonia, the country girl. In the struggle between the sexes envisaged by Willa Cather, Ántonia seems to have gotten the upper hand:

> I could see the little chap, sitting here every evening by the windmill, nursing his pipe and listening to the silence; the wheeze of the pump, the grunting of the pigs, an occasional squeaking when the hens were disturbed by a rat. It did rather seem to me that Cuzak had been made the instrument of Ántonia's special mission. This was a fine life, certainly, but it wasn't the kind of life he had wanted to live. I wondered whether the life that was right for one was ever right for two![18]

This last comment brings into question the entire feasibility of a city-country union. Willa Cather seems to have doubts as to whether the two modes of life can ever be rendered compatible. In addition, it also recalls her distrust of marriage in general. The marriage of the Cuzaks is as idyllic a union as she was ever to portray in any of her novels, and yet even here there is the suggestion not only of female dominance but of marriage as being inevitably frustrating.

The human fertility of the Cuzak homestead is matched by the fertility of the soil. The years of backbreaking labor spent tending the crops has at last yielded a rich fruit. Ántonia is especially proud of her orchard, which has been planted in the painstaking way that orchards are in Willa Cather's novels: every tree had to be watered by hand after a hard day's labor in the fields. The result is a yearly apple crop that far surpasses that of any of their neighbors. At the center of all this fertility is a symbol of civilization. Years before, Ántonia had told Jim she was homesick for the garden behind her father's house in Bohemia which had had a table and green benches in it where they could entertain their friends and talk about such things as music and woods and God and when they were young.[19] This garden image seems to stand in her mind for exactly the right relation between human beings and the nature in which they are placed, a nature modified and well stocked with benches so that civilized people need not get their clothes dirty when they discuss philosophical problems and wish to sit down. Now Ántonia leads Jim to the center of her orchard, and there he finds a grape arbor with seats along the sides and a warped plank table.[20] She has reproduced in the middle of her ideal farm her own idea of the civilized garden. Jim's detailed description of it enhances its importance:

> We sat down and watched them. Ántonia leaned her elbows on the table. There was the deepest peace in the orchard. It was surrounded by a triple enclosure; the wire fence, then the hedge of thorny locusts, then the mulberry hedge which kept out the hot winds of summer and held fast to the protecting snows of winter. The hedges were so tall that we could see nothing but the blue sky above them, neither the barn roof nor the windmill. The afternoon sun poured down on us through the drying grape leaves. The orchard seemed full of sun, like a cup, and we could smell the ripe apples on the trees. The crabs hung on the branches as thick as beads on a string, purple-red, with a thin silvery glaze over them. Some hens and ducks had crept through the hedge and were pecking at the fallen apples. The drakes were handsome fellows, with pinkish grey bodies, their heads and necks covered with iridescent green feathers which grew close and full, changing to blue like a peacock's neck. Ántonia said they always reminded her of soldiers— some uniform she had seen in the old country, when she was a child.[21]

This passage contains a cluster of images, all of which contribute to the agricultural image used also in *O Pioneers!*, that of the garden of the world. Several ideas are at work here. First, there is the idea that at the center of all this fertility of farm and family is a place of quietness, a place which contains the deepest peace which human beings can know. The still center is protected from the outside world by a triple barrier which excludes not only strangers (the wire fence) but also extremes of heat and cold, with their connotation of everything else which man finds unpleasant. But aside from shutting out, it also shuts in; it confines the inhabitants of the garden so they cannot tell what is going on in the outside world; they can't even see their farm or windmill, the symbols of the way in which they earn their living. Thus the garden becomes another of those images of sanctuary and retreat which we have seen as giving so important a clue to Willa Cather's attitude toward life. The orchard resembles a cornucopia; it is full like a cup, and the fragrance of its fruit hangs over it. The concept of plenitude finds further development in the idea of roundness, when the crab apples on the trees are compared with beads on a strong. Finally Ántonia's comparison between the iridescent shimmeringness on the necks of her ducks and the uniforms of soldiers she had seen as a child in Bohemia suggest that the aesthetic response to life has been carried from Europe to America, but instead of being aroused by an artificial and destructive product of civilization, it is now tamed and rendered beneficent by being brought closer to nature, and is simulated by such a harmless and thoroughly natural creature as a barnyard fowl.

In the middle of this earthly paradise stands its Eve, the now victorious Ántonia. She has triumphed over adversity and over nature; she has wrestled with life and imposed an order on it, her order, just as she has imposed order on the wilderness of Nebraska by converting part of it into a fruitful farm with a garden at its center. In her double role as founder of a prosperous farm and progenitor of a thriving family she becomes the very symbol of fertility, and reminds us of Demeter or Ceres of old, the ancients' goddess of agriculture. Willa Cather herself points up the comparison, and it is of value to her to do this, for she makes an earth-goddess of Ántonia; the mortal who struggles with the adverse powers of nature and conquers them becomes the type of all successful human endeavor and passes over into the realm of myth. That Willa Cather quite deliberately makes an earth-goddess of Ántonia is seen in the following passage:

> She lent herself to immemorial human attitudes which we recognize by instinct as universal and true. I had not been mistaken. She was a bettered woman now, not a lovely girl; but she still had that something which fires the imagination, could still stop one's breath for a moment by a look or gesture that somehow revealed the meaning in common things. She had only to stand in the orchard, to put her hand on a little crab tree and look up at the apples, to make you feel the goodness of planting and tending and harvesting at last. All the strong things of her heart came out in her body, that had been so tireless in serving generous emotions.
>
> It was no wonder that her sons stood tall and straight. She was a rich mine of life, like the founders of early races.[22]

And what becomes of the other protagonist in the story, Jim Burden? When he revisits his past by returning to Black Hawk, it gives him no clues to his identity or to the meaning of life such as he has found in the Cuzak farm. He is not able to build on his past as Ántonia is on hers:

> My day in Black Hawk was disappointing. Most of my old friends were dead or had moved away. Strange children, who meant nothing to me, were playing in the Harlings' big yard when I passed; the mountain ash had been cut down, and only a sprouting stump was left of the tall Lombardy poplar that used to guard the gate. I hurried on.[23]

The town no longer means anything to him, although the country still does. It has changed too much; the children and the trees are gone. The town families he had known had had no roots, since the community in which they lived had given them none, and so they had passed on to other places. But there are parts of the country that haven't changed at all. Jim takes a long walk out of town and stumbles upon an old road, the first road built from Black Hawk to the north, in fact the very same road over which Ántonia and he had traveled on the first night of their arrival in the Midwest. The road becomes a symbol of the unchanging quality of the countryside, and carries him back to the region of childhood memories:

> I had only to close my eyes to hear the rumbling of the wagons in the dark, and to be again overcome by that obliterating strangeness. The feelings of that night were so near that I could reach out and touch them with my hand. I had the sense of coming home to myself, and of having found out what a little circle man's experience is.[24]

The wheel has come full circle, and the same road which had first brought him to Black Hawk now carries him away from an unsatisfying present and into a nostalgically remembered past. Nothing could illustrate better than this final contrast between the Cuzak farm and Black Hawk the difference between country and town, Ántonia and Jim, the yea-saying and nay-saying attitudes toward life. Both had been set down in the Middle West without any previous training which would help them, both had once literally traveled down the same road, but their circumstances and temperaments were different. Ántonia now prefers the country because it gives her a greater chance to fulfill herself; Jim because it has changed less than the city and because it is linked with the past, to which he turns because it is all he has:

> For Ántonia and for me, this had been the road of Destiny; had taken us to those early accidents of fortune which predetermined for us all that we can ever be. Now I understood that the same road was to bring us together again. Whatever we had missed, we possessed together the precious, the incommunicable past.[25]

Perhaps the best way of summing up the meaning of *My Ántonia* is to recapitulate the story of each of the three sections in terms of the dominant imagery. The first part, concerning the struggle of the Burdens and the Shimerdas with the wild land, is described in terms of animal imagery; as in *O Pioneers!* the central symbol is the unbroken colt. This represents inchoate material waiting to have form imposed upon it, vitality ready to be harnessed by order. Ántonia too is waiting to have form imposed upon her; by her father, by the Burden family, and by the Harlings, form being in this context the stamp of civilization itself. The imposition of form on wild nature is a difficult thing, as those who do not have the strength to achieve it find out; Mr. Shimerda fails at the task and kills himself, while even Ántonia barely survives. But she does survive.

In the book's second part the dominant image is the plough. Both Ántonia and the land are now ready to be creative and fertile; to produce children and crops. This section contains the struggle between town and country traditions, with Ántonia absorbing both: she first learns from and then emancipates herself from the Harlings. Unlike her father, she is able to triumph over adversity—in her case, an unfortunate love affair.

In the third section of the book the dominant image is the earth-goddess in the garden of the world. This section shows the final fruition of both woman and land, which comes about because Ántonia is able to combine the vitality of nature with the order of civilization, both in her own life and in the life of the land. In this section Jim Burden meets adversity and is inspired by Ántonia.

The importance to her career of Willa Cather's two prairie novels can hardly be overestimated. In them she gives the fullest expression she ever gave to one of her major themes, the meaning of the European experience in America. The exact significance of America differs in the two prairie novels. In *O Pioneers!* America functions as pure raw material; it is the land where the creative will best can operate. *My Ántonia* does not contradict this, but the emphasis has shifted; America is now the land in which "Europe" can reach its finest flower. For Willa Cather as for many other nineteenth-century people Europe and America stood for pairs of opposites: Europe was tangibly the past, America tangibly the present; Europe stood for order, America for chaos. The two are connected, since the present is always visibly chaotic and needs to have order imposed upon it by applying the lessons learned in the past. The most important antithesis of all, however, was that America stood for nature whereas Europe represented civilization. The difference between the two novels is that in *O Pioneers!*, even while Alexandra is struggling to conquer it, it is the wildness of nature which is being celebrated, the untamed vitality of the frontier, whereas in *My Ántonia* the vitality and the discipline of civilization are combined to form a new synthesis, which provides the basis for a settled agricultural society like that eulogized by Horace and Vergil.

I have shown that at a certain point in her career Willa Cather gradually ceased looking to the world of art for subject matter and began seeking it in the world of nature. But this did not mean that she gave up her belief in the world of art as a source of value. Because she did not her former cultural ideal came into conflict with her present one, for the world of urban sophistication has little in common with the world of simple homely virtues associated with the countryside. This conflict between cultural ideals was by no means peculiar to Willa Cather but was part of a much more general conflict present in the minds of nineteenth-century Americans concerning their ideas about themselves; it revolved around the question of whether they owed their allegiance to the concept of primitivism, or the concept of civilization and the stages of society. According to primitivism, since nature is seen as the source of all value, the closer a man lives to nature the better off he is, physically, mentally, and morally. According to the concept of the stages of society, all men progressed through certain stages of development proceeding from the most primitive to the most civilized, starting with the nomadic and proceeding upward through the pastoral and agricultural until finally they reached the industrial and commercial stages. These last two—the agricultural and industrial-commercial—correspond to the rural and urban stages, which I have discussed under the headings of country and town. In the nineteenth century the two turn up over and over again as contrasting ideals as to how life should be lived, the best literary expression of this being in the novels of James Fenimore Cooper.[26] As we have seen, Willa Cather herself vacillated between the two, as indeed Americans traditionally have done. In *O Pioneers!*, she merely states the case for both sides, without making any choice between the two. But in *My Ántonia* she resolves the conflict in the direction of a highly civilized and sophisticated rural civilization, and this remains her ideal for the rest of her career, although in her later books (starting with her very next novel) she believes it to be an ideal impossible of achievement.

But this highly civilized and sophisticated rural way of living which she celebrates is actually a little too good to be true. It is doubtful whether anybody could achieve that particular combination of urban-bred sensibility and rural rootedness and strength which she envisaged. When this is seen as combined with a hierarchal three-generation family unit in which the roles are assigned and the whole is sustained by ritual, ironically enough the place where it is most likely to be found is not in the country at all but in the city. Such a pattern is common among orthodox Jewish families who (like the Cuzaks) are not too far removed from their immigrant ancestors. But this is hardly where Willa Cather looked for her heroines.[27]

The concepts of primitivism and civilization have an all-pervasive influence on Willa Cather's fiction. They affect, for instance, her presentation of her heroines. In *O Pioneers!* she emphasizes the heroine as a solitary individual; in *My Ántonia* she emphasizes the heroine as part of a group, first as a member of a family and then as its head. Similarly the differing treatment of the prairie in the two books likewise shows the influence of the two concepts. In *O Pioneers!* the land being eulogized is the entire Great Divide; Willa Cather tells us, "Alexandra's house is the big out-of-doors."[28] In *My Ántonia* the center of attention has been narrowed down to the family living on the family farm; in other words, the homestead. This shows Willa Cather dealing in literary terms with a vitally important historical reality. The entire trans-Mississippi region was settled in the post–Civil War period by farmers called homesteaders; in fact, the Homestead Act of 1862 was conceptually based on just such a family unit as the Cuzaks.

O Pioneers! forms a sharp contrast to *My Ántonia* in structure as well as subject matter. In structure the earlier book has a superimposed form while the form of the latter is largely organic and arises from the cycle of the seasons. The organizing principle of *O Pioneers!* is the theme of the creative will directed, first toward the world of nature, then toward the world of man; the organizing principle of *My Ántonia*, as we shall see later, is the vegetation myth. Of the two *O Pioneers!* has the tighter structure, popular opinion to the contrary. In *My Ántonia* the part tends to be greater than the whole: one remembers fine but isolated passages such as Jim Burden's killing of the rattlesnake or the description of the plough against the sun.

To study the spirit behind the form of an artistic work is a fascinating albeit highly speculative occupation. In the case of the two prairie novels some light is shed on structure by what we know of Willa Cather's biography and temperament. What she was trying to do in *O Pioneers!* was evidently to show that the power of love, although it can succeed with the land, must fail when it comes to people. But this is highly idiosyncratic, and reflects her own inner fears rather than any universal human truth. What she was trying to do in *My Ántonia* was somewhat different. Leaving the vegetation myth aside for a moment, a part of the book's form is still superimposed. Willa Cather has constructed the novel as a series of snapshots or vignettes, each of them commemorating some important event. Since we know that she tended to omit struggle and conflict from both books, as well as the direct presentation of evil, it seems that her vignettes are meant to present only life's happy and successful moments, and such as showed the triumph of the will. If this is true, she was willfully failing to see life steadily and see it whole, or to give an artistically convincing representation of the entire human scene as she knew it.

In spite of its flaws, *O Pioneers!* on the whole is a successful portrait of an important American historical era. In the larger sense, it can be regarded as a kind of allegory on Western man and his entire history. It shows him—as he has historically been—as much more successful in dealing with his physical environment than with his fellow man: Alexandra's saga follows a success-failure pattern as she moves away from relatively simple problems and toward the more complex. I find it necessary to make separate judgments on the two parts of the book. In the main I believe Willa Cather is aesthetically and historically right when she takes the wild frontier as a symbol of the challenge offered to heroic souls by the precariousness of human existence, and sees the westward expansion in nineteenth-century America as a working out of the romantic aspiration toward a better life. But I believe she is dangerously idiosyncratic in seeing spontaneous relations between the sexes as being as uniformly dangerous and unrewarding as she makes them out to be. This view reflects her own particular upbringing and temperament—particularly the latter—and it severely limits her art. Nevertheless, in spite of its limitations, *O Pioneers!* is a convincing novel; in it Willa Cather comes as close as she ever does to a frank and square confrontation of the conflicts inherent in human life. But this is all she does; she faces them but is unable to resolve or transcend them. And even in *O Pioneers!* she turns her face away from the conflict before the book is over.

My Ántonia, in some ways more successful than *O Pioneers!*, in other ways is less successful; it is more affirmative but less honest. If in the first book Willa Cather gives a frank portrayal of her gloomy and one-sided view of human relations, in the second she is willing to falsify the material she has at hand in order to make the final triumph of the heroine appear almost effortless. *O Pioneers!* is the more original in form, with its brilliant linking of plots to project the success-failure motif; *My Ántonia* is more conventional in theme, if not in content, since it comes at the end of a long tradition of literary works written in praise of husbandry. It is an agrarian idyl, and its real subject is man's right relation to nature. The right relation turns out to be, not that defined by primitivism, but that of the agrarian tradition, a version of the concept of civilization which held that the stages of society culminate in the settled agricultural level, and that any further development in the direction of the city is a step downward.

In the largest sense the structure of *My Ántonia* is based on the vegetation myth. The core of this age-old mystery, as we have said, is the taking of the cycle of the seasons as the pattern for all recurrent rhythmical processes in nature, including human death and birth. It regards birth as rebirth and holds that, although death is inevitable, every person is "born again" through his children; the individual dies but the community lives on. *My Ántonia* is about this mystery of death and birth. Mr. Shimerda dies in the dead of winter, and when Ántonia is reborn as the head of a group of her own she is described in terms of the sensuous summer imagery and the garden of the world. In a sense when Mr. Shimerda dies, a good part of his daughter dies too; all her more civilized attributes wither away. She gives up her fine manners and becomes coarse and crude like her brother Ambrosch. She is reborn to civilization when she goes to town to live and relearns nice ways of doing things from the Harlings. Finally, after learning all she has to learn, she is ready to take her place in society by starting a family of her own and is reborn once again into the human community.

If we compare the two prairie novels in terms of their use of vegetation myth, we find that *O Pioneers!* deals with the death of nature and *My Ántonia* with its rebirth. *O Pioneers!* presents fertility of the soil and sterility in human beings; *My Ántonia* shows fertility of both the soil and human beings. Thus, in a profound sense *My Ántonia* is the most affirmative book Willa Cather ever wrote. Perhaps that is why it was her favorite.

But we have seen that as an author Willa Cather could not face certain facts of human experience—as, in *My Ántonia*, the problem of apparently motiveless evil involved in Larry Donovan's seduction and abandonment of Ántonia. It is also true that in her work as a whole she could not accept the emotional profundity of the vegetation myth as for the most part she did in this novel. In brief, she could accept fertility in crops more easily then in human beings, the reason being her fear of physical passion and the dependence upon others which it entails. This is evident even in *My Ántonia*, which all of her novels most celebrates fecundity. As far as the reader is concerned, Ántonia's family is produced ready-made. Never once is a pregnancy or birth directly presented in Willa Cather's novels; what we do see is the corn growing. This implies that she only half understood the vegetation myth; she understood the cycle of the seasons but did not understand its application to the life of human beings and to their recurrent crises of birth, love, and death. She substituted in its stead, as we shall see in her later novels, an almost Platonic belief in essences, and the desire to freeze the world in the grip of form once the ideal is achieved.

NOTES

[1]*My Ántonia* (Boston, 1918), p. xiv. Hereafter referred to as "MA."
[2]MA, p. xiv.
[3]See Willa Cather's remark reported in E. K. Brown, *Willa Cather: A Critical Biography* (New York, 1953), p. 202: "A comment on *My Ántonia* that Willa Cather made in an interview she gave in Lincoln a few years after the book came out shows that in her use of Jim as narrator she had been trying to achieve two effects that were not really compatible: Jim was to be fascinated by Ántonia as only a man could be, and yet he was to remain a detached observer, appreciative but inactive, rather than take a part in her life." This clearly implies that Willa Cather considered Ántonia to be the central object.
[4]MA, p. 241.
[5]MA, p. 354.

[6]MA, p. 355.
[7]MA, p. 388.
[8]Mildred Bennett, *The World of Willa Cather* (New York, 1951), p. 47.
[9]MA, p. 200.
[10]MA, p. 205.
[11]MA, p. 156.
[12]MA, p. 205.
[13]MA, p. 370.
[14]MA, p. 394.
[15]MA, p. 396.
[16]MA, p. 403.
[17]MA, p. 404.
[18]MA, p. 413.
[19]MA, p. 269.
[20]MA, p. 384.
[21]MA, p. 385.
[22]MA, p. 398.
[23]MA, p. 416.
[24]MA, p. 419.
[25]MA, p. 419.
[26]Cf. Henry Nash Smith, *Virgin Land* (Cambridge, 1950), pp. 59–71. See especially his discussion of *The Pioneers*.
[27]On the other hand, it may explain Willa Cather's close and continuing friendship with the Menuhins, parents of the violinist Yehudi, in the nineteen-thirties.
[28]*O Pioneers!* (Boston, 1913), p. 84.

Richard Giannone

MY ÁNTONIA

The crier soon came, leading that man of song
Whom the Muse cherished; by her gift he knew
The good of life, and evil—
For she who lent him sweetness made him blind.   —*Odyssey*

Willa Cather's classical work, *My Ántonia* (1918),[1] shows the expansion of her now recognizable uses of music. There is, as always, music as medium of the inner spirit. Again, music voices the alternating beauty and brutality of the untamed Nebraska land and indicates the severe conditions under which the frontiersmen live. Among characters, both major and minor, musical ability or musical insensitivity go hand in hand with Cather's favor or disfavor. In the case of certain figures, Mr. Shimerda and Leo Cuzak, for example, music is intimately linked with their fortunes. Collectively, musical spirit connotes a constructive view of life; and this commitment to living is configured in two musical patterns: the dance, which vivifies an inner rhythm, and the violin, which represents the cultural progress born of man's positive, creative energy. Finally, music becomes the metaphorical equivalent for Ántonia's greatness, her capacity for love and her inner spirit. If there is no "clear reason"—as Thea Kronborg would say—to account for the Bohemian girl's immediate and lasting response to life, it is because her *joie de vivre* cannot be conveyed in words. It is more a rhythm than a reason that the narrator gives. Ántonia's vitality is felt and thus rightly represented through a sensuous form. Music in *My Ántonia* captures what is ineffable in the heroine: her warmth, naturalness, spontaneity, freedom, strength, and her haunting presence in the memory of those who knew her.

The spokesman for those who remember Ántonia Shimerda is Jim Burden, the narrator, whose aesthetic responsibility is to recast for himself and then for the reader "the precious, the incommunicable past." As a memoirist, Jim relies heavily on music to catch an exultant moment in his personal history. Music helps Jim arrive at one of his most important insights into human experience: the shared intensity

From *Music in Willa Cather's Fiction* (Lincoln: University of Nebraska Press, 1968), pp. 107–23.

of childhood is only lived and once lived, lost. Insofar as the past can be regained it is through imaginative shaping, through art which endows remembrance with a new emotional form. Like his boyhood in Nebraska, music exists in time, and the inevitable end of its beauty, its insupportable pleasure, gives music a nostalgic quality which is congenial to Jim's mind and which is in keeping with the heightened sense of loss he gives to his memoir. Music helps by recalling specific occasions to him, but it performs a higher service by providing a form flexible enough to hold his rather intuitive observations and the impressionistic episodes which make up the book. In fine, music acts on Jim as a mnemonic evocation of Ántonia and life on the Divide.

Willa Cather did use music to connect two temporal or spatial orders in works before *My Ántonia*. *Alexander's Bridge* has something of this technique in the retrospective sections, but it was not developed into a principle of composition. *My Ántonia*, then, in addition to incorporating previous uses of music, adds a new one and brings music from the center of moral interest which it held in *The Song of the Lark* to a position of structural determination. Music amounts to the "sheath" or "mould" for recollection—the form by which art could "imprison for a moment for shining, elusive element which is life itself," as Cather put it in *The Song of the Lark*. The relation of music to form in *My Ántonia* is first suggested by Jim Burden's description of the way he wrote his memoir of Ántonia and Nebraska: " '*I didn't take time to arrange it; I simply wrote down pretty much all that her name recalls to me. I suppose it hasn't any form.*' " There are several controlled patterns in the novel, like the seasonal cycle, which imply more exactitude than Jim realizes; but one pattern, music, while ordered with diligence, reveals a pliant, associational coherence which Jim would allow as proper to his subject.

II

The novel spans thirty-one years. It opens in the fall of 1885 when Jim Burden, ten years old, coming from Virginia to Nebraska, meets Ántonia Shimerda, who is fourteen and has emigrated with her family from Bohemia; and the book closes with their reunion in the fall of 1916, when Ántonia is established in Nebraska as the mother of a large family. As Jim Burden recalls his first arrival on the Nebraska prairie, the land's "empty darkness" (7), mystery, and monotony return to his memory. Nature hostilely greets the apprehensive immigrants, American and European alike, with a vast sameness whose fearfulness is intensified by the absence of human touch. "There was nothing but land," as Jim remembers Nebraska, "not a country at all, but the material out of which countries are made." The frontier gives one the feeling of being "outside man's jurisdiction"; and though at first overwhelmingly expansive, this new world does offer the boy an immensity into which he can be assimilated. "Between that earth and that sky I felt erased, blotted out" (8). The ambivalent rapport he feels with the frontier comes to Jim more comprehensively a short time later through the land's music, its voice, the wind. Sitting in the middle of his grandmother's garden, he "could hear it [the wind] singing its humming tune up on the level" (18) and "could see the tall grasses wave" under its gentle pressure. This music is especially audible in spring, as when the lark's song heralds the earth's floral bounty:

> It was a beautiful blue morning. The buffalo-peas were blooming in pink and purple masses along the roadside, and the larks, perched on last year's dried sunflower stalks, were singing straight at the sun, their heads thrown back and their yellow breasts a-quiver. (127–128)

As the land's roughness is gradually smoothed by human hands, the yield from tilled soil seems audible.

> July came one with that breathless, brilliant heat which makes the plains of Kansas and Nebraska the best corn country in the world. It seemed as if we could hear the corn growing in the night; under the stars one caught a faint crackling in the dewy, heavy-odoured cornfields where the feathered stalks stood so juicy and green. (137)

Nature's other mood is also interpreted in music. The singing wind has a "bitter song" as well as a soothing hum. This is its winter mood, a mood with a stark message in its melody:

> When the smoky clouds hung low in the west and the red sun went down behind them, leaving a pink flush on the snowy roofs and the blue drifts, then the wind sprang up afresh, with a kind of bitter song, as if it said: "This is reality, whether you like it or not. All those frivolities of summer, the light and shadow, the living mask of green that trembled over everything, they were lies, and this is what was underneath. This is the truth." (173)

The bitter wind-song rises to the surface of Jim's association when he is musing about Mr. Shimerda's suicide. As he thinks of the lonely man, he "could hear the wind singing over hundreds of miles of snow" (101). Against this harsh, melodic accompaniment, Jim's thoughts form vivid pictures of "all that Ántonia had ever told me about his life before he came to this country; how he used to play the fiddle at weddings and dances" (101–102). But for Mr. Shimerda that music was silenced some time ago. Surely his sensitive ear heard in the wind-song the harsh truth that happiness is a lie. His life is proof of the message. That is why he shot himself.

It is the dark background of hardship and hostility that defines the special place of music in prairie life. In a world which is largely a composite of deprivations, music becomes an important consolation, providing an occasion for camaraderie, for a reassuring moment of community amid isolation and solitude. When Jim thinks of the savage descent of winter on Black Hawk, the little town into which he and his grandparents moved after three years in the country, he recalls how "a hunger for colour came over people" (174), how they used to linger outside the Methodist Church "when the lamps were lighted early for choir practice or prayer-meeting," held there by "the crude reds and greens and blues" of its "painted glass window," and his memory associates music with the effort to parry the bleakness of the outside world, to bring that world within man's jurisdiction—in short, to humanize it. Thrown back on their own devices by nature, the pioneers sang and played in their infrequent hours of leisure. These sounds are the memorable man-made sounds on the desolate plains; they are the soft, human rejoinders to nature's strident howls and the "hungry, wintry cry" (68) of coyotes.

A number of musical occasions highlight Jim's memoir. Russian Peter's "gaudily painted harmonica" (37) and the tunes that "were either very lively or very doleful" revive the thought of Russian Peter's tragic life. Those days in Jim's youth when "lives centred around warmth and food and the return of the men at nightfall" (66) were enlivened every Saturday night by musical entertainment. Otto Fuchs, the Burdens' amiable handyman, lingers in Jim's memory as one of the "good fellows" (67) who had kept the faith with many things, and the feature of Fuch's personality which Jim remembers most is his "good baritone voice" which he lent to folk songs and which "always led the singing when he went to church services at the sod school-house."

The events in Jim's memory which are most clearly linked to the lost happiness of boyhood are mostly musical. There are, in particular, those Saturday nights at the Harlings' when, as he puts it, "one always felt at ease." In that cheerful home, which was " 'like Heaven' " to Ántonia and Jim, the natural impulse for musical expression was nourished.

> Frances taught us to dance that winter, and she said, from the first lesson, that Ántonia would make the best dancer among us. On Saturday nights, Mrs. Harling used to play the old operas for us—"Martha," "Norma," "Rigoletto"— telling us the story while she played. Every Saturday night was like a party. (175)

In retrospect the "jolly evenings at the Harlings' " (156) are a significant part of the unregainable happiness of childhood. Jim's recollections of those evenings are filled with music and with amateur musicians. "There was usually somebody at the piano" (158): Julia Harling practicing seriously; Frances playing after Julia until dinner; Sally drumming "the plantation melodies that Negro ministrel troupes brought to town"; and even the smallest child, Nina, playing the Swedish Wedding March. As Jim's mature memory turns to the vivacious household, the musical associations are so strong that its mistress is caught in a musical attitude: "I can see her at this moment: her short, square person planted firmly on the stool, her little fat hands moving quickly and neatly over the keys, her eyes fixed on the music with intelligent concentration" (158).

Music is also a tie between the prairie and the outside world. Through this universal medium the settlers learn something of the metropolitan life from which they are separated. At the Saturday night gatherings of traveling salesmen in the parlor of the Boys' Home—"all the commercial travellers in that territory tried to get into Black Hawk for Sunday" (170) in order to stay at the Boys' Home, "the best hotel on our branch of the Burlington"—the man who traveled for Marshall Field's "played the piano and sang all the latest sentimental songs." And one could count on talk about "actors and actresses and musical prodigies" (183).

When an Italian family, the Vannis, come to Black Hawk and begin giving dancing lessons and holding dances in their tent pavilion, the young people eagerly welcome this escape from the humdrum routine of life. "At last there was something to do in those long, empty summer evenings, when the married people sat like images on their front porches, and the boys and girls tramped and tramped the board sidewalks . . . " (196). Now music breaks the dark silence which settles on a small Nebraska town. Music improves the conditions of life.

> That silence seemed to ooze out of the ground, to hang under the foliage of the black maple trees with the bats and shadows. Now it was broken by lighthearted sounds. First the deep purring of Mr. Vanni's harp came in silvery ripples through the blackness of the dusty-smelling night; then the violins fell in—one of them was almost like a flute. They called so archly, so seductively, that our feet hurried toward the tent of themselves. Why hadn't we had a tent before? (196)

Music whets youth's appetite for life and brings out the dormant impulse for gaiety; when it has music, youth also has its happy hour.

In the scenes at the Vannis' pavilion, Willa Cather does more than dramatize how music transforms frontier life; she uses it to make certain observations about the social structure in a prairie town. In these instances, music redefines the social system of a prairie town. In Book II, "The Hired Girls," Jim goes out of his way to indict the haughty and narrow small-town mind and tells of a "curious social situation in Black Hawk" (197), the class distinction small-town mores created when Bohemian and Scandinavian country girls went into service with town families. "The daughters of Black Hawk merchants had a confident, unenquiring belief that they were 'refined,' and that the country girls who 'worked out,' were not" (199). Moreover, Black Hawk boys were supposed to marry Black Hawk girls, and "the country girls were considered a menace to the social order. Their beauty shone out too boldly against a conventional background" (201). Jim considers the attitude of the townspeople "very stupid" (200), and in proof of the equality—superiority, rather—of the foreign-born girls to the native Americans—cites the "'popular nights'" at Vannis' tent, which "brought the town boys and the country girls together on neutral ground" (203). Since dancing has nothing to do with artificial social superiority and everything to do with natural charm, Black Hawk's young men were willing to "risk a tiff with their sweethearts and general condemnation for a waltz with 'the hired girls'" (197). But no matter how strongly the town blades are attracted, their mothers have no need to be alarmed—"The respect for respectability was stronger than any desire in Black Hawk youth" (202). Music gives the hired girls a status which society denied. Even those who live by this decorum of suppression, the clerks and bookkeepers, even they could not help but feel the happiness from such musical heartiness.

Throughout *My Ántonia* music, musical talent, and musical interest are honorific qualities and designate a constructive commitment to life. Music implies a spirited and sensitive nature. Where that nature expresses itself spontaneously and freely, one finds joy and harmony; and in general, where there is music, there is happiness. Conversely, where there is no music or where music is forced or where the musician is constrained, there is profound unrest. In giving the music motif a negative treatment, Cather wishes to underscore the positive and restorative value of musical expression. There are a number of examples of this technique in the novel. The most conspicuous one is the development of Ántonia's father, Mr. Shimerda, in whose isolation and cultural yearnings Jim sees shadows of himself.

Mr. Shimerda, as his daughter reveals and as his actions confirm, immigrated to America against his will. " 'He not want to come, nev-er!' " Ántonia tells Jim. " 'My mamenka make him come" (89-90). He was altogether unsuited to the demands of the rugged Nebraska frontier, and he felt his inadequacy deeply, all the more deeply because he was a sensitive man. Unlike his quarrelsome wife, he had come to terms with life in the old country; and for him, acclimation to the new world is degeneration. The horror to Jim of this misplaced gentleman is conspicuous. Jim observes: "I suppose, in the crowded clutter of their cave, the old man had come to believe that peace and order had vanished from the earth, or existed only in the old world he had left so far behind" (86). In that "old world . . . left so far behind," Mr. Shimerda has been a musician. Unlike the other musicians in the novel, he seems to have had some training though we are never sure just how much (Ántonia, for example, recalls her father's lively discussions of music). He shares with the other musicians in My Ántonia an inborn talent and inner warmth which make their music humanly compelling even if it is artistically deficient by the highest standards. His refinement and culture, the two features of his nature which Cather emphasizes through his musical talent, isolate him on the great plains and deepen his tragic condition. After crossing the ocean, the Bohemian retains the form of his old life. To compensate for the disorder of his new life he rigorously attends to the orderliness of dress; and to defy the mysterious and uncultured world—or, perhaps, to cling to the old—he refuses to play his violin. Mr. Shimerda's renunciation of music signals desperation; psychologically, his decision denies the possibility of happiness. With music goes his desire for life. At the center of his soul there is deadness where there was once great, vigorous life. In Ántonia's words:

> "My papa sad for the old country. He not look good. He never make music any more. At home he play violin all the time; for weddings and for dance. Here never. When I beg him for play, he shake his head no. Some days he take his violin out of his box and make with his fingers on the strings, like this, but never he make the music." (89)

Mr. Shimerda's abstention from music, which he valued above his other cultural interests, points up the sharpness of his misery and the completeness of his detachment from the human community. The final tribute to the old gentlemen is, suitably, a musical one—a tender interruption of the silence he sought. Otto Fuchs leads the mourners in a hymn, "Jesus, Lover of My Soul," at Mr. Shimerda's grave. The hymn offers a compassion which the prairie withheld from the man, and Charles Wesley's reverent words balance the emotional farewell of the Shimerda family with a tribute to precisely the kind of "helpless soul" Mr. Shimerda was. And the comfort for which the hymn asks is a deeply human one. The final words do not violate our good impression of the Bohemian gentleman as do the family's manners and pietism.

> Thou of life the Fountain art,
> Freely let me take of Thee;
> Spring Thou up within my heart!
> Rise to all eternity![2]

The alienation of the artistically sensitive person in this cultural outpost comes up a second time in the novel. In Book III, which covers Jim's university years at Lincoln, Willa Cather once again observes through music the artist in society. Where she dramatized the tragic consequences of the artist's plight with Mr. Shimerda, in the third book she portrays the comic, almost farcical, dimension of artistic life on the prairie.

Lena's neighbor across the hall is a Polish violin teacher, a Mr. Ordinsky. Fundamentally he feels the way Mr. Shimerda does about the cultural life in Nebraska. But where Mr. Shimerda turns within and becomes shy and retiring, Ordinsky turns on society without and becomes bold and rather hilariously pompous. Formal even in his shabbiness, Ordinsky becomes arrogant to the extent that society is hostile to music. With his waistcoat held together by safety pins he stalks about remarking how " 'the noblest qualities are ridiculed' " in " 'a place like this' " and asserting the primacy of " 'delicacy' " and " '*noblesse oblige*' " (286–287). There is something pathetically hopeless about this man. His seriousness about music is admirable of course, and his affectation are not without charm; but his "furious article, attacking the musical taste of the town" (287) and his calls for " 'chivalry' " and " '*amour-propre*' " are futile gestures. His vain show before the " 'coarse barbarians' " (288) is embarrassing and only confirms the incongruity of art in this society; but still, beneath Ordinsky's mad histrionics is the lamentable circumstance of a society which is unprepared either to receive or aid the few artistic members who seek to improve it. Such a state of affairs either prohibits a violinist from playing or, if he performs in spite of the hostility, turns him into a doubtful and absurd sort, the man in motley. Ordinsky's own flamboyant hauteur finishes the job society starts.

At the end of the novel the full symbolic value of the violin becomes clear when Willa Cather relates it to Ántonia's heroic career. When Jim returns to Black Hawk many years later, Mr. Shimerda's violin, "which Ántonia had always kept" (347), sings again, this time in the deft little hands of Leo Cuzak, Ántonia's son and the youngest musician in the novel. The previously opposing values of divided worlds, Europe and America, are reconciled in the promise of Leo's success; and the old world's ideals and joys which are embodied in the musical instrument are preserved in Leo himself. Willa Cather stresses the point by insisting upon the Bohemian-ness of the young boy. Like his brothers and sisters, he understands and speaks Bohemian, and yet he seems comfortably placed in the new world, the pleasures of which he fully appreciates. When Leo plays, it is as if cultural progress, held in check while the settlers contended with the tough, daily tasks, moves forward from where it left off.

Little Leo seems equal to the responsibilities of a cultural custodian. He is playful, lively, sensitive but still bold, and he has those "deep-set, gold-green" eyes (348) which characterize such heroic Catherian creations as Thea Kronborg and Professor St. Peter. Moreover, he is instinctively a musician. Old Mr. Shimerda's instrument, as Jim Burden notes, is too big for Leo, "but he played very well for a self-taught boy" (347). What was literally dead, what Mr. Shimerda had cultivated and loved in Prague, has been reborn—and it is the violin, first put aside and then taken up again, which represents the process of transformation and regeneration in *My Ántonia*.

III

The most sustained and revealing development of music in *My Ántonia* occurs toward the end of Book II, "The Hired Girls," in the seventh through twelfth chapters which cover the events from late winter to spring of 1892. The section is pivotal because it brings to a close Jim Burden's high school education and Ántonia Shimerda's education in the ways of town life and leads up to "the summer which was to change everything" (193) for the two friends, when Ántonia's vitality lapses into irresponsibility. Both narrator and heroine are entering adulthood. Jim leaves for the University of Nebraska in the fall; Ántonia begins to assume moral independence. Music, the metaphor for freedom and vitality, elicits signs of their emotional growth.

The principal musical occasion in this section is the Blind d'Arnault interlude. This sequence, which might seem disproportionately long and extraneous, like the grotesque Russian story of Pavel and Peter's involvement with a bridal party who were thrown to the wolves, holds special importance for an understanding of Ántonia's magnificent capacity for life. The mulatto's performance, initially described as a welcome break in a desolately monotonous winter on the prairie, through Jim's appreciation enlarges into a metaphorical description of Ántonia's inner nature, of the burning fire of life that warms her spirit, of the "inner glow" that never fades.

The occasion is one of those Saturday-night gatherings of commercial travelers in the comfortable parlor of the Boys' Home which Mrs. Gardener, the owner, arranged around a grand piano. For Jim and Ántonia the presence at the hotel of Blind d'Arnault, the Negro pianist who is to give a concert in the Opera House on Monday, promises particularly gay music on this cold March night. His arrival in the parlor does brighten the musical atmosphere. In fact, his music generates a festivity which exceeds Jim's expectation. D'Arnault begins by leading the men in "'some good old plantation songs'" (184) and ends with fiery dance music that brings Ántonia and her friends from the adjacent dining room to spin with the gentlemen visitors in the parlor. Jim finds in Blind D'Arnault's piano-playing a talent capable of arousing the animal as well as spiritual impulses in man. The mulatto is, really, the nonpareil of musicians in *My Ántonia*. He has to an extraordinary degree the instinctive musical facility that Mr. Shimerda and Leo Cuzak have in more normal measure. If Leo plays by ear, then d'Arnault plays by body. He literally possesses the instrument. We are told that when, as a child, he first touched a piano, he "coupled himself to it, as if he knew it was to piece him out and make a whole creature of him" (188). He is described as a sheer, sensory mechanism, a mechanism that is not so much designed to receive sensory information from the external world as to transmit the impulse that comes from within. What comes from within is a basic, sensuous rhythm of unusual strength. His body emanates that rhythm.

> When he was sitting, or standing still, he swayed back and forth incessantly, like a rocking toy. At the piano, he swayed in time to the music, and when he was not playing, his body kept up this motion, like an empty mill grinding on. (184)

Mrs. Harling has told Jim about Blind d'Arnault, and he relates the case history of this "nervous infirmity," as he calls it. D'Arnault was born on a plantation in the Far South. He had been blind almost since his birth, and the nervous motion of his body became apparent when he was old enough to walk. When he was six he began running off from home, blind though he was, to stand outside the Big House and listen to Miss Nellie, the plantation's mistress, practicing on the piano. One time when she went out of the room, the blind child made his way into the house and to the source of the sounds that held him spellbound. With the keyboard at his finger tips, the boy began to play passages from pieces Miss Nellie had been practicing but which had already taken so definite a form within the blind child's brain that the "pattern . . . lay all ready-made on the big and little keys" (188). Melody, harmony, modulation are the conditions of the child's responses to the world. The tactile and auditory terms that Jim uses to describe the child's approaching the piano insist upon the irrational hypersensitive nature of Blind d'Arnault's mind.

> Through the dark he found his way to the Thing, to its mouth. He touched it softly, and it answered softly, kindly. He shivered and stood still. Then he began to feel it all over, ran his fingertips along the slippery sides, embraced the carved legs, tried to get some conception of its shape and size, of the space it occupied in primeval night. (187)

In his dark universe there is but the light of music. Music bridges his world and the outside world. It is expression and identification. With an uncanny musical instinct come his gifts of absolute pitch and accurate memory. Everything about the mulatto prodigy—his being a blend of races, his blindness, his spastic touching and keen hearing—contributes to the total impression that he is elemental musical sensation itself. "It was as if all the agreeable sensations possible to creatures of flesh and blood were heaped up on those black-and-white keys, and he were gloating over them and trickling them through his yellow fingers" (189). When he play, his body and inner being undergo a transformation. He is divested of consciousness in the

way that Thea Kronborg loses hers. In both instances the body becomes an unconscious, effortless medium for art. The word Willa Cather uses in *The Song of
the Lark* is "vessel"—"In singing, one made a vessel of one's throat and nostrils and
held it on one's breath, caught the stream in a scale of natural intervals." The term
describes the still emptiness of the artist's consciousness and body, and it fits Blind
d'Arnault. He is a vessel, ten yellow fingers through which trickle musical sensations.

The fascination with the pianist's past and the warm response to his stirring, if
crude, music are, first of all, comments on the narrator. We see in Jim Burden a
preference for strong emotion. That preference makes his account of Blind d'Arnault a celebration of an emotional genius which triumphs over barriers of mistaken
judgment and physical infirmity. Jim, we observe, is growing into a more generous
attitude toward human behavior than society or even his charitable grandparents
could teach him. Reason and logic, he begins to learn through Blind d'Arnault's
music, are less helpful at times than are emotions and intuitions. Jim's record of the
impromptu concert presupposes a capacity to respond to something elemental, like
the blind pianist's interior fire, and a capacity to realize that spiritual vigor of this
kind makes its claims above ordinary standards of judgment, like the quality of
musicianship, for example. This sensitivity to the irrational and irreducible in man is
requisite for Jim as celebrator of Ántonia, whose distinction, like the pianist's,
remains beneath appearance and whose success, again like d'Arnault's music, cannot be measured by conventional rules. The heart or a mind with supersensory
impulses is required.

Recognizing that d'Arnault's music with its frenzied and wonderful qualities
invites a special kind of spiritual response and therefore defines a way of perceiving
human attributes, we can go on to consider Ántonia's connection to that music. On
that Saturday night in March her reaction to his playing is not different from that of
her friends Tiny, Lena, and Mary Dusak. They all enjoy the lively waltzes and, with
Mrs. Gardener away in Omaha, enjoy the generally free atmosphere of the hotel.
The strong rhythm from the piano floats into the dining room of the hotel where
Ántonia and the other country girls are listening and has a contagious effect on
them. "In the middle of a crashing waltz, d'Arnault suddenly began to play softly,
and, turning to one of the men who stood behind him, whispered, 'Somebody
dancing in there.' He jerked his bullet-head toward the dining-room. 'I hear little
feet—girls, I 'spect'" (189). The Marshall Field's man, Kirkpatrick, looks over the
transom and sees the country girls waltzing. He insists that they join the "'roomful
of lonesome men on the other side of the partition'" (190). Then, "at a word from
Kirkpatrick, d'Arnault spread himself out over the piano, and began to draw the
dance music out of it, while the perspiration shone on his short wool and on his
uplifted face" (191). This "glistening African god of pleasure" generates waves of
musical excitement. When the dancers pause to change partners, he urges them
not to "'let that floor get cold,'" and he plays until his manager stops him by shutting
the piano. The excitement his music has aroused is strong enough to keep Jim and
Ántonia stirred up for some time afterward. "I walked home with Ántonia. We
were so excited that we dreaded to go to bed. We lingered a long while at the

Harlings' gate, whispering in the cold until the restlessness was slowly chilled out of us" (192).

In the fuller context of Ántonia's story, especially the sections treating the arrival of the Vannis' dancing pavilion in June of 1892, the Blind d'Arnault passage relates closely and specifically to the heroine. As music pieces d'Arnault out and makes "a whole creature of him" (188), so it brings Ántonia into a new awareness of herself. D'Arnault's music signals the awakening of something strong and passionate in Ántonia which the subsequent dances at the tent and the Firemen's Hall kindle. The dances mark Ántonia's rapid progress toward an understanding of herself. Dancing broadens the margins of her life and desire beyond the pleasant but narrow confines of the Harling house. Given her natural exuberance, Ántonia has only to find rich soil in order to bloom. And so she does. "The Vannis often said that Ántonia was the best dancer of them all" (205). Jim tells us later that when spinning onto the floor with Tony "you set out every time upon a new adventure" (223).

Dancing also sets Ántonia out on a new adventure, a moral adventure for which she is not prepared. She becomes preoccupied with the pavilion and is absorbed in the idea of following her desire. She hums dance tunes all day and "at the first call of the music, she became irresponsible" (205)—remiss in her household chores and careless in her personal relations. Sudden freedom and pleasure carry Ántonia away, as first great pleasures can, and rather than surrender her new liberty she quit her job with the Harlings to work for the Cutters. "'I guess I want to have my fling, like the other girls'" (208), she announces to Mrs. Harling, whose concern for the girl's "'reputation'" is genuine. As things turn out, that fling creates a special seclusion, not the freedom Ántonia expected. With the Cutters she is caught in an atmosphere of emotional tension and lives under a threat of physical harm. And her premature independence is expressed in a style which separates her from Jim's and Mrs. Burden's sympathy. Ántonia's clothes become showy, cheap imitations of Mrs. Gardener's flashy mode. The country girl cannot control every situation with the ease she displayed in the Harling kitchen and yard among children and generous adults. Evil assumes subtler forms than Ántonia can cope with and misfortune follows. Wick Cutter's devious attempts to seduce her and Larry Donovan's success in doing so qualify the prize of freedom for which Ántonia fought and are the comeuppance for self-reliance not grounded in experience. But another qualification is in order here so that we do not judge Ántonia more strictly than Willa Cather does. The Cutter and Donovan affairs arise from no serious fault in Ántonia. She suffers because of virtue: she is too innocent, too trusting, too kind to suspect the sly intention of Cutter and the confidence game Donovan specializes in. Her response to both situations reveals deeply sympathetic traits. The Cutter experience does not teach her to be suspicious but, admirably, not to be so vain; and the illegitimate child Donovan fathers becomes for Ántonia a possibility for great love. Besides quickening a desire within Ántonia, Blind d'Arnault's music suggests the heroine's blindness and foreshadows the reckless spree her lack of foresight brings about. Finally, Blind d'Arnault's crashing music reminds us of a

passion which vitalizes even Ántonia's erratic behavior and which transforms isolation into independence, sorrow into joy.

The Blind D'Arnault passage is the pulsating center of *My Ántonia*. Occurring
as it does in the very middle of the novel, it gives off the emotional—the musical—
impulse which reverberates throughout. We are led up to this outpouring of music
and spirit by a series of references to Mr. Shimerda's violin, the Saturday musicales
at the Harlings', and Ántonia's own enjoyment of music, especially the kind she can
dance to. We are led away from this generative center by the dances at the Vannis'
tent and the Firemen's Hall and by Leo's tender playing of his grandfather's violin.
The treatment of Blind d'Arnault's performance is ambivalent. His music invokes
ignorance, indiscretion, hot-headedness; but it draws out freedom, fancy, courage.

The spiritual kinship Willa Cather establishes between d'Arnault and Ántonia
brings us directly to the novelist's revelation of those musical souls whose "yearnings
. . . first broke the silence of the world," to return to one of her first statements
about the power of music. Cather penetrates behind surface difference to show
spiritual likeness. The pianist's kind of music corresponds to Ántonia's kind of life in
that both are intense and passionate, following something primal, almost primordial.
"No matter how many wrong notes he struck, he never lost the intention of a
passage, he brought the substance of it across by irregular and astonishing means"
(189). Ántonia has the same talent. She knows what is morally right instinctively,
without the aid of code or commandment; she converts defeat into triumph. Seen
in this way, d'Arnault's gift of absolute pitch matches Ántonia's absolute love, and
his retentive memory suggests her power to bring together the disparate experiences of Europe and America, country and city.

To read the d'Arnault passage as a musical commentary on Ántonia is not to
reduce that passage to a delimiting metaphor; such a reading, rather, reveals the
richness and intensity of Ántonia's life and also something of Willa Cather's masterly
use of musical figure. The evaluative summation of d'Arnault's life and musical
accomplishment runs a parallel course to Ántonia's life: from imitation to originality,
from confinement to release, from excitement to expression, from frustration to
self-expression.

> As a very young child he could repeat, after a fashion, any composition that
> was played for him. No matter how many wrong notes he struck, he never
> lost the intention of a passage, he brought the substance of it across by
> irregular and astonishing means. He wore his teachers out. He could never
> learn like other people, never acquired any finish. He was always a Negro
> prodigy who played barbarously and wonderfully. As piano-playing, it was
> perhaps abominable, but as music it was something real, vitalized by a sense
> of rhythm that was stronger than his other physical senses—that not only filled
> his dark mind, but worried his body incessantly. To hear him, to watch him,
> was to see a Negro enjoying himself as only a Negro can. It was as if all the
> agreeable sensations possible to creatures of flesh and blood were heaped up
> on those black-and-white keys, and he were gloating over them and trickling
> them through his yellow fingers. (188-189)

Like d'Arnault, Ántonia has a kind of blindness, and it is a deficiency which, like his, produces compensating benefits. Ántonia says: " 'The trouble with me was, Jim, I never could believe harm of anybody I loved' " (344). As the pianist's blindness sharpens his auditory and tactile awareness, Ántonia's inability to believe anyone unworthy of love creates an over-balance of love. Surely she is all the more heroic because she cannot comprehend evil and because she cannot hate. Homer's passage on the harpist, Demokodos, which I have used for this chapter's epigraph, tells us how we must judge Ántonia—by her great talent, love, for that is how she judges others. He who lent her sweetness did make her blind.

IV

Finally, music has a broad associational importance for the special kind of heroic life Ántonia represents. While music helps to bring back to Jim's mind the Nebraska past and his relationship with Ántonia, it also serves as a bridge to a still more distant past—the European past. Mr. Shimerda's music, unheard in America but frequently heard in Europe, is altogether of that distant world. But for Ántonia that world is not lost. She transplants its traditional values. The past is a shaping part of her present. In her inner ear the music of Prague lingers in various forms. It comes to her from nature. When she hears the katydid sing, for example, the recollection of a village beggar woman who sang songs for a warm place near the fire evokes her European childhood. " 'I ain't never forgot my own country' " (238). Her country, in a way, is still heard.

> "In summer, when they [flowers] were in bloom, he [Mr. Shimerda] used to sit there with his friend that played the trombone. When I was little I used to go down there to hear them talk—beautiful talk, like what I never hear in this country." (236)

In her own household at the end of the novel there is music as there was at the Harlings' place and in her Prague home. Impressively, music is deeply rooted in the Cuzaks' everyday life.

The impromptu concert after the festive dinner Ántonia prepared to honor Jim's homecoming is a beautiful tribute to her special musical nature. As the flourishing orchards represent the interior quality of Ántonia's genius, her profound repose, the musicale marks the familial quality of her greatness, her large love. Yulka, one of the Cuzak girls, accompanies Leo's playing of the violin; and though her effort is less successful than Leo's, Yulka succeeds in the way that counts. Music fills the parlor with expression and love. During the duet, little Nina gets up from her corner and begins to dance in the middle of the floor, and no one would think of being so ungenerous as to check the child's spontaneous demonstration of emotion. The assumptions in the air of Ántonia's world are deeply human, and they go back to all the good things she herself discovered in music when she was young and which she lives by when old—feeling, freedom, rhythm, openness, and love. No wonder Jim "was conscious of a kind of physical harmony" (349) among the people around Ántonia. It is in the music of the air. Again a soul has touched a soul; again a rainbow bridge is raised into the kingdom of the soul.

Ántonia is not a musical artist as is the great Thea Kronborg. But then Willa Cather's ultimate interest in Thea's artistic eminence is more than a fascination with a fight to become a great lyric singer. Cather sees the artistic life as one aspect of the universal striving for selfhood and meaning. So, too, does she see in Ántonia's struggle and domesticity an aspect of the artistic. These lives represent two expressions of the inextinguishable human spirit.

Still, so much about Ántonia *is* musical. Her life is musical in the final harmony she achieves with the world around. In its spontaneity and its direction, the music of Ántonia's life is attuned to the whole music of nature, a music which ranges from the frailest katydid's thin, rusty chirp up to the earth's symphonic florescence. Ántonia's power and perfection come from the unison achieved between her life and all of life—a concord between the cadence of the universe and of her spirit. The measure of her artistry is the harmonic activity around the farm. The place abounds with life. Numerous children and animals run about; the land flourishes; and the orchards are laden with autumn fruitfulness. All this physical growth goes back to a spiritual growth in Ántonia. Beauty and youth are gone. Only an "inner glow" remains. But "whatever else was gone, Ántonia had not lost the fire of life" (336). That fire within warmed her in the winter of adversity and precipitated her growth as a person. She made of her foreign ancestry a cultural asset and heritage of family life; she made of her stay in town an opportunity to refine the farm life of her family; she made of her illegitimate child a fine, loved daughter; she made of foreign American soil a home. Her gift is a perennial transformation of want and weakness into pleasure and strength.

NOTES

[1]*My Ántonia* (Sentry Edition; Boston: Houghton Mifflin, 1961). All references are to this text.
[2]*Franklin Square Song Collection*, selected by J. P. McCaskey (New York: Harper and Brothers, 1881), p. 133.

William J. Stuckey

MY ÁNTONIA:
A ROSE FOR MISS CATHER

Critics who are most committed to defending Willa Cather's integrity as an artist seem to have developed a talent for talking about *My Ántonia* out of both sides of their mouths. For though Miss Cather's admirers have found much to praise in the individual parts of this book, they have turned up a fairly large number of serious flaws as well. It is generally acknowledged, for example, that the book is very loosely organized, that many incidents have no apparent function in the novel, and that though it is supposed to be about Ántonia, most of the five books that make up the novel are about the narrator, Jim Burden. Even more damaging has been the critics' admission that, in spite of Jim Burden's assertion that he would have liked to have had Ántonia for a wife, there is little in the novel to support this. Indeed, one critic has said that there is an emotional emptiness in Jim and Ántonia's relationship.[1]

The conclusion of *My Ántonia* has also given some critics pause, for although it is this section that does most to create the beautiful symbolic Ántonia, there is the feeling among some readers that this is a tacked-on happy ending and, further, that the method of creating this beauty is not altogether honest.[2] Instead of pursuing the implications of their insights, however—by asking how these flaws may be squared with the rest of the novel—critics have either set them aside or found a means of explaining them away.[3] And so, the general impression one gets from reading Miss Cather's critics is that *My Ántonia* is a beautiful book celebrating agrarian values, but that it is not one that will bear much looking into.

This attitude is hardly a compliment either to Willa Cather or to *My Ántonia*, for though it may help preserve the popular view that *My Ántonia* is an inspired novel about a vital, dynamic earth mother living on the Nebraska frontier, it keeps us from exploring the contradictions beneath the surface story. And surely, unless those contradictions are faced, we cannot say with much conviction what this novel actually is about.

One way to square these contradictions with the surface events of the story is to see that though *My Ántonia* is ostensibly about Ántonia, actually, technically, it is about what Ántonia *comes to mean* to Jim Burden.

From *Studies in the Novel* 4, No. 3 (Fall 1972): 473–83.

This is not a trivial distinction, as I shall try to show, for though there is much in the novel that cannot be fully brought into a single design, much of it can be seen as a consistently playing down, even a denying of what Ántonia is, and a playing up of what Jim Burden is finally able to make her into. And so it might be said that *My Ántonia* is not so much the story of Ántonia's agrarian success, as it is Jim Burden's success in converting her into a symbol of a way of life that he approves of. This is not to say, of course, that the details of Ántonia's life are not an important part of Jim's story. They are. But they are also the raw materials from which Jim Burden is able to select those things that can be made to fit *his* picture of Ántonia. In the process, some of this raw material has to be suppressed. And it is this suppression, particularly in the conclusion, that strikes some readers as dishonest. But if one sees how this suppression follows logically from what has gone before, then it will seem no more or less dishonest than the rest of the book.

The general pattern of Jim Burden's success comes from his desire to convert Ántonia into a beautiful image of agrarian life and Ántonia's resistance to that conversion—a pattern that might be sketched somewhat as follows: at first Jim is attracted to Ántonia's warmth and vitality, but at the same time repelled by the grosser aspects of her behaviour; later, while still drawn to her, he is further repelled by her growing crudeness and, still later, by the way she is attracted to other men. It is not masculine jealousy that Jim appears to feel, but some deep sense of outrage and frustration. He likes Ántonia and wants to approve of her, but her manners and her animal vitality prevent him from doing so. As a consequence, Jim's relationship with Ántonia shifts back and forth between liking and disgust.

The high point of Jim's disgust comes after a fight between Jim and Wick Cutter, a would-be seducer of Ántonia. After the fight, Jim says that he hates Ántonia and that he never wants to see her again. Shortly thereafter (and apparently without being reconciled with her), Jim goes away to the University at Lincoln. There, from reading Vergil, he comes to understand that without vital, earthy girls (like Ántonia, though he does not specifically name her) there would be no poetry. This insight appears to be a turning point in Jim's relationship with Ántonia, for when he goes home and discovers that she has been seduced by a cheap ladies' man named Larry Donovan and has borne his child, he is not shocked or disgusted. Instead, he is able to think of Ántonia in a wholly idealized way. When he goes East to Harvard Law School, he carries with him a warm and happy image of his childhood friend.

In the concluding section of the novel, Jim rounds out his beautiful portrait of Ántonia. He has returned to Nebraska after an absence of twenty years and has found in Ántonia's life nothing to shock or dismay him. Indeed, he is able to see in her and in the beautiful family and the fine orchard and fertile farm she has created a symbol for the source of civilization itself.

The pattern I have described starts at the beginning of the novel, shortly after Jim and Ántonia meet. Jim, of course, does not know Ántonia very well and is not as deeply attracted to her as he is later to become, but he "snuggles" down with her in the prairie grass and admires the beauty of the landscape. He thinks Ántonia "quick and very eager" and remarks that it was "wonderfully pleasant" there with the blue sky over them and the gold tree in front. Then Ántonia spoils the beauty of the occasion by making a gesture that Jim regards as too familiar. She offers him "a little chased silver ring she wore on her middle finger. When she coaxed and insisted" that he take it, Jim "repulsed her quite sternly." He remarks, "I didn't want her ring, and I felt there was something reckless and extravagant about her wishing to give it away to a boy she had never seen before."[4] These are to be Ántonia's most exasperating qualities—her extravagant vitality and her improper behaviour, for the early Jim can be wholly content with her only when her vitality is checked by what he sees as appropriate formal gestures.

The same problem occurs again in the "rattlesnake incident," except that instead of being overly friendly, Ántonia is now being overly oppressive. Just previous to this incident, Ántonia has been "taking a superior tone" with Jim and he resents it. It is not that he wants Ántonia's affection. What he wants is for her to behave toward him the way a girl should behave toward a boy. The encounter with the snake, which Jim kills, terrifies Ántonia, and Jim's bravery in killing it chastens her into paying him the deference he feels is his due. "She liked me better from that time on, and she never took a supercilious air with me again. I had killed a big snake—I was now a big fellow" (p. 35). This incident is handled rather lightly and Jim's wish to be treated as a "big fellow" is no doubt humorously meant. Still, it is significant that Jim's dissatisfaction, here again, is due to Ántonia's refusal to take what he regards as a proper attitude toward him. And, also significant, she pleases him only when she expresses that attitude.

There is in the novel, as I have said, a good deal that cannot be assimilated to this pattern. Our concern, however, is with Jim the image-maker, not with Ántonia, the raw material on which the image draws. Still, the things that Jim chooses to tell about his grandparents and about their home, about the town of Black Hawk and the townspeople, and especially what he says about Ántonia's family, fall more fully into place when one sees how they are related to this pursuit of a forced image of excellence. Take, for example, the way Jim creates for us an image of his grandparents. There are a number of characters in the book that are treated with astringent realism, but the Burdens are handled as gently as if they were two valuable old woodcuts. They are homely, to be sure, for they are country people, but they are spotlessly beautiful. Their manners and dress, the way they treat Jim and the hired hands, their relations with their neighbors, the way they conduct their household—all possess a kind of aloof serenity. The Burden grandparents, it seems, have achieved a perfection of form that Jim wants Ántonia to have.

Jim's trouble lies, of course, in his initial failure to see that Ántonia will not be able to learn that form from his grandparents. But then Jim is not concerned with reasons. He merely sees how imperfect Ántonia and her family are and he displays their imperfections with harsh clarity. The Shimerdas are pictured by Jim as dirty, disorganized, inept, and ill-mannered. Whereas the Burden grandparents never exhibit any unattractive emotions, the Shimerdas appear to do nothing but quarrel, whine, steal, and beg. Only Mr. Shimerda, the Austrian violinist, keeps up an attractive exterior and significantly is the only one among the Shimerdas who deeply appreciates the Burdens' good manners. Indeed, he finds their well-ordered house a civilized refuge in an otherwise savage world. When Mr. Shimerda takes his life, Jim has the feeling that the old violinist's soul visits the Burdens' house before departing for the next world. Jim thinks that had Mr. Shimerda been able to live in the Burdens' house, "this terrible thing would never have happened" (p. 68).

As Jim gets to know Ántonia better, his difficulty with her reduces to the unpleasant fact that she prefers to be more like her family than like his.[5] That is why Jim grows angry with Ántonia when she takes her family's side in a fight with one of the Burdens' hired hands, and that is why he is so repelled by her when she imitates her brother's crude table manners. It does not occur to Jim to admire Ántonia's loyalty to her family or to see that table manners are not a reliable indication of human worth. Here again, what is important to Jim is how Ántonia behaves and, at this point in the novel, he cannot accept her behaviour.

Essentially the same thing is brought out, but in a positive manner, on the one occasion in the early part of the book when Ántonia deeply pleases Jim. A number of things have happened just before this to make Jim vow he will never be friends with the Shimerdas again, but then Ántonia (unaccountably) comes to work for Jim's grandmother and now that Ántonia is under the Burdens' roof Jim is delighted with her. "We were glad to have her in the house," Jim says. "She was so gay and responsive that one did not mind her heavy, running step, or her clattery way with pans." And Ántonia pleases Jim by expressing her liking for the Burden household. "I like your grandmother," she tells him, "and all things here." Jim comes back, "Why aren't you always nice like this, Tony?" (pp. 92–93).

If Tony had remained in the Burden household or, later, had stayed in the cultivated Harling household (where she continues to be a "nice" motherly hired girl), Jim might have been able to keep her high in his estimation, but Ántonia's old wilfulness reasserts itself along with her animal vitality. She insists on going to the notorious Saturday night tent dances and this indecorous behaviour causes her to lose her position with the Harlings. Perversely, it seems to Jim, Ántonia goes to work for Wick Cutter, an infamous woman chaser. Mrs. Harling predicts that Ántonia will "have a fling" at the Cutters that she "won't get up from in a hurry" (p. 137). As it turns out, Ántonia does have her fling, but it is Jim who has trouble getting up. In an attempt to protect Ántonia's honor from Wick Cutter, he gets his eye blackened and his lip cut. This experience deeply depresses him. He says that he hates Ántonia for having let him in "for all of this disgustingness" (p. 162).

This incident perhaps more than any other one gives us an important insight into Jim's attachment to Ántonia. His interest is not the conventionally romantic one that some readers have tried to find (and which Miss Cather to some extent encourages). Jim does not love Ántonia as a man would. His feeling for her is that of a child who "hero-worships" an older person. He wants to admire and look up to Ántonia and, of course, he is inevitably disappointed. It never occurs to Jim to question his demands on Ántonia. He is too preoccupied with his ideal of her.

The solution for getting Ántonia permanently enshrined in Jim's admiration is not directly presented in the novel. Jim simply goes off to the university at Lincoln, acquires a certain distance from her, along with an insight by way of Vergil into the poetic worth of primitive women, which hardly prepares us for his ability to accept so readily behaviour from Ántonia (her "elopement" with Larry Donovan and the illegitimate baby) that would have shocked him earlier. But the problem for the skeptical reader is that Jim does not really accept what Ántonia has done. He avoids it or, more accurately, his author arranges matters so that none of the potentially unpleasant details are allowed to get through to Jim. He learns of Ántonia's affair indirectly, and through a woman who likes Ántonia very much and who therefore puts her situation in an attractive light. His only contacts with Ántonia's baby, moreover, are in a photographer's studio where he notices a picture of it ("one of those depressing 'crayon enlargements' often seen in farm-house parlours"), and, later, when given a quick look by Ántonia's sister (p. 207). Then when Jim sees Ántonia again, he sees her alone, out-of-doors, under a beautiful sky and against a backdrop of trees and shocks of wheat. Ántonia almost spoils the beauty of this meeting by talking about her little girl, but Jim, who perhaps is clinging fast to his revelation from Vergil, quickly lifts the conversation to a higher plane.[6] "Do you know, Ántonia," he says, "since I've been away, I think of you more often than of anyone else in this part of the world. I'd have liked to have you for a sweetheart, or a wife, or my mother or my sister—anything that a woman can be to a man. The idea of you is part of my mind.... You really are a part of me" (p. 208).

Jim has at last succeeded in getting Ántonia detached from the disappointing realities of her life and converted into a beautiful picture he can carry East with him when he goes off to Harvard.

It takes twenty years for the full idealization of Ántonia to take place. And during that time she has had the opportunity not only to increase in her ability to reflect Jim's ideal, but to take on the ability to reflect the timeless pattern of civilization as well. She is married now, the mother of eleven children, the mistress of a fertile farm and a well-ordered household. She can no longer spoil Jim's ideal of her, for she is, from Jim's point of view, a completed, a finished person. And he is only a visitor in her house, a status that gives him the distance and detachment necessary to his idealization. Gone are both the appearance and the necessity for seeing anything unpleasant in Ántonia's life; instead are manifestations of the rural virtues that Jim associates with his grandparents and their beautifully managed old farm: cleanliness, order, decorum. The only vestige of the Shimerda household is, happily, the violin that once belonged to Ántonia's unhappy father, which two of Ántonia's children play, with less than moderate success. For it is not the fine arts that Ántonia comes to symbolize for Jim Burden, but the domestic ones. He is able to see her permanently at last, as the maker of formal gestures which, he says, "we recognize by instinct as universal and true" (p. 228).

From the standpoint of ordinary human behaviour, Jim Burden's interest in Ántonia is unconvincing. This is implied in E. K. Brown's suggestion that Miss Cather might better have employed a feminine point of view.[7] Perhaps. But this is like saying she might better have given us a different Ántonia. We have no way of knowing what Ántonia might have been (or, indeed, whether she would have been) had Miss Cather chosen to create her from a different point of view. All we have is what we have been given. Nor need we believe that Jim Burden is a real man in order to accept the fact that Miss Cather used him to create *her* Ántonia. Jim Burden, convincing or not, is the special consciousness out of which Ántonia has been brought before us and we cannot separate the two.

Most writers, whether deliberately or not, try to keep the special consciousness out of which a novel comes from showing—perhaps because the process of writing fiction is an evasion as well as an affirmation. In *My Ántonia* Miss Cather did something most unusual. She not only allowed this special consciousness to show; she put it in the forefront of her story and, whether she meant to or not, made it the chief focus of attention. She did that, I believe, out of psychological as well as artistic necessity.

We can, perhaps, see better why Jim Burden is necessary if we compare him with a similar but significantly different narrator—Nick Carraway of *The Great Gatsby*. Nick Carraway and Jim Burden are, in a sense, narrative devices for making "objective" a special kind of romantic sensibility. Both novels include a heroine who is the embodiment of that sensibility—Daisy Buchanan and Ántonia Shimerda—and both are made to reveal their romantic significance through the subjective response of a character who may also be said to have "created" them. But there is an important difference between Fitzgerald's treatment and Willa Cather's. Fitzgerald has two narrators, one romantic, one realistic. Gatsby, the romantic, creates Daisy romantically. Nick, the realist, communicates Gatsby's romantic creation and supplies, along with it, a realistic portrait of Daisy. We are not meant to share Gatsby's vision of Daisy, but rather to understand it and to admire the vitality and the sense of wonder that such a vision implies. Miss Cather, on the other hand, combines in one character, Jim Burden, romantic vision and realistic skepticism. Burden tries to make us see Ántonia (and her unpleasant family) in an unillusioned way, but he also wants to make us accept certain illusions about Ántonia as well. Jim's problem (which is also Miss Cather's) is that he cannot get Ántonia into romantic focus until he is far enough away to keep from seeing the things that make her seem unromantic. An essential difference, then, between these two novels is that Fitzgerald, while technically writing "objectively" about a romantic vision, still keeps that vision mysterious; whereas Miss Cather, who wishes to give direct expression to that vision, shows us much about her heroine that is unromantic. This is, in part, a failure of technique.[8]

A failure of technique in a writer of Willa Cather's talent is more than a technical failure, of course. It is a failure of sensibility as well. For what is significant about Jim Burden is not that he is a clumsy device the reader must somehow see around, but that Miss Cather chose to use him in the first place and that she kept on using him even when it must have been apparent that he was not working. But technique, if I may shift the perspective somewhat, is often the result of compromise between what the writer wishes to say and what, given the material he has to work with and the nature of his sensibility, he is able to write. In this sense, the point of view from which a novel is told is the writer himself, or as much of him as we can ever know.

Willa Cather, when pressed by critics who complained that *My Ántonia* was not a novel, maintained that it was not intended as such. It was, she said, simply about people she had once known.[9] Technical failures cannot be so easily explained away. *My Ántonia*, though evidently based on the facts of Willa Cather's life, obviously is fiction. Still, it is more autobiographical than Willa Cather's other fiction, not just because it closely follows those facts (often in a pointless way) but because it reveals a side of her that does not show itself so visibly in her other novels. Jim Burden is, in an important sense, Willa Cather, and *My Ántonia* demonstrates the way Miss Cather's imagination set about converting the raw materials of experience into art. For her, the creation of fiction was not the striking of a balance between personal feeling and the facts of experience (or, as T. S. Eliot has said, of intensifying the world to fit one's feelings). For Miss Cather, it was the imposing of her strong and intensely personal feelings upon a sometimes intractable world. The much admired image of the "plough against the sun," for example, illustrates specifically the way her imagination worked. The plough that Jim and the hired girls see magnified into heroic size against the setting sun can stand as a symbol for the real world; the sun, for the writer's vision which lifts up that world and intensifies it to match the writer's feelings. This imaginative process, however, is partly a romantic heightening, partly a matter of excluding what is ugly or extraneous.

The extent to which this process was a characteristic of Willa Cather's mind is revealed in a remark made by Elizabeth Shepley Sergeant, a friend of hers. "There was so much that Willa Cather did not want to see and saw not," but "what she did see she had selected instinctively and in that instinctual sharing of it she gave it a sort of halo of brightness."[10] Willa Cather, her friend makes clear, did not want to see unpleasant things in places or in people she liked, and she was not able to see anything to admire in what she disapproved of. When she wrote, she was capable of being mercilessly realistic about what she despised. What she loved, she had to beautify. That is what great art meant to Willa Cather: making things beautiful.[11]

Willa Cather's talent for beautifying worked best when it was called upon to deal with things remote, with landscapes, village streets, houses, groups of people, or single persons detached from relationships with others and caught in a characteristic attitude. It was the surface of life and isolated moments of exalted emotion that gave Willa Cather her most satisfying clues to the meaning of experience.[12] Jim Burden's problem with Ántonia was Willa Cather's problem as well, possibly because Ántonia was based upon someone in her own past whom she had known too personally to romanticize completely. It was only when, like Jim Burden, she had put time and distance between her and her past, after having lived long enough in Pittsburgh and, later in New York, that she could see it in the beautiful way her imagination required.[13]

It is commonly said that in turning away from stories about artists and New England aristocrats, which had preoccupied her in earlier years, and directing her attention to the Nebraska frontier on which she had grown up, Willa Cather was heeding the advice of Sara Orne Jewett to deal with the life in her own particular corner of the world.[14] But Miss Cather's imaginative return to Nebraska was as much an escape as it was a return, for the failures and defeats, the emotional sterility of pioneer life that she had depicted with such bitterness in her earliest fiction, are not really faced in *My Ántonia*.[15] It is simply there, in inert passages of unassimilated realism (the story of Pavel and Peter, Mr. Shimerda's suicide, the death of the tramp who flings himself into a harvesting machine), preserved like a fly in the amber of Willa Cather's mellifluous prose. Had she really gone home again, had she come to grips with what it was in frontier culture (and perhaps in herself) that destroyed sensitive people or turned them into sterile dilettantes, *My Ántonia* might have been a moving tragedy rather than a potential tragedy with a tacked-on happy ending.[16]

However aware Willa Cather may have been of the tragic implications of her material, she was not capable of writing that kind of book. Her method was to reject failure by rejecting life and by finding in the past, her own and later—in works like *Death Comes for the Archbishop* and *Shadows on the Rock*—in the remoter lives of historical personages, materials out of which she could construct beautiful images of life. *My Ántonia* to some extent escapes the deadly beautifying process. There is in it still a sense of life but it is life struggling to resist the embalming of art.

The story of Jim Burden's struggle and final success with Ántonia is, then, the story of an artist who triumphs over life by converting it into an art object. This, of course, is what all artists do, but Miss Cather has taken it a step farther; she has put the artistic process into the center of her story. A novelist like Fitzgerald or Hemingway or Henry James (to name a writer Miss Cather is said most to resemble) uses art to catch the very feel of life itself. At the end of novels like *The Great Gatsby, A Farewell to Arms* and *The Portrait of a Lady* (a James novel that illustrates, I believe, how little of the essential James is in Willa Cather) there is a final opening out of the fictional world into the world of reality. Gatsby is delivered from his cocoon of illusion into the frighteningly real world of men. Frederic Henry walks out of romance into the cold and sobering rain, and Isabel Archer is at last made to see the ugly truth her romantic imagination had concealed from her.[17] These conclusions, of course, are still fictions, but the intent one senses behind them is to make them resemble the world of actual experience.

The intent one senses behind the conclusion of *My Ántonia*, on the contrary, is to lift Ántonia out of her "real" world into a world of changeless art. The Ántonia of the final pages of this novel—the vital, irrepressible Ántonia—has become at last the beautiful tomb of Jim Burden's past.[18]

NOTES

[1]Most of the critics who discuss this book at any length make essentially this complaint, but see especially E. K. Brown, *Willa Cather: A Critical Biography* (New York: Alfred A. Knopf, 1953), p. 199.

[2]See David Daiches, *Willa Cather: A Critical Introduction* (New York: The Crowell-Collier Co., 1962),

p. 45, and John H. Randall III, *The Landscape and the Looking Glass* (Boston: Houghton Mifflin Co., 1960), p. 148.

[3]Randall, for example, argues that the novel has a double protagonist (Jim stands for the head, Ántonia for the heart), which only formally relates Jim's sterility to Ántonia's vitality and does not resolve the basic contradictions in the novel (p. 107). For a subtler attempt to resolve the contradiction see Terence Martin, "The Drama of Memory in *My Ántonia*," *PMLA*, 84 (March 1969), 304–11.

[4]*My Ántonia* (Boston: Houghton Mifflin Co., 1954), p. 20. All quotations are from this edition. Subsequent page references are given in the text.

[5]Years ago an elderly Bohemian woman of my acquaintance told me she thought the portrait of the Shimerda family highly unfair. I never agreed with this criticism until recently when, on rereading the novel, I found hardly a detail about the Shimerdas, particularly Mrs. Shimerda, that does not express either contempt or superiority—or both. Mr. Shimerda is more gently treated, but he is an ineffectual dandy whose most redeeming quality besides his cleanliness appears to be his appreciation of the Burdens' superiority.

[6]The importance attached to this insight from Vergil is suggested by Jim's statement that "this revelation seemed" to him "so inestimably precious," that he "clung to it as if it might suddenly vanish" (p. 175).

[7]P. 201

[8]Willa Cather said that in using Jim Burden as her narrator she had been trying to achieve two effects: "Jim was to be fascinated by Ántonia as only a man could be, and yet he was to remain a detached observer, appreciative but inactive, rather than take a part in her life." Brown, p. 202.

[9]Brown, p. 199.

[10]*Willa Cather: A Memoir* (Philadelphia and New York: J. B. Lippincott Co., 1935), p. 46. Miss Sergeant tells a great many anecdotes that illustrate Willa Cather's stubborn refusal to accept anything that contradicted her own feelings. See especially pp. 36–37 and 163–64.

[11]This is apparent to anyone who has read very much of Willa Cather's fiction or her drama criticism. But see Randall's discussion of the influences of Walter Pater on her, pp. 1–6.

[12]A close friend of Willa Cather's tells an ancedote that illustrates this quality in Miss Cather. As preparation for writing *Sapphira and the Slave Girl* she visited her old home in Virginia. She found the house so "ruinous and forlorn" that she "did not go inside the house, but only stood and looked down at it from a distance. All these transformations instead of disheartening her, seemed to light a fierce inner flame that illuminated all her pictures of the past." Edith Lewis, *Willa Cather Living: A Personal Record* (New York: Alfred A. Knopf, 1953), p. 183.

[13]Randall, pp. 58–64.

[14]Ibid., p. 60.

[15]Ibid., pp. 21–33.

[16]Daiches, p. 45.

[17]It seems ironic, considering the influence James is supposed to have had on Willa Cather, that the aestheticism of James's villain Gilbert Osmond should resemble that of Miss Cather's hero Jim Burden.

[18]Elizabeth Sergeant recalls that during a visit Miss Cather made to Miss Sergeant's apartment (this was during the time she was working on *My Ántonia*), Miss Cather "suddenly leaned over—and this is something I remembered clearly when *My Ántonia* came into my hands at last in 1918—and set an old Sicilian apothecary jar of mine, filled with orange-brown flowers of scented stock in the middle of a bare, round, antique table. 'I want my new heroine to be like this—like a rare object in the middle of a table, which one may examine from all sides'" (p. 139).

Edward J. Piacentino

IMPRESSIONISTIC CHARACTER PORTRAITURE IN *MY ÁNTONIA*

My Ántonia, although not a work within the elitist domain of *avant garde* fiction of the early twentieth century, is generally acknowledged to be Willa Cather's masterpiece. Regarded as a classic of modern American fiction, a novel with an irresistibly enduring appeal, *My Ántonia* has been widely and sometimes ingeniously discussed, and, as one might expect, there are almost as many divergent views of the novel and its merits, artistic and otherwise, as there are critics who have explored it. H. L. Mencken, in a contemporary review that appeared in *Smart Set,* lauded it enthusiastically, saying that *My Ántonia* "shows an earnest striving toward . . . free and dignified self-expression, high artistic conscience, . . . [and] civilized point of view";[1] and his generous appraisal helped to establish a positive tone that much of the subsequent criticism of the novel would later echo.

My Ántonia is respected highly because it demonstrates the impressive imaginative sensibility of Willa Cather functioning as a serious and conscientious craftsman of distinguished magnitude. Miss Cather herself, at different points in her career, made pronouncements clearly suggesting that she perceived the novel genre to be an art form. In one of her more famous pronouncements, found in her oft-quoted essay, "The Novel Démeublé," Cather remarked, "Out of the teeming, gleaming stream of the present it [the novel] must select the eternal material of art."[2] She then went on to say that she hoped some of the younger writers of her time would "attempt to break away from mere verisimilitude, and following the development of modern painting, to interpret imaginatively the material and social investiture of their characters; to present their scene by suggestion rather than enumeration."[3] Thus since Cather was an advocate of the suggestive, or as it is sometimes called, the impressionistic method, an important dimension of her artistry, Dorothy Tuck McFarland has accurately recognized, "lies primarily in her power to create with words vivid pictorial images that are imbued with an ineffable quality of felt reality . . ."[4]

If as she viewed it, the purpose of the novel was to be selective and hence suggestive for the intention of evoking feeling—the "quality of felt reality"—then

From *Midamerica* 9 (1982): 53–64.

this may in part explain the reaction of Justice Oliver Wendell Holmes, who, when reading *My Ántonia* in 1930, twelve years after the initial publication, wrote that the book had "unfailing charm . . . , a beautiful tenderness. . . . It is a poem made from nature"[5] or that of Cather's official biographer, E. K. Brown, who noted that "everything in the book is there to convey a feeling, not to tell a story, not to establish a social philosophy, not even to animate a group of characters. The feeling attaches to persons, places, moments."[6]

Because to Willa Cather the transference of feeling was of the utmost importance in a novel, she seems to have consciously adopted a stylistic strategy in *My Ántonia* that closely approximates the general method of the lyric poet: the evocation of feeling through concrete images and image patterns; however, in carrying out her intention, she turned over the narrative responsibility to Jim Burden, who, in becoming the first-person retrospective narrator of *My Ántonia*—the controlling character through whom the events are filtered—also serves as Cather's author-surrogate. From the information revealed in the introduction of *My Ántonia*, we recognize that Jim is not a writer by profession; rather he is a lawyer employed by one of the great western railways and a writer by avocation only. As many of the novel's commentators have observed, Jim is a romantic, an idealist, a middleaged malcontent who, although dissatisfied with the state of his present life, is a character with an astute poetic sensibility.

As Cather's surrogate-author, an imaginative idealist, then, Jim often describes Ántonia and some of the other foreign immigrants who settle the Nebraska Divide impressionistically, frequently almost poetically, rather than resorting to the techniques of photographic, representational realism.[7] In his portrait of Ántonia, particularly, as well as his portraits of some of the other foreign-born settlers, but to a lesser degree, Jim presents a series of vivid details, chiefly apt impressionistic natural images to accentuate some of their dominant attributes and personality traits and to convey his personal impressions of and attitudes toward these characters—a practice which importantly influences the way the reader, too, ultimately perceives them.

Of all the characters Ántonia—Jim's beloved embodiment of the agrarian ideal—is mainly depicted in terms of natural, land-related images.[8] In Jim's description of her, Ántonia's eyes are delineated figuratively, within an idyllic frame of reference, as "big and warm and full of light, like the sun shining on brown pools in the wood."[9] "Her skin," Jim continues, "was brown, too, and in her cheeks she had a glow of rich, dark colour. Her brown hair was curly and wild-looking" (p.23). The qualities of warmth and light importantly connote the very vitality, the vigor that is so frequently associated with Ántonia's character throughout the novel, and anticipate the ingredients essential to the earth-goddess image Ántonia projects in the last section of the book. The color brown that dominates this passage clearly has affinities with the land itself, bringing to mind the rich hue of the soil and thus serving to reinforce Ántonia's relationship to the land.

In addition, there are several recurring imagistic references to Ántonia's brown skin that seem to re-emphasize her close kinship to the land. In one such reference accenting Ántonia's vitality, Frances Harling, using a figure of speech drawn from a product of the land itself, tells Grandmother Burden, " 'She had such fine brown legs and arms, and splendid colour in her cheeks like those big dark red plums' " (p. 153). And in the first of several reunion scenes between Jim and Ántonia, when she is twenty-four years old and back on the family farm with a child born out of wedlock, Jim avidly recalls, "I took her hands and held them against my breast, feeling once more how strong and warm and good they were, those brown hands, and remembering how many kind things they had done for me" (p. 322). And finally when Jim returns to the Divide and confronts Ántonia after a twenty-year absence, Ántonia, though a middle-aged veteran of an arduous life and the matron of a large family and a fertile and productive farm, is viewed by him impression-istically: "Ántonia came in and stood before me; a stalwart, brown woman, flat-chested, her curly brown hair a little grizzled" (p. 331). Even though physical change is evident to Jim as he views her at this time, still to him " . . . Ántonia had not lost the fire of life. Her skin, so brown and hardened, had not that look of flabbiness, as if the sap beneath it had been secretly drawn away" (p. 336). In every instance cited, the vital dark brown hue of Ántonia's skin remains dominant and constant, an emblem of the qualities of endurance and fecundity reflected in the land itself, the same land to which she has cast her destiny. In short, such recurring color imagery implicitly establishes the strong link between Ántonia and the land and thus high-lights the endearing naturalness and durability of her character—qualities which Jim (as well as Cather) seems to admire.

Ántonia's "curly," "wild-looking" hair can by association also be shown to correspond to the land, particularly its qualities of spontaneity and freedom—seemingly unwieldy, natural attributes—that Jim often assigns to the land in his descriptions of it.[10] Such attributes are usually viewed positively, almost idealistically, by Jim; and in Book II, the Black Hawk section, he emphasizes this attitude by pointing out the strong harmony that exists between Ántonia and Mrs. Harling, the cultured Norwegian lady for whose family Ántonia temporarily works and with whom she shares so many similarities: "They had strong, independent natures, both of them. They knew what they liked, and were not always trying to imitate other people. They loved children and animals and music, and rough play and digging in the earth. . . . Deep down in each of them there was a kind of hearty joviality, a relish of life, not over-delicate, but very invigorating" (p. 180).

This invigorating quality of Ántonia's personality—in part suggested by her eyes, described in terms of fire imagery as "fairly blazing with things she could not say" (p. 25)—is described in the first section of the novel when Jim relates her manner of temporarily arousing her father from one of his frequent states of depression: "Tony ran up to him, caught his hand and pressed it against her cheek. She was the only one of his family who could rouse the old man from the torpor in which he seemed to live" (p. 41).

Another facet of Ántonia's personality—her stability and fortitude—suggestive more of a man than of a woman—personality traits that become pragmatic for her to adopt in the spring following her father's suicide, is also presented impressionistically through the use of apt natural images. "Her neck," Jim remarks, "came up strongly out of her shoulders, like a bole of a tree out of the turf" (p. 122).

Book V, the final section of My Ántonia, represents the culmination of Jim Burden's impressionistic rendering of the heroine, the quintessence of Ántonia's idealization within a mythic perspective as an "earth goddess, mother earth, the madonna of the cornfields," to use James Woodress's designation.[11] The image of Ántonia as earth goddess fittingly reveals, John H. Randall III observes, "the final fruition of both woman and land, which comes about because Ántonia is able to combine the vitality of nature with the order of civilization, both in her own life and in the life of the land."[12] In Book V, to be sure, Ántonia is portrayed in her greatest glory. She is the mother of a large and happy family and the matron of a fertile and prosperous farm, the very epitome of her vitality and triumph which serves as a counterpoint to Jim's own failure and unhappiness. In this section, moreover, Ántonia's maternal care and control of her children are viewed figuratively by Jim in terms of animal imagery which suggests that Ántonia, in her role as mother, acts naturally, almost instinctively: "She pulled them [her children] out of corners and came bringing them like a mother cat bringing in her kittens" (p. 332). In addition, Jim sees several of her children as displaying some of the same exuberant vitality which he has always associated with Ántonia herself. For example, one of her sons, whom Jim meets when he nears the Cuzak farm, is described as "fair-skinned and freckled, with red cheeks and a ruddy pelt as thick as a lamb's wool, growing down on his neck in little tufts" (p. 330). Another of her sons, Leo, as he runs up to his mother, is impressionistically seen by Jim as "like a little ram" as he "butted her playfully with his curly head" (p. 333). And finally when Ántonia's children emerge from the fully stocked fruit cave, as Jim and Ántonia patiently wait outside, Jim's impression of them—an impression in accord with the fertility myth—is that they are "a veritable explosion of life out of the dark cave into the sunlight" (p. 339).

Such strikingly impressionistic descriptions of Ántonia's children and her relationship with them are just several of many indicators in the novel that serve to shape the reader's attitude toward the Cuzaks so that what he sees of them is, in fact, strongly affected by Jim's own impressionable sensibility.

As Jim concludes his visit at the Cuzak farm, though he fully realizes that Ántonia is "a battered woman now, not a lovely girl" (p. 353), he at the same time recognizes that "she still had that something which fires the imagination, could still stop one's breath for a moment by a look or gesture" (p. 353). This climactic portrait of Ántonia is significant, for in lucidly reinforcing the image of Ántonia as a symbol of fertility, Jim perceives and comprehends the harmonic relationship she has with the land, an association, James Woodress acknowledges, that relates Ántonia "to the old story of man and the earth."[13] As Jim nostalgically discloses, "She had only to stand in the orchard, to put her hand on a little crab tree and look up at the apples, to make you feel the goodness of planting and tending and harvesting at last. All the strong things of her heart came out in her body, that had been so tireless in serving generous emotions. . . . She was a rich mine of life . . . " (p. 353). In referring to Ántonia as a "mine of life," Jim chooses an appropriate metaphor which interestingly relates back to Ántonia's association with the land at the novel's outset when she and her family lived in a dugout cave hewn from the very earth itself.

Though Jim Burden also portrays some of the other foreign immigrants through sometimes provocative impressionistic images which serve to establish certain distinguishing characteristics in aiding the reader to gain insight into their personalities, none is idealized to the extent that Ántonia has been. And in fact as many critics of *My Ántonia* have noted, many of these characters, especially Lena Lingard, though they exhibit some of the heroine's vitality—since they too spend their first years on the Divide on family farms—they, unlike Ántonia, eventually permanently withdraw from the land, the very source of their vitality.

Of the two Norwegian girls that Jim portrays most fully, Lena Lingard and Tiny Soderball, Lena is, through the imagery used to describe her, shown to be the very antithesis of Ántonia.[14] Lena, one of the hired girls whom Jim affectionately admires and to whom he is enamored for a brief period during his college years at the University of Nebraska, is consistently described in very light color tones that contrast to the brown tones so often associated with Ántonia. Lena, whose first name derives from the Greek appelation, Helena, meaning torch or light one, is aptly named and thus is described as a "plump, fair-skinned girl . . . , demure and pretty" (p. 159). "Her yellow hair," Jim observes, "was burned to a ruddy thatch on her head; but her legs and arms, curiously enough, in spite of constant exposure to the sun, kept a miraculous whiteness . . ." (p. 165). Another physical feature that Jim stresses about Lena is her eyes, "candid eyes, that always looked a little sleepy under their long lashes . . . " (p. 163). Lena, we learn, is repeatedly depicted in relation to soft, gentle, delicate things—silks, satins, fine clothes—and when Jim meets her at the Harlings, he makes note of her being attracted to the "cheerful rooms with naïve admiration" (p. 163).

Yet Jim's relationship with Lena is far from Platonic; he is charmed, in a romantic sense, by her beauty, by her radiance, and by her delicate nature. And while still living in Black Hawk, Jim has a recurring dream about Lena, a dream that reflects his erotic view of her. When he describes this dream, he does so using natural, light-related imagery: "I was in a harvest-field full of shocks, and I was lying against one of them. Lena Lingard came across the stubble barefoot, in a short skirt, with a curved reaping-hook in her hand, and she was flushed like the dawn, with a kind of luminous rosiness all about her. She sat beside me, turned to me with a soft sigh and said, 'Now they are all gone, and I can kiss you as much as I like' " (pp. 225–226). If the soft, romantic imagery is not enough to create the impression Jim seeks to convey and to establish a contrast with Ántonia, his afterthoughts about this dream make the contrast intended blatantly clear: "I used to wish I could have this flattering dream about Ántonia, but I never did" (p. 226).

Later, when Jim carries on a brief romantic affair with Lena in Lincoln, where she has set up her own dress-making shop, he again describes her, using predominantly gently soft, natural, light imagery. For instance, when Jim used to meet Lena in downtown Lincoln after his morning classes, she seemed to him "as fresh as the spring morning" (p. 280), and frequently her delicate vitality would be enhanced by the jonquils or the hyacinth plants she carried with her. The tone of her voice he views as "soft," "with her caressing intonation and arch naiveté" (p. 281). To hear Lena's voice, moreover, becomes a pleasant diversion for Jim, for she "was almost as candid as Nature" (p. 281). "Lena," Jim further muses, "was never so pretty as in the morning; she awakened fresh with the world every day, and her eyes had a deeper colour then, like the blue flowers that are never so blue as when they first open" (pp. 281–282).

Lena, the converse of Ántonia, like Jim, leaves the land, becoming, James Woodress points out, "a Benjamin Franklin type who works hard, builds a business, prospers, and remains devoutly attached to the work ethic."[15]

Some of the other characters whose physical traits, particularly the color tone of their skin, are enhanced in part through natural imagery, are not given extended portraits; albeit a strong resemblance exists between the images used to describe them and their dominant personality traits. In several of the descriptions of Mr. Shimerda, Ántonia's father, for example, some fine suggestive touches can be recognized in the images Jim selects to delineate him. In the first scene in which Jim describes Mr. Shimerda's physical features, he observes that "he was tall and slender, and his thin shoulders stooped" (p. 24). While his hands are "white and well-shaped" (p. 24), "his eyes were melancholy, and were set back deep under his brow. His face [Jim continues] was ruggedly formed, but it looked like ashes—like something from which all the warmth and light had died out" (p. 24). Mr. Shimerda's listlessness, his broken spirit, is suitably complemented by the image of ashes, the waste product of a consumed fire. The vital elements of warmth, light, activity— some of the very qualities of life embodied in his daughter Ántonia—are noticeably absent in him. In fact, Mr. Shimerda seems to have lost all purpose for living; he is sick and very despondent. When Ántonia and Jim confront him late one afternoon as he is hunting rabbits on the prairie, Jim observes that he "looked at Ántonia with a wintry flicker of a smile" (p. 41), a well chosen metaphor to capture the old man's depressed spirit as well as the overbearing inertia characterizing his present life.

Another character whose personality is partially disclosed through natural imagery is Otto Fuchs, an Austrian immigrant who is the Burdens' hired man. When first seen by Jim on the night of his arrival at the train station in Black Hawk, Otto is viewed as resembling a desperado, someone who "might have stepped out of the pages of *Jesse James*" (p. 6). A former cowboy, stage driver, bartender, and miner, who "had wandered all over the great Western country and done hard work everywhere" (p. 67) and who "had drifted back to live in a milder country for a while" (p. 12), Otto is an adventurer, a lover of the outdoors, "one of those drifting case-hardened labourers who never marry or have any children of his own" (p. 84). Furthermore, Otto seems a man of firm constitution, ready and apparently completely able to use his fists, his brute strength, when necessary. Interestingly, one of his favorite pastimes is to tell tales of titillating escapades about his experiences in the Black Tiger Mine and "about violent deaths and casual buryings, and the queer fancies of dying men" (p. 111). Otto's physical features fittingly give the impression of just such a man. As Jim readily perceives at the time of his first encounter with Otto, "the ends of his moustache were twisted up stiffly, like little horns. He looked lively and ferocious.... A long scar ran across one cheek and drew the corner of his mouth up in a sinister curl. The top of his left ear was gone, and his skin was brown as an Indian's" (p. 6). Several natural images stand out in this passage: his moustache shaped like animal's horns, presumably a bull's, and his brown skin tone; both of these references serve to suggest Otto's ruggedness and durability, his assertive nature, and his untamed vitality, a vitality that may be representative of the prairie land of the Divide itself. Though his fierceness and aggressiveness have for the most part been subdued while in the employ of the Burdens, these traits, so important to his sense of being, may, Jim implies, assert themselves again—this time in the wilds of the Colorado mountains. When the Burdens decide to leave the land (a harmonious agricultural existence), rent their farm, and move to Black Hawk, the necessary stimulus is provided; and Otto and Jake Marpole depart for "the Wild West" (p. 144), seeking further adventure as silver prospectors.

And lastly, Mr. Cuzak, Ántonia's husband, a Bohemian immigrant with a similar background to Mr. Shimerda, Ántonia's father, is, like the other characters examined thus far, a person whose physical constitution and lively personality are in part accentuated by natural imagery. When Jim first sees Mr. Cuzak, he states that "he moved very quickly, and there was an air of jaunty liveliness about him. He had a strong, ruddy colour, thick black hair, a little grizzled, a curly moustache, and red lips" (p. 356). Furthermore, he has "strong teeth" and a "hard hand, burned red on the back and heavily coated with hair" (pp. 356–357). Such details as his liveliness, ruddy skin color, grizzled hair, and generally weathered demeanor—either when considered individually or as a collective unit—can be associated with the primitive naturalness of the land itself, a quality, it should be recalled, previously illuminated in Ántonia's character through markedly similar image clusters.[16] Of some slight interest as well is Mr. Cuzak's habit of glancing sidewise at people to whom he speaks, an idiosyncrasy that Jim implies is sincere, innocent, and almost habitually instinctive as the behavior of an animal. As Jim remarks, Mr. Cuzak "always looked at people sidewise, as a workhorse does at its yokemate.... This trick did not suggest duplicity or secretiveness, but merely long habit, as with a horse" (p. 358).

Though farm life is not the kind of existence the city-bred Cuzak necessarily preferred, still he has managed to adapt, having learned to live in a relatively happy harmony with his wife and children. As Jim reflects, "Cuzak had been made the instrument of Ántonia's special mission" (p. 367), a mission of a woman, her husband simply acknowledges, with " 'such a warm heart' " (p. 367).

Edith Lewis, a life-long friend of Willa Cather, noted in her commemorative biography on the author that Cather felt My Ántonia "was the best thing she had done—that she had succeeded, more nearly than ever before, in writing the way she wanted to write."[17] In adopting as one facet of her artistic strategy, her philosophy of composition, the imagistic method in order to delineate personality traits of some of the characters impressionistically—characters who make up the dramatis personae of My Ántonia, Cather ably demonstrated that she could give solid substance to her precept: "that in writing novels as in poetry, the facts are nothing, the feeling is everything,"[18] feeling, we have seen, that can be most effectively evoked and artfully transmitted through carefully selected and skillfully wrought imagery. True to her own high standards of artistic integrity, true to her conception that the novel is an art form, Willa Cather, in the discerning judgment of Dorothy Tuck McFarland, created in *My Ántonia* a novel with a "seemingly artless surface [but which actually] is ... the result of the most careful artistry."[19]

NOTES

[1] H. L. Mencken, rev. of *My Ántonia*, by Willa Cather, *Smart Set*, Feb. 1919. Quoted in *Willa Cather and Her Critics*, ed. James Schroeter (Ithaca: Cornell University Press, 1967), p. 8.

[2] Willa Cather, "The Novel Démeublé," in *Willa Cather on Writing: Critical Studies of Writing as an Art* (New York: Alfred A. Knopf, 1949), p. 40.

[3] Ibid.

[4] Dorothy Tuck McFarland, *Willa Cather* (New York: Frederick Ungar Publishing Co., 1972), p. 3.

[5] Quoted in James Woodress, *Willa Cather: Her Life and Art* (New York: Pegasus, 1970), pp. 182–183.

[6] E. K. Brown, *Willa Cather: A Critical Biography* (New York: Alfred A. Knopf, 1953), p. 206.

[7] Significantly, Willa Cather, like many outstanding twentieth-century practitioners of the novel form, including such notables as James Joyce and William Faulkner whose major novels exhibit poetic qualities, began her literary career as a poet, her first published book being *April Twilights* (1903), a collection of thirty-seven lyric poems. James Woodress in *Willa Cather: Her Life and Art*, p. 104, notes that Cather had been writing and publishing poems since she was a student at the University of Nebraska. And some of her poems appeared in magazines such as *Home Monthly*, the *Courier*, the *Library*, the *Critic*, *Lippincott's*, *Harper's Weekly*, and *Youth's Companion*.

[8] John J. Murphy, "Willa Cather: The Widening Gyre," in *Five Essays on Willa Cather: The Merrimack Symposium*, a volume which he also edited (North Andover, Mass., Merrimack College, 1974), p. 55, only generally points out that Ántonia is described in "earthy imagery."

[9] Willa Cather, *My Ántonia* (Boston: Houghton Mifflin, Co., 1954), p. 23. Subsequent references to *My Ántonia* will be to this edition, and page numbers will appear parenthetically in the text of the essay.

[10] David Stouck, *Willa Cather's Imagination* (Lincoln: University of Nebraska Press, 1975), p. 48, notes that Ántonia's "wild, impulsive, and generous nature is so much a part of the untamed landscape." Stouck, moreover, sees freedom as a key element in Jim's landscape descriptions in Book I. Note especially the description on pp. 19, 29, and 48. Also observe Jim's description of Ántonia and her sister Yulka while they are with him on a winter sleigh ride: "The great fresh open, after the stupefying warmth indoors, made them behave like wild things" (p. 64).

[11] James Woodress, "Willa Cather: American Experience and the European Tradition," in *The Art of Willa Cather*, eds., Bernice Slote and Virginia Faulkner (Lincoln: University of Nebraska Press, 1974), p. 51.

[12] John H. Randall III, *The Landscape and the Looking Glass: Willa Cather's Search for Value* (Boston: Houghton Mifflin, Co., 1960), p. 145. Randall's analysis of Ántonia as a fertility goddess is the most thorough and persuasive interpretation of this facet, particularly his treatment of the vegetation myth in relation to the seasonal cycle that structures the novel. Also, see Evelyn Helmick, "The Mysteries of Ántonia," *Midwest Quarterly*, 17 (1976), 173–185.

[13] Woodress, "Willa Cather: American Experience and the European Tradition," p. 51.

[14] What Philip L. Gerber in *Willa Cather* (Boston: Twayne Publishers, 1975), p. 104, says about Tiny Soderball is also suitably applicable to Lena Lingard: "... her story is one of a series of separate panels whose effect is to illuminate Ántonia's triumph."

[15] Woodress, "Willa Cather: American Experience and the European Tradition," p. 49.

[16] See *My Ántonia*, especially p. 23.

[17] Edith Lewis, *Willa Cather Living: A Personal Record* (New York: Alfred A. Knopf, 1953), p. 107.

[18] Cather, *Willa Cather on Writing*, p. 84.

[19] McFarland, p. 40.

Mary Kemper Sternshein

THE LAND OF NEBRASKA
AND ÁNTONIA SHIMERDA

Setting is a necessary element of any novel, but only a few authors have made a Great Plains setting an integral part of their stories. The Great Plains setting of novels has served mainly as a backdrop. This backdrop is lowered into place in the first chapter of the book and remains there throughout the novel without becoming obtrusive or interfering with the plot. When used like this, the Great Plains setting never becomes a part of the novel. None of the features of the land are worked into the novel, so the reader is never aware of the changes in the land or the seasons' coming and going. Setting is as automatic as capitalizing the first letter of the first word of a sentence—it is done as a matter of course and then forgotten.

Not all authors are guilty of this sin of omission. Willa Cather, in her novel *My Ántonia*, chooses the Nebraska territory as her setting. She does not stop with that choice. As the novel progresses, the land plays an important part, perhaps the most important part, of the story. The land is as important as any of the characters in the novel. To illustrate this point, land, images of the earth, plowing, harvesting, the cycle of the seasons are used in the novel *My Ántonia* by Willa Cather to parallel the growth and development of Ántonia Shimerda, one of the characters.

The land of Nebraska is revealed to us through the eyes of Jim Burden. He sees Nebraska after dark as he rides to his grandparents' home in a wagon. The only land to which Jim can compare this new territory is his old home, Virginia. Jim notices immediately that there are no mountains here—only land and sky. As a matter of fact, after more thought, Jim decides

> There was nothing but land: not a country at all, but the material out of which countries are made. . . . I had the feeling that the world was left behind, that we had got over the edge of it, and were outside man's jurisdiction. . . . Between that earth and that sky I felt erased, blotted out.[1]

When Jim goes to bed, he doesn't say his prayers because he is still awed by the magnitude of this new country. He's even a little frightened by its size.

From *Heritage of the Great Plains* 16, No. 2 (Spring 1983): 34–42.

The following morning, Jim's feelings completely change. The light of day helps to make this new country familiar and inviting. Jim now sees

> ... that the grass was the country, as the water is the sea. The red of the grass made all the great prairie the colour of wine-stains, or of certain seaweeds when they are first washed up. And there was so much motion in it; the whole country, seemed, somehow, to be running (13).

Thus, the very things which bothered Jim the previous night in the dark on the way to his new home now delight him. He does not mind the absence of the mountains—he notices the grass and how it blows in the wind resembling waves. The waves of grass are moving so swiftly that they seem to run; they are free.[2] Jim describes other parts of the country as having this feeling of freedom. Once he says "The road ran like a wild thing ..." (16). Later he feels that ". . . sunflower-bordered roads always seem to me the roads to freedom" (21). All of Jim's observations point to one thing. Human beings have not made much of a mark on the frontier of Nebraska. Jim does not include in his descriptions acre after acre of cultivated fields or wooden A-frame houses. The Burdens have the only wooden house. The other houses are made of sod. The roads are not paved; they're not even graveled. Dirt roads snake from one farm house to the next. The country seems almost as young as Jim.

Jim isn't the only newcomer to the country of Nebraska. Ántonia Shimerda comes to Nebraska with her family. We first hear of Ántonia while Jim is traveling on the train. The conductor tells Jim about a young girl who can not speak English. We assume that she is foreign. The conductor continues to kid Jim about the girl who is "as bright as a new dollar."

> "Don't you want to go ahead and see her, Jimmy? She's got the pretty brown eyes, too!"
> This last remark made me bashful ... (16)

When Jim first sees Ántonia, she is "clutching an oilcloth bundle." Once again, Jim pushes this disturbing idea—a girl—into the back of his mind. He was not impressed after his first meeting with her. She was different from any other girl he had met.

The Burdens' paid a neighborly visit to the Shimerdas' where Jim meets Ántonia formally this time. In the daytime, Jim notices that Ántonia is actually pretty. She does have big eyes; they are also brown and full of light like the sun. Ántonia runs up to Jim, coaxingly holds out her hand, and runs up the hill. Ántonia laughs as her skirt blows in the wind. After she, Jim, and Yulka have their first English lesson there on the hill, Ántonia impulsively gives Jim her ring (20).

It is easy to see, within the first few pages of the novel, how the country of Nebraska and Ántonia are similarly described. Both instill a feeling of apprehension in Jim when he sees them for the first time in the dark. When seen in the sunlight, both Nebraska and Ántonia have beautiful qualities. They are both free and uncontrolled. They are both impulsive and untamed, yet they are generous, also.

Nebraska is not always this inviting and friendly to people. In winter, the entire country freezes solid. It is barren of all forms of life. Snow is everywhere, and it often drifts up and around the houses; an act which necessitates tunneling out. Winter in Nebraska isn't cruel or mean, but it is hard and bitter.

> Winter comes down savagely over a little town on the prairie. The wind that sweeps in from the open country strips away all the leafy screens that hide one yard from another in summer, and the houses seem to draw closer together. . . . The pale, cold light of the winter sunset did not beautify—it was like the light of truth itself. When the smoky clouds hung low in the west and the red sun went down behind them, leaving a pink flush on the snowy roofs and the blue drifts, then the wind sprang up afresh, with a kind of bitter song, as if it said: 'This is reality, whether you like it or not. All those frivolities of summer, the light and shadow, the living mask of green that trembled over everything, they were lies, and this is what was underneath. This is the truth.' It was as if we were being punished for loving the loveliness of summer (115–116).

Many times families were cut off from town or from neighbors for months. Individual families must manage on their own. They must be resourceful enough to keep morale high and to make the best of the situation. The Shimerda family does not have this resourcefulness necessary to survive intact through the winter. Mr. Shimerda, Ántonia's beloved father, commits suicide shortly after Christmas. Following her father's death and subsequent funeral, Ántonia could, herself, turn bitter toward life. As signs of spring appear on the Nebraska prairie, Ántonia becomes more reconciled to her father's death.

Spring bounces in like a new puppy (79). The Shimerdas "spring clean" and alleviate many of their uncomfortable problems. They have a new four-room cabin, a windmill, a hen house, and chickens. They even have a milk cow. Their fields are ready to be planted. Ántonia still retains her tendency to respond to questions in a sharp and biting manner. She pumps Jim for information about planting corn and then very rudely insults his grandfather. She very haughtily remarks that Jim's grandfather is not Jesus. He doesn't know everything (80). As winter finally melts into spring, most of these cutting remarks melt from Ántonia's mind and another season approaches.

As spring advances into summer, Ántonia and the land of Nebraska become even closer together. Ántonia has accepted her father's death, but she knows that he killed himself partially because the country was too inhospitable to him. It was not cultivated as he was. Ántonia begins to work the land with a vengeance. She does not go to school like the other children in the territory do. She stays home and works "like mans" (81). She runs her own team of oxen and works just as long and hard as her brother does to cultivate this wild, free land. She does regret her inability to go to school because Jim catches her crying on the way to the barn one day (81). Even though her father has instilled in her a strong desire for education, she somehow knows that the land must be tamed before time can be spent with trivialities and extras like school. The death of Ántonia's father also killed the civilized, educated facet of the Shimerda family. When Ántonia begins to work in the fields like a man, her "civilized attributes wither away."[3] Her genteel manners and social veneer are stripped away, leaving a woman just as coarse and crude as any male field hand. Thus, as the land of Nebraska is being stripped of the red grass by the plow, Ántonia is also being stripped of her initial attributes as she works in the fields.

When Ántonia moves to town as a hired girl, she loses much of her contact with the land. Of all the seasons discussed during Ántonia's stay in town, winter is most predominant. Even Jim notices that winter in town is different than winter on the farm.

> Winter lies too long in country towns; hangs on until it is stale and shabby, old and sullen. On the farm the weather was the great fact, and men's affairs went on underneath it, as the streams creep under the ice. But in Black Hawk the scene of human life was spread out shrunken and pinched, frozen down to the bare stalk (120).

The winter drags in town. There is nothing to do to relieve the monotony as there was on the farm. All the young people of Black Hawk become involved with music and dancing at the dancing pavilion. Ántonia especially enjoys dancing and tries to go to the pavilion as often as she can. She has "relearned" her civilized social manners while she works at the Harlings.[4] Her intense joy of dancing helps her to lose her job with the Harling family. Her ability to enjoy herself in the dancing pavilion also begins to change her reputation slightly. In the winter in a city, people need diversion. Ántonia becomes a diversion. All of the city boys like to dance with her, yet they know and she knows that no serious relationship will develop (133).

Only once during her stay in Black Hawk does Ántonia ever revert back to the feelings and thoughts she had when she was young. Ántonia and two other girls are in the country picking wild flowers. They meet Jim there. Jim notices that Ántonia has been crying. The flowers have made her homesick; her homesickness has made her miss her father. She reminisces for a few minutes and then asks Jim about her father's spirit once more. Jim reassures her that her father's spirit is happy. Then, amid the spring blossoms, the new green leaves, the butterflies, bees, and singing birds, Jim reflects that "Ántonia seemed to me that day exactly like the little girl who used to come to our house with Mr. Shimerda" (154). In this springtime setting, "Ántonia had the most trusting, responsive eyes in the world; love and credulous-ness seemed to look out of them with open faces" (154). When Lena Lingard interrupts Ántonia's solitude and reminiscing, Ántonia returns once again to the gay, carefree hired girl on an outing picking wild flowers. The weather subtly changes, too. It becomes hot; almost unbearably hot. The heat was so great "that the dogwoods and scrub oaks began to turn up the silvery underside of their leaves, and all the foliage looked soft and wilted" (155). The attitudes of both Ántonia and the weather have changed, however subtly, when reminded of the present.

The very last thing that Ántonia, Jim, and their friends see that day is an ordinary plough standing alone in a field. The vision is beautiful. The plough entirely fills the red-orange circle of the sun. Jim describes the picture.

> Magnified across the distance by the horizontal light, it stood out against the sun, was exactly contained within the circle of the disk; the handles, the tongue, the share—black against the molten red. There it was, heroic in size, a picture writing on the sun (159).

The plough stands for more than the material object it represents. It is a symbol of a whole way of life; it stands for a settled agricultural civilization.[5] Human beings are beginning to conquer and tame the country of Nebraska. Seeing ploughs and cultivated fields is more common than seeing the red grass which grew on the prairie. The cultivation process is not nearly complete at this point, though, just as Ántonia's new-found manners do not do her any good until she begins to use them in her favor.

A large break in time separates us from Ántonia and Jim. Jim leaves Nebraska, finds a job in the East, and marries. When he returns to Black Hawk years later, he comes during a hot summer. He has been somewhat disillusioned by life, and he has returned to Nebraska to revive and to relive memories of things he thought were important. He hears the story of Ántonia's child from Mrs. Steavens. Ántonia packed to leave Nebraska for Denver one day in March. It was a raw, cold day, and it was raining. Ántonia herself fluctuated between being happy at the news and sad about leaving the country for good (201). When Ántonia returns to her family disgraced, the weather once again foreshadows her future. When she arrived, "It was one of them lovely warm May days, and the wind was blowing and the colts jumping around in the pastures . . . " (203). For the remainder of the summer and the fall, Ántonia works in the fields, plows, and tends livestock. The weather remains mild and calm just as Ántonia remains quiet and steady. Ántonia no longer "puts on airs" or brags about anything. She suffers through pain quietly by herself. She only goes to town when it is unavoidable. Summer and fall are placid times.

Ántonia's next incident is also foreshadowed by the weather. A heavy snow-storm falls as Ántonia struggles to drive her cattle home. This is the third heavy snow in the book. During the first, Mr. Shimerda shot himself. During the second heavy snow when Jim and Ántonia lived in Black Hawk, Ántonia begins dancing with the young men in town and creates a reputation different from the one she maintained while living on the farm. During this third storm, Ántonia's child is born. Mrs. Steavens stops her story at this point, and the next morning, Jim meets Ántonia once again out in the fields on the farm. The season is summer. The day is hot. As the sun sets, the moon vies for brilliancy in the sky.

> In that singular light every little tree and shock of wheat, every sunflower stalk and clump of snow-on-the-mountain, drew itself up high and pointed; the very clods and furrows in the fields seemed to stand up sharply. I felt the old pull of the earth, the solemn magic that comes out of those fields at nightfall (209).

Ántonia and the land of Nebraska are once again paralleled. After having her child, Ántonia decides to stay on the farm and work the land. As she plants corn, plows, tends livestock, etc., she begins to regain her self-esteem and self-confidence. She's ready to pick up where she left off years ago and make the best of her life. In this respect, the land is doing the same thing. The plants are standing tall and straight, high and pointed. Regardless of the size of the plant, each is striving to reach as high as it can. With an atmosphere like this created at the end of Book Four, the reader feels optimistic about Book Five. He hopes that Ántonia will remain content and stable since she has returned to a life she loves and knows well.

We don't see Ántonia again for twenty years. As Jim walks through her yard to the house, this is the view he sees.

> ... the forest of tall hollyhocks ... The front yard was enclosed by a thorny locust hedge, and at the gate grew two silvery, mothlike trees of the mimosa family. From here one looked down over the cattle-yards, with their two long ponds, and over a wide stretch of stubble which they told me was a ryefield in summer. ... behind the houses were an ash grove and two orchards: a cherry orchard, with gooseberry and currant bushes between the rows, and an apple orchard, sheltered by a high hedge from the hot winds (220).

Jim seems slightly surprised at finding so much cultivation of the land. He is also mildly surprised at the number of children Ántonia has had. Both the land and Ántonia have been bountiful and produced well after they were "tamed." Neither the land nor Ántonia's spirit will ever be truly conquered, but both have been tamed enough to be malleable. Ántonia and the land are so much a part of each other now that it would not be inappropriate to classify Ántonia as an earth mother. Everything she does becomes fruitful and multiplies. Jim even says:

> She was a battered woman now, not a lovely girl; but she still had that something which fires the imagination, could still stop one's breath for a moment by a look or gesture that somehow revealed the meaning in common things. She had only to stand in the orchard, to put her hand on a little crab tree and look up at the apples, to make you feel the goodness of planting and tending and harvesting at last (228–229).

Ántonia herself has realized how important the land is to her. She commented on this occasionally throughout the book, but only after the birth of her first child does she really feel a close bond to the land. She comments that she could never live in a city because "I like to be where I know every stack and tree, and where all the ground is friendly" (208). "I belong on a farm. I'm never lonesome here like I used to be in town. You remember what sad spells I used to have, when I didn't know what was the matter with me? I've never had them out here" (223). Ántonia is content with her life; she no longer fights against it or tries to find pleasure elsewhere. She has helped to cultivate and tame the land so that her children may now engage in the frivolities of education, music, and other fields in the humanities.

The reader should never believe that the spirits of the land or of Ántonia have been dampened or destroyed. The indomitable, wild, free spirits both exist at the end of the novel. There is one spot of land that has never been cultivated and never will be. The red grass of Nebraska still grows there, wild and free. Mr. Shimerda's grave is this spot. Jim described it well.

> . . . instinctively we walked toward that unploughed patch at the crossing of the roads as the fittest place to talk to each other. . . . The tall red grass had never been cut there. It had died down in winter and come up again in the spring until it was as thick and shrubby as some tropical garden-grass (207–208).

Ántonia also has preserved her wild and free spirit, but she has done so in a slightly different manner. Leo, her twelve year old son, represents this freedom of mind and spirit. Leo is as Ántonia was when she first came to Nebraska. Ántonia says of him "That Leo; he's the worst of all. . . . And I love him the best . . ." (218). He is a mischievous little boy who enjoys almost everything—especially being alive. Leo is also the one child of Ántonia's who represents Mr. Shimerda's artistry. Leo is the person who plays his grandfather's old violin. Even Leo's description is one conducive to wild freedom. Jim says

> . . . he really was faun-like. He hadn't much head behind his ears, and his tawny fleece grew down thick to the back of his neck. His eyes were not frank and wide apart like those of the other boys, but were deep-set, gold-green in colour, and seemed sensitive to the light (226).

Jim's description goes even further, though, and tells us of Leo's innermost thoughts. When Leo wakes up before the rest of the family, Jim thinks,

> He seemed conscious of possessing a keener power of enjoyment than other people; his quick recognitions made him frantically impatient of deliberate judgments. He always knew what he wanted without thinking (228).

Leo, then, typifies the person Ántonia was as a child. He will have the opportunities Ántonia did not have. Leo can pursue any desire he wishes.

The novel ends at this point, after having securely tied the ends of the story together. Ántonia is finally seen as an earth mother; she and the earth become synonymous with each other. They eventually compliment each other and serve the same function. Although both the land and Ántonia are "tamed" by their experiences with life, neither has lost a strong sense of freedom. The novel ends on this note. The feeling of wildness and freedom will never be taken away from either the land or from Ántonia's family. They are too much a part of each other.

NOTES

[1] Willa Sibert Cather, *My Ántonia* (Boston, Houghton Mifflin Company: Riverside Press Cambridge, 1918), p. 7. Subsequent references to this work will be given within the text of the paper in parentheses.
[2] David Stouck, *Willa Cather's Imagination* (Lincoln: University of Nebraska Press, 1975), p. 48.
[3] John Herman Randall III, *The Landscape and the Looking Glass* (Boston, Houghton Mifflin Company: Riverside Press Cambridge, 1960), p. 149.
[4] Ibid.
[5] Ibid., p. 135.

Patrick W. Shaw

MY ÁNTONIA: EMERGENCE
AND
AUTHORIAL REVELATIONS

In one of the saner commentaries concerning *My Ántonia,* Terence Martin notes the twenty-year gap between Books IV and V. He does not elucidate the hiatus, but he does inadvertently suggest its importance when he states that Jim's absence from Nebraska and the intervening life "afford little but material for conjecture and inference."[1] The narrative blank space is more important than Martin makes it appear, but indeed we do conjecture and infer when faced with the missing decades. Primarily, we ponder the superficially simple but ultimately complex question of what exactly is the process Jim undergoes, and consequently, what does the entire novel "mean"? We watch Ántonia change substantially—see her experience times of searching calm, bitchy hoydenism, sexual debauchery, physical and psychic pain, and maternal tranquility. These changes are graphic in the narrative design: Ántonia's screaming attack on Jim in chapter XVIII, Book I; her dehumanizing labors in chapter III, Book IV; and her serene beauty throughout Book V. In contrast, we notice very little commensurate growth or change for Jim. Viewed against Ántonia's near epic struggles, he appears strangely flat, peculiarly immutable. Since his place in the narrative is at least equal to hers and since Cather does not typically offer contrastive characters without giving each adequate stature (as with the bishops Latour and Vaillant), Jim's apparent lack of development does perplex.

Evelyn Helmick tries to solve the riddle by tracing Jim's personality back to "primordial matriarchial mysteries."[2] She explains *My Ántonia* generally and the pivotal Cuzak section particularly in terms of these ancient Greek rites and locates Jim's gradual movement toward self-awareness in the realm of Ántonia's matriarchy. Helmick is certainly correct in recognizing the presence of myth in the novel, and her offering of the Eleusinian Mysteries to account for questions raised by Jim's befuddling personality does illuminate. Cather, however, does not force us quite so far afield in search of answers, because her entire narrative is replete with light sources of its own. We might recall that she once belittled her own art with the comment that she wished she had a hundred dollars for each of the faults in *My Ántonia;* but such self-deprecating humor suggests the effort she made to mask

From *American Literature* 56, No. 4 (December 1984): 527–40.

how careful she was in composing the novel and how close it was to her own psyche. Ultimately we discover that her myths are domestic and her mysteries solvable from internal clues.

Ironically, a good place to commence looking for answers is in the apparent vacuum of the lost twenty years, because the essential change which Jim undergoes, his moral or psychological growth, occurs during this time. Jim reaches no final goals nor absolute conclusions, because Cather, as we shall see, denies linear progressions and terminal events; but Jim does experience a definite quest. It begins literally when he leaves Virginia as a child and it enters the metaphysical or transcendent stage when he returns to Ántonia after twenty years. Because his psychic changes are indeed ultimately mysterious, as Helmick suggests, Cather wisely chooses to let the metamorphoses occur out of sight, off stage; and only by examining the varied symbolic and thematic elements Cather so meticulously gives us on stage can we by indirection come to understand just what Jim seeks, how he changes, what precipitates the changes, and finally how he begins to arrive at the peace and apperception that have so long evaded him. By examining the subtlety of Cather's design, both dramatically and metaphysically, we realize that the twenty-year lacuna contains a spatiotemporal reality which engulfs, alters, and finally explains *My Ántonia* and, by extension, Willa Cather.

First, let us look at the concrete, internal clues which Cather offers. She uses a number of motifs in *My Ántonia,* but lying at the heart of her design is the theme of submergence-emergence. She names this central motif early when she marks the "subterranean habit"[3] of the owls and prairie dogs. Thereafter she develops the subterranean concept along all levels of conceptualization, from the simple visual to the transcendent. As expected, the subterranean motif is first discernible in the realistic, seemingly trivial details of the narrative: the black and white badger that lives in grandmother Burden's garden and that requires an occasional chicken sacrifice (p. 17); the prairie dogs and "brown earth-owls" that share the underground (p. 29); and the "monstrosity" rattlesnake that descends the burrows and fattens on the rodents (p. 45). These and similar animals appear so frequently that they soon become a subliminal part of the narrative background against which we view Jim and Ántonia. Conventionally, these animals could easily be interpreted in terms of the dualistic cosmology, the good-evil dichotomy, as so readily suggested by the black-white badger; but Cather is not a conventional symbolist or imagist and does not limit her imaginative use of the animals solely in that way.

From the animals we move to a more subtle but still literal aspect of the motif: the subterranean life of the people. Most apparent on this level is the dugout where we first encounter the Shimerdas. Grandmother Burden sets the tone for our response when she says she hates to think of the Shimerdas "spending the winter in that cave of Krajiek's" (p. 20). Reality proves even harsher than grandmother's cave image implies, for we soon discover that the Shimerdas' first American home is nothing but "a door and window sunk deep in the draw-bank" (p. 22) and that the family survives in less comfort than the animals from which the concept of the buried life derives. The animals submerge and emerge in natural life cycles, but the

Shimerdas' predicament suggests the buried life or death-in-life. Ironically the Burdens themselves are temporally not far removed from such troglodytic existence. The residue of the Burdens' past life still shows in the basement kitchen, painted "as it used to be in the dugouts" (p. 9) and in the adjoining long cellar which Jim explores but tentatively. The subterranean motif continues even more graphically when the blizzard strikes and the men have to dig a "tunnel through the snow . . . with walls so solid that grandmother and I could walk back and forth in it" (p. 93). Juxtaposed with the digging of the tunnel is Mr. Shimerda's suicide, which culminates in the ever present grave that stands like "a little island" on the prairie and that is the "spot most dear" to Jim (p. 119). His fascination with the grave suggests also that at this stage of his life Jim relates more to submergence than emergence. His own life impulses remain buried for many years, and the crossroads location of the grave implies the choices lying before him.

The literal placing of Mr. Shimerda into the earth (planting, as the old cowboy Otto Fuchs might say) begins our entrance into the metaphysical or unconscious realm of Cather's motif. On this level the most pervasive element is the prairie itself and the plants it nurtures. We note that though Jim originally feels that the prairie is "nothing but land" (p. 7), the earth roundabout is in fact very productive. Wasteland images occur in the "muddy little pond" and "rusty willow bushes" (p. 14), but the pages are dominated by emblems of natural growth: the cornfield, the sorghum patch, the box-elder, and the red grass that dyes the landscape the eucharistic "colour of wine-stains" (p. 15). And within the controlled growth of grandmother's garden are the "big yellow pumpkins" (p. 16), which in retrospect stand as an early emblem of Jim's own emergence or transcendence in that the pumpkins initiate for him the desire to "float off" into the sky with the sun which produces them (p. 16). Finally, we see the fruit cave of Book V, the cellar from which Ántonia's children tumble with glee—"a veritable explosion of life out of the dark cave into the sunlight" (p. 339) and a positive counterpoint to the depressing hole in which we first meet Ántonia. Here the emergence and symbolic rebirth are so startling that even stolid Jim becomes dizzy. Terence Martin sees this particular image as being strained, which it certainly is. Yet the strain seems intentional, for by this stage of the novel Cather wants to place tension upon the image to emphasize the literal-metaphysical associations, the animate-inanimate relationships. Just as badgers and pumpkins spring from the secret permutations of the earth, so spring children and self-realization.

The emergence Cather most wishes to emphasize is the movement from darkness to light, a point she makes via reiterated light images. Beginning in the very first lines of the Introduction, where the train "flashed" through "bright-flowered pastures," the imagery continues in grandfather Burden's "snow-white beard" (p. 12), in the "shining white bark" of the cottonwoods (p. 21), and in the "sunflower-bordered roads" (p. 28). Indeed, light symbols permeate the novel. We are here most concerned, however, with the light which Cather casts upon Ántonia, since Jim emerges from his darkness into the brightness of her humanism. This spiritual emergence is foreshadowed by the first description Cather gives of Ántonia's eyes, which are "big and warm and full of light, like the sun shining on brown pools in the wood" (p. 23). The eye/sun image repeats in the major symbol concluding Book IV. Near father Shimerda's grave, Jim and Ántonia are saying goodbye for what they think may be the last time, just prior to the twenty-year hiatus. They linger on the prairie until tears appear in Ántonia's "bright, believing eyes" (p. 321) and the sun begins to set. Simultaneously, the "moon rose in the east," and for several minutes "the two luminaries confronted each other across the level land, resting on opposite edges of the world" (p. 322). The luminaries symbolize Jim and Ántonia, with Cather's ironic reversal of conventional sun-moon symbolism. Though the passive moon is usually feminine in symbology and the dominant sun masculine, here the sun is Ántonia, with her powerful, warming light, and the moon is Jim, who reflects but does not yet emit light.[4] At this moment on the prairie, as in the two decades immediately following, Jim and Ántonia are physically worlds apart, though spiritually unified. The entire eye/sun image is the light which Cather gives to help us illuminate the darkness of the missing twenty years. As with the cave image, the symbolism may appear strained; but Cather is not the predictable symbolist, and as before, she places tension on the image to make it convey the psychological complexity of the Jim/Ántonia union.

Cather's intent with the "luminaries" passage is perhaps further appreciated if we realize that the lines present not an isolated piece of symbolism but are a continuation of a motif she inaugurates at the outset of Jim and Ántonia's life together. Literally within minutes of their first meeting, Ántonia offers Jim "a little chased silver ring she wore on her middle finger" (p. 26). Typical of his submerged personality at this stage, he refuses the ring because he is subconsciously aware of what it emblematizes. "I didn't want her ring," he says emphatically, and goes on to chide Ántonia's reckless behavior in wanting to betroth herself "to a boy she had never seen before" (p. 27). Even at this early age Jim innately fears commitment, not only to the pubescent Ántonia but more so to life's natural forces, which she so graphically represents. Ironically, while she lives destitute in the dark cave and Jim dwells in the reflected light of Burden wealth, he is the one who inhabits the darkness of his own doubts and timidity. Though intelligent and educated, and though he is appointed her tutor immediately after the ring episode, Jim and not Ántonia dwells in subterranean ignorance. He does not emerge until near the end of the novel, when as a middle-aged knight of American industry he makes his pilgrimage back to Ántonia, the source of his true enlightenment.

Thus the silver ring episode culminates in the sun-moon image of Book IV. We recall that during the latter passage Jim finally confesses his love for Ántonia—or at least comes as close to confessing as he possibly can. Even if he cannot utter the word "love" to the Bohemian girl he has been warned against, he does admit that he would like to have her "for a sweetheart, or a wife, or my mother or my sister—anything that a woman can be to a man" (p. 321). These disparate roles indicate not only Jim's emotional confusion but also the multiplicity of Ántonia's character, the cosmic femininity she symbolizes. At the moment of Jim's confession, the "pale silver" moon rises, with Cather's choice of adjectives echoing the silver ring which Ántonia has previously offered. Whereas Jim rejected the symbolic union she proposed so long ago, here he notes that the sun and moon join to form a "singular light" (p. 322) that emblematizes the spiritual union which has taken place over the years. Jim, at the end of Book IV, is not yet conscious of the union, but the mysterious forces of the union sustain him through the silent twenty years and carry him back to Ántonia in the very next book.

In "The Forgotten Reaping-Hook: Sex in *My Ántonia,*" Blanche H. Gelfant emphasizes various sexual symbols and concludes that Jim is a pusillanimous character fearful of sexual encounters, one who sublimates or represses his sexual drives so that they ultimately find expression in his penetrating the virgin prairie with his railroad. Gelfant believes that Jim's sexual fear makes of him "a wasteland figure who finds in the present nothing to compensate him for the loss of the past, and in the outer world nothing to violate the inner sanctum of memory."[5] Aside from the unfortunate train/penetration metaphor, Gelfant's argument is persuasive; but she seems finally to oversimplify both his character and Cather's narrative design and to apply Eliot's terminology too hastily. As we will see, Freudian sex theory does not easily explain Cather.

What Cather wishes to suggest is not that heterosexual love is some horror to be avoided via escape into the past but that certain forms of love transcend lust or carnality and, for that matter, time. Typical of Jim, he does not fully comprehend this transcendent love at its instant of manifestation, but during the twenty years that he will be physically separated from Ántonia the love develops as inexorably as the other natural processes which permeate and inform the narrative. We are reminded, perhaps, of Andrew Marvell's term "vegetable love" from another context, though with Jim and Ántonia the love is anything but carnal. Thus, when he subsequently returns to her, his emergence from darkness is commencing, for he begins to accept and understand this magical, mysterious love. The love emanates indeed from "the precious, the incommunicable past" (p. 372), but it does not suggest that Jim wishes to retrogress or that life is circumscribed by yesterdays. The love comes from the past literally in that it began at a biologically earlier stage in his growth, but it exists in a continuum. It sustains him permanently, even if at times he is almost totally ignorant of its existence. Here we must recall that one of Jim's final observations in the novel concerns the future: his promise to himself to "tramp along a few miles of lighted streets with Cuzak" (p. 370). The literal trail to the past—"a bit of the first road that went from Black Hawk out to the north country" (p. 370)—is still discernible, but the streets of the future are lighted, and they are the byways that Jim anticipates with enthusiasm.

In Book V Cather continues and extends the images and motifs of the earlier books to emphasize Jim's realization of the "miracle" (p. 331) that has been gestating for twenty years. Light images once again characterize Ántonia: white cats, light kitchen, shining range, white aprons, and the recurring yellow pumpkins. She has completed her emergence physically from the dugout and psychologically from the dependence that has previously mired her in darkness. Throughout the early parts of the novel she has been in thrall to her father, her sullen brother Ambrosch, the scoundrel Larry Donovan, and even to Jim himself. But in Book V, she has worked herself free, has risen toward the light like one of the rugged prairie sunflowers that are so frequently mentioned. No longer dependent, she is the one upon whom others depend, and in that ironic freedom she attains a transcendent beauty as difficult for the superficial view to reveal as is the beauty of the snakes, owls, and other natural prairie life. Despite her many batterings and her physical unattractiveness, she retains the mysterious beauty, the "fire of life" (p. 336) which has for so long beckoned to Jim. In the closing lines of Book IV, Jim departs from Ántonia in "intrusive darkness"; but in Book V he emerges into the light that she emits, there to become aware of his own purpose, his own self. He is abiding by natural laws as inexorable as those which determine that the sun will generate light and energy and that the moon will be illuminated out of darkness by that light.

The fact that at the conclusion of the novel we are still uncertain what Jim has realized about himself and that his personality still remains tantalizingly imprecise is in keeping both with Cather's overall design and with the specifics of the twenty-year break. As E. K. Brown says, "Everything in the book is there to convey a feeling, not to tell a story,"[6] and indeed the entire narrative operates on a delicate balance between realism and surrealism, with the prairie forming a solid background but with the personalities of the foreground actors being far more nebulous. Like the prairie flowers that bloom a day and are gone, our understanding of the characters' psyches is ephemeral. Ultimately and ironically, this element of Cather's design is also "'realistic,'" for such vagueness is the best we can expect when analyzing human personalities. Percy Lubbock fixes the truism for us by noting that in reading a novel, all we can hope to attain is "a cluster of impressions, some clear points emerging from a mist of uncertainty."[7] So it is with Cather's narrator. Jim himself does not fully understand the mysterious transformations that have occurred during these silent years in which natural processes change him. For Jim it is the cocoon time, and he can no more explain it to the reader than the prairie can explain its grasses or the moon its light. What Jim can do, however, is to create the "feeling" Brown notes and trust that the patient reader can share it. We can appreciate the subtlety of Cather's design even more, perhaps, if we remember something that William Carlos Williams liked to point out about the reader of literature: the reader can comfortably perceive the past and future, but "he never knows and never dares to know . . . what he is at the exact moment that he is."[8] It is this poetic conundrum of the ephemerality of our own mortal perceptions and the ironic transference between reader and fictive character that Cather manages so well and that makes some readers uncomfortable in her presence.

Clearly, then, an understanding of Cather's adeptness with symbols and motifs yields an appreciation of her artistic sophistication. Equally important, by realizing how clever and subtle Cather can be with literary devices, we in turn gain insights into the artistic psychology which generates the technique, for Cather herself is a study in submerged and emergent elements. Such insights can best be organized in terms of several persistent questions that have traditionally plagued Cather: (1) why does she use the male persona as spokesperson; (2) why does she emphasize the child; and (3) why does she seemingly worship the past?

To answer the first of these questions—and ultimately the remaining two— we must commence by recognizing the psychosexual conflicts implicit in *My Ántonia*. Deborah G. Lambert states the situation best when she characterizes Cather as "a lesbian writer who could not, or did not, acknowledge her homosexuality and who, in her fiction, transformed her emotional life and experiences into acceptable, heterosexual forms and guises."[9] The resulting bifurcation of the artistic self is evident in *My Ántonia,* for in the Jim-Ántonia juxtaposition we see the twin selves that were suppressed within Cather. Jim Burden and Ántonia Shimerda are externalizations of Cather herself, emerged from the depths of her very private personality.[10] Through the chemistry of her art Cather tries to separate the two, but ultimately she cannot do so and the male-female personas appear as literary Janus—or, to adopt Mark Twain's terminology, extraordinary twins.

Jim is but nominally masculine, a condition which Cather unconsciously emphasizes by surrounding him with stereotypical males such as Jesse James, whose biography so impresses the young Jim; Otto Fuchs, himself a character who could have "stepped" from the pages of that same biography (p. 6); and the lustful Wick Cutter, who literally tries to rape Jim and whose name so appropriately connotes both emasculation and defloration. Even when compared to meek Anton Cuzak, the great impregnator, childless Jim is conventionally lacking. He shields his feminine sensitivity, however, with the armor of success in the masculine world of law and high finance. Thus protected from fault and accusation, he is transformed into Cather the artist—careful, premeditative, and safe. On the other hand, Ántonia presents the conventional male traits in feminine disguise. She is the quintessential but paradoxically masculine woman, the Bohemian secret-self Cather longed to express. Lambert correctly notes that Ántonia reveals "the consequences of Cather's dilemma as a lesbian writer in a patriarchal society" (p. 677). In her roles of cook, gardener, mother, and wife she conforms to the code of the stereotypical frontier woman, thereby masking the mannish qualities which she has exhibited throughout the first four books of the narrative. Just as no one can get at Jim through his Big Business shield, no one can possibly fault Ántonia in her Earth Mother guise. Even her sins are sins of love and motherhood, and in her astonishing fecundity she fulfills not only her assumed female purpose but compensates for her one premarital misstep. With each new baby she legitimizes and relegitimizes the bastardry of her firstborn. Like Hester Prynne, she pays her dues, and by Book V she has long since moved into able and absolution out of adultery. It is not difficult to see the childless, husbandless, doubtful Cather seeking her own salvation via Ántonia, trying to appease the prairie society which intellectually and geographically she could reject but which psychologically was always with her.

We need look no farther than Sinclair Lewis' *Main Street* (1922) to be reminded of the village virus that was so epidemic and to which intelligent young women such as Cather were especially susceptible. Never able to free herself completely of the virus, Cather nevertheless could create a healthy fictive persona which vicariously assuaged her sexual guilt and proved to the world that she could be the good girl, the prairie female personified—a bit rebellious and unlucky but in the final accounting bathed in the redeeming light of motherhood and legitimacy. Moreover, by juxtaposing this idealized frontier female with Jim, the successful capitalist who incidentally is articulate enough to write a book, Cather managed the extralegal, truly spiritual marriage, the integration of selves that was in fact impossible. In *Freudianism and the Literary Mind,* Frederick J. Hoffman refers to exogamy, the galvanizing fear of incest we inherit from our most primitive ancestors.[11] The term conveniently explains the taboo with which Cather struggled in the Jim-Ántonia characterizations. Because they represent the dual halves of Cather's psyche, the brother-sister of her unconscious, she could not allow them any physical intimacy. They had to remain pure of each other, else she unconsciously sanctioned the most forbidden of sexual "crimes." Hoffman goes on to point out that James Joyce, her contemporary, was able to write openly about incest and homosexuality because he was "not enchained or imprisoned by the power of his unconscious life" (p. 149). Cather was not exactly imprisoned by her unconscious life either, but above all else she remained a daughter of the Nebraska village and was more prudent than Joyce in exposing the painful dichotomy between the private self and the social self. Her art, consequently, is both syntonic and asyntonic, a paradox we see manifested in her intermingling of narrator and heroine.

As for the question of Cather's preoccupation with children, we cannot deny that they do dominate *My Ántonia.* Jim, Ántonia, and her sibling initiate the action, and the outpouring of Cuzaks concludes it. The children, however, are more than simple embodiments of authorial sentimentality of escapism. They are central to the subterranean-emergence motif we have discussed and are another key to understanding Cather's own psychic perceptions.

Freud's theory that children are innately and naturally "perverse" in their refusal to conform to what society defines as proper behavior casts some light on Cather's use of children. In discussing infantile sexuality Freud elucidates the child's innate perversity, a quality brought about by the fact that "the psychic dams against sexual transgressions, such as shame, loathing and morality" have not yet been formed.[12] For the artist this quality makes the child an ideally suitable emblem of the guiltless exploration of all erotic possibilities. Unconsciously sensing that eroticism should express itself in various forms, not just genitally or heterosexually, the child develops naturally through oral, anal, and genital stages of eroticism, a process Hoffman refers to as "the blessed anarchy of childhood" (p. 99). Particularly apropos to our immediate purposes is Freud's note that the pregenital phases cannot be "designated *masculine* and *feminine"* since the gender distinctions form only later in the genital stage (*Basic Writings,* p. 597). Unfortunately, the individual enters adulthood during the genital stage of development, and what was once an innocent "perversity" becomes a destructive genital fixation with definite male-female gender differentiations. In short, selfish pleasure must surrender to the demands of reproduction in order to guarantee the species, and reproduction is unavoidably a heterosexual-genital demand. Freud sees the resulting conflict between natural erotic pleasures and social prerequisites as the major cause of neuroses; and for Freud, neuroses were destructive.

Cather separates from Freudian doctrine on this point. Her view of neuroses is more accurately reflected in the thinking of Norman O. Brown, who in *Life against Death* disagrees with Freud and sees neuroses, with their "fixation on perversions," as positive demonstrations of "the refusal of the unconscious essence of our being to acquiesce in the duality of flesh and spirit."[13] Brown agrees with Freud that the genital orientation produces undesirable side effects, but he categorically rejects what he terms Freud's "'rude, persistent demand for the bodily origin of spiritual things" (p. 25). He finds comfort in the fact that despite all that "parental discipline, religious denunciation of bodily pleasure, and philosophic exaltation of the life of reason" have been able to do, the human animal remains unconvinced that its "pleasure-seeking" childhood impulses are wrong; and neuroses are the positive signs of our stubborn refusal to say good-bye to the lost paradise of childhood (p. 31).

As we have already noted, Cather could not in her own life reify her subconscious desires, could not shake free of "parental discipline" and "religious denunciation"; but in her fictive children she intuitively projects both the sexual freedom inherent in the preadult stages of erotic development and the natural freedom from death awareness that ultimately constricts the adult. Significantly, though Ántonia truly loves the apron-clad and dutifully attendant girls of her brood, her favorite child is Leo the faun, a child epitomizing the sexually free, uninhibited spirit—the "perverse" and socially rebellious soul. For Cather, therefore, the child is not only a literary symbol of innocence and exuberance, not only the "image of inviolability" that Blanche H. Gelfant recognizes in "The Forgotten Reaping-Hook" (p. 76). For Cather the child is an artistic extension of the essential design of the narrative, an image of sexual guiltlessness and of the time when sexual pleasures could be pursued and enjoyed, free of what Brown terms "the tyranny of genital organization" (p. 29). Childhood is not a stage to which Cather simplemindedly wishes to return, like a badger retreating into the dark burrow. It is instead a perpetual element of the human psyche which helps make the rigors of life bearable and from which the artist-as-child can draw. As Frederick J. Hoffman reminds us, the entire life of the individual and of the race is encapsulated in the child, and the artist naturally turns to the child for inspiration (p. 19). From the child in her, Cather received both her artistic imagination and answers to questions arising from her own "perverse" sexuality.

Shifting from Cather's children to her concept of time is more a matter of nuance than of substantive distinction, for just as childhood's natural and innocent perversity is lost to adulthood's demand for sexual organization and species continuity, so commensurately is the child's freedom in time sacrificed to the adult's imposition of chronological schemes—with similar adverse consequences. As Karl Malkoff phrases it, using Freudian-Brownian theories in his analysis of contemporary verse, "Instead of experiencing unending nowness, we locate ourselves at some specific point along a continuing line."[14] Unlike Freud and many of the other novelists of her era (such as Katherine Anne Porter and Scott Fitzgerald, who saw moral debts, like monetary ones, rolling out of the vaults of the past with ruinous surcharges having accrued) Cather intuitively rejected the linear perspective. She could not readily conceive of the "me" of the present forever fleeing some "me" of the past down an inescapable tract of time. Untypically, her view of the past was neither Freudian nor puritan. It was—and the term seems more apropos than hazardous—childlike in its positive and benign trustfulness.

Again Norman O. Brown helps elucidate my point. Until recently we had little choice about temporal theories. Historical-linear time seemed the *sine qua non* of existence. Freud subscribed to this view and concluded that our desire to retain the past means that we consequently search for the past in the future, thereby enmeshing ourselves in neuroses. However, Einsteinian physics and other post-Freudian developments have forced reexamination of the historical time concept. Brown borrows from these new theories to hypothecate the existence of a consciousness emancipated from the historical-linear idea and therefore freed of the learned complexes that frustrate and repress us. If we can be set loose from the birth-life-death syndrome, which demands conformity and biological reproduction, then the individual is subsequently free to exist "not in time but in eternity" (*Life against Death,* p. 94). Such an articulation of time is precisely what the child enjoys innately, before socialization squelches the natural, harmonious impulses. With no awareness of mortality and no fear of death, and thus blissfully ignorant of the compulsion to reproduce its kind, the child is released into eternity. As we can see, then, what Cather wanted to convey with her fictive children was not slavish nostalgia or escapism but an integrated attempt to reunite herself psychologically with nature, to lessen the culturally imposed strictures of historical time and sexual dogma. If, somewhat mystically through an imagination drawing heavily from childhood and the past, Cather could enter eternity (as Brown suggests is indeed possible), she thereby freed herself from the complexes that first create and then feed upon guilt and repression. Such a desire was impossible to reify completely, but it is nonetheless perceptibly at work in her fiction.

NOTES

[1] "The Drama of Memory in *My Ántonia,*" *PMLA,* 84 (1969), 308.

[2] "The Mysteries of Ántonia," *Midwest Quarterly,* 17 (1976), 178.

[3] *My Ántonia* (Boston: Houghton Mifflin, 1954), p. 30. All further references to this work appear in the text.

[4] A good example of the moon used as a feminine symbol can be found in the poetry of Sylvia Plath. For a discussion, see Judith Kroll, *Chapters in a Mythology* (New York: Harper & Row, 1976).

[5] Gelfant, *American Literature,* 43 (1971), 63–64.

[6] *Willa Cather: A Critical Biography* (New York: Knopf, 1953), p. 206.

[7] *The Craft of Fiction* (New York: Viking, 1957), p. 1.

[8] *Imaginations* (New York: New Directions, 1971), p. 89. Quoted by Karl Malkoff pp. 64–65. See note 14.

[9] "The Defeat of a Hero: Autonomy and Sexuality in *My Ántonia,*" *American Literature,* 53 (1982), 676.

[10] See, for instance, Leon Edel, "Willa Cather and *The Professor's House,*" in *Psychoanalysis and American Fiction,* ed. Irving Malin (New York: Dutton, 1965), pp. 215ff. Edel discusses the application

of psychology to biography. His point, supported by analysis of *The Professor's House*, is that Cather revealed her own suppressed fears and doubts in her fiction. Such an argument is hardly startling today, but it does serve to reiterate the point that Cather, more protective of her private life than most writers, exposed more of her inner self than she knew.

[11] *Freudianism and the Literary Mind*, 2nd ed. (Baton Rouge: Louisiana State Univ. Press, 1957), p. 18.

[12] *The Basic Writings of Sigmund Freud*, ed. and trans. A. A. Brill (New York: Modern Library, 1938), p. 592.

[13] *Life against Death* (New York: Vintage Books, 1959), pp. 31–32.

[14] *Escape from the Self* (New York: Columbia Univ. Press, 1977), p. 5. Malkoff's summary of Freud's and Norman O. Brown's thinking, while not directly applied to Cather, coincides with my own ideas and is quite informative.

Judith Fetterley

MY ÁNTONIA, JIM BURDEN AND THE DILEMMA OF THE LESBIAN WRITER

I

In "To Write 'Like a Woman': Transformations of Identity in Willa Cather" (forth-coming in *Journal of Homosexuality*), Joanna Russ claims Cather as a lesbian writer and essays to understand the central situation in many of her novels and stories as an indirect expression of a lesbian sensibility. Not unlike most readers of Cather, I have long thought *My Ántonia* both a remarkably powerful and a remarkably contradictory text and have long suspected that its power was connected with its contradictions.[1] Russ' thesis, while controversial,[2] is hardly startling once stated; and it provides an admirable framework within which to understand this connection and thus the meaning of Cather's text. As Deborah G. Lambert has demonstrated, *My Ántonia* is a watershed book for Cather, marking the transition between her ability to write as a woman about women and her decision to write as a man about men.[3] In *My Ántonia*, the transition and transformation are still in process and the process is incomplete. What marks *My Ántonia*, then, as a central, if not the central Cather text, is not so much the evidence it contains of Cather's capitulation to convention, but rather the evidence it contains of her deep-seated resistance to such capitulation. It is, if you will, the force-fed loaf but partially chewed. As such, it defines the nature of Cather's situation as an American writer who is a lesbian writer. And in defining so sharply that situation, *My Ántonia* enables us to grasp the essence of Cather's art and of her achievement.

II

In Book IV, the Widow Steavens informs Jim of the fate of their Ántonia: "My Ántonia, that had so much good in her, had come home disgraced. And that Lena Lingard, that was always a bad one, say what you will, had turned out so well, and

From *Gender Studies: New Directions in Feminist Criticism*, edited by Judith Spector (Bowling Green, OH: Bowling Green State University Popular Press, 1986), pp. 43–59.

was coming home here every summer in her silks and her satins, and doing so much for her mother. I give credit where credit is due, but you know well enough, Jim Burden, that there is a great difference in the principles of those two girls. And here it was the good one that had come to grief!"[4] One might well ask where the Widow's certainties are coming from, what principles are determining the comfortable clarity of her moral universe. How is it that she can so easily distinguish the good woman from the bad one? Surely, Ántonia's goodness comes straight from her conventionality; she is all that one could ask for in the way of traditional womanhood. She is smart as a whip, but will never attend school; eager and quick to learn the language of her new country, she will always speak broken English with an accent which marks her as foreign; eventually she will speak no English at all; nurturant in the extreme, she saves even the insects, making a nest in her hair for the protection of the sole surviving cricket. Above all, she identifies with men and against women. She is passionately devoted to her father whom she ennobles, in a moment of extraordinary disclosure, for having married her mother when he could have bought her off. Since Ántonia herself will recapitulate her mother's experience, her idealization of her father and denigration of her mother is as painful as it is predictable. She pads about after Charley Harling, "fairly panting with eagerness to please him" (p. 155); and she equally "pants" after Jim and his approval, hoping that "maybe I be the kind of girl you like better, now I come to town" (p. 154). With Lena she is cold and distant because Lena "was kind of talked about, out there" (p. 164); Tony is not one to give a sister the same uncritical support she gives men.

In Book II, we learn that Tony is all heart: "everything she said seemed to come right out of her heart," and this is the source of her power (p. 176). In Book IV, we learn the limitations of the power of "heart." "The trouble with me was," she later explains to Jim, "I never could believe harm of anybody I loved," thus indicating how radical is her severance of head from heart (p. 344). Tony's "all heart, no head" approach to life leads her directly into the arms of Larry Donovan, for whom she performs the conventional female function of becoming the mirror in which one is seen as large ("His unappreciated worth was the tender secret Larry shared with his sweethearts," p. 305); against her better judgment, she participates in the mythology of the transforming power of women's love: "I thought if he saw how well I could do for him, he'd want to stay with me" (p. 313). The arms of Larry Donovan open directly onto the realm of the seduced and abandoned and "my" Ántonia is "poor" Ántonia now. Though Jim professes anger at this convention, there is a direct connection between the qualities he values in Ántonia and her abandoned state, between being "good" and being "poor." At the end of Book I, Jim murmurs, "Why aren't you always nice like this, Tony?" (p. 140). Previously, she has not been so nice: "Ántonia ate so noisily now, like a man" (p. 125), and "like a man" she works, competing daily with Ambrosch and boasting of her strength. From the "fate" of acting like a man and losing "all her nice ways" (p. 125), Grandmother Burden "saves" her, getting Ántonia a job in town serving the Harlings. Tony's salvatory tenure at the Harlings is abruptly terminated, however, by another incursion of not-niceness. Forced to choose between working for the Harlings and going dancing, Tony "set[s] her jaw" and leaves: "A girl like me has got to take her good times when she can. Maybe there won't be any tent next year. I guess I want to have my fling, like the other girls" (p. 208). To which Jim responds, "Tony, what's come over you?" Tony is unrecognizable when not "nice," that is, when she uses her head to have some fun and puts herself, her desires and her needs before the approval and service of others.

But, of course, Tony's "badness" is only a temporary deviation from her trajectory towards apotheosis as earth mother, in which image she is fully delivered up in Book V, fittingly titled "Cuzak's Boys." Defined not only as the mother of sons but as the mother of the sons of her husband, so completely does "niceness" require the elimination of self, Antonia admits, in an aside reminiscent of Aunt Polly, "That Leo; he's the worst of all. . . . And I love him the best" (p. 335). Obviously, in boys badness is goodness. Though "a rich mine of life" to others, Ántonia is herself somewhat depleted. She is a battered woman, whose grizzled hair, flat chest and few remaining teeth reflect the toll exacted of one who plays the role of earth mother.

This is a role which Lena, "coming home here every summer in her silks and satins, and doing so much for her mother," has firmly refused, eliciting thereby the Widow's fiery denunciation of her as "bad." From the moment she first appears at the Harlings' back door, Lena presents a marked contrast to Ántonia. While Tony pants after approval in broken English, Lena moves through the world with "perfect composure" and perfect English (p. 160). Unlike Tony, Lena is "crazy about town" (p. 164) because she sees it as the way up and out, and up and out Lena intends to get. "Through with the farm" and through with family life and resolutely anti-marriage, Lena is determined to be economically and personally independent; she has come to town to learn a profession. Lena's clear head is clearly harnessed to her vision of her own self interest and, while she "gave her heart away when she felt like it, . . . she kept her head for her business and had got on in the world" (p. 298). Though Lena's success is in itself sufficient to draw the Widow's ire, her definition of "good" requiring an element of failure in which head is submerged in heart and self is deferred to other, the personal focus of the success is equally enraging. It's bad enough that Lena wants to take care of herself; worse yet is her desire to take care of her mother. To Ántonia's male-identification and glowing commitment to father-right and brother-right, Lena opposes the image of a woman-identified-woman whose hidden agenda is rescuing her mother. Lena's resistance to marriage derives from her perception of it as bad for women—too much work, too many children, too little help: "she remembered home as a place where there were always too many children, a cross man and work piling up around a sick woman" (p. 291). Further, "it's all being under somebody's thumb" (p. 292), and when that somebody is cross or sullen, "he'll take it out on her," wives serving for men, as Lena knows, as live-in-victims (p. 162). On the same occasion in which Tony builds a shrine to her father for actually having married a girl he seduced, Lena reveals the heart of her hidden agenda: "I'm going to get my mother out of that old sod house where she's lived so many years. The men will never do it" (p. 241). Not only does Lena identify with her mother; she sees her mother identifying with her: "She'd get away from the farm, too, if she could. She was willing for me to come" (p. 161). The handkerchiefs Lena would buy for her mother carry the letter "B" for Berthe, not "M" for mother.

III

Though the moral universe of the Widow Steavens is simple, that of the text of *My Ántonia* is not. At several points and in several ways, *My Ántonia* fails to confirm or ratify the Widow's easy differentiation. Indeed, to read *My Ántonia* is to be visibly confronted with a series of contradictions, to be forced to raise a series of questions, and to be required to realize that these contradictions and questions, as they are central to the act of reading the text, are central to the text's meaning. One such question emerges from Jim's final apotheistic tribute to Ántonia: "It was no wonder that her sons stood tall and straight. She was a rich mine of life, like the founders of early races" (p. 353). But where are these sons? Even a cursory examination of *My Ántonia* reveals nothing to support the validity of Jim's assertion; on the contrary, it reveals much that subverts it. If one examines the various men who appear in *My Ántonia,* the cumulative picture is one of weakness, insubstantiality, and self-destruction. Sons in *My Ántonia* are neither tall nor straight nor well-fed. Either they are being starved to death or they are constitutionally incapable of assimilating offered nourishment or both or more. Emblematic is the nameless tramp whose story Tony recounts in Book II. Arriving out of nowhere, he offers to run the threshing machine and minutes later jumps into it head first. Tony's response emphasizes the peculiar maleness of this behavior: "What would anybody want to kill themselves in summer for? In threshing time, too! It's nice everywhere then." And besides, she adds, "the machine ain't never worked right since" (pp. 179, 178). Bewildered Tony may well be as to the cause of this behavior but hardly as to its existence; her own father, in an act which anticipates the demise of Wick Cutter, has blown his head off because life is simply too much for him. He becomes daily less substantial until there remains only enough energy to mark the fact of his existence by the violence of its termination. Consumptive rather than consuming describes the men in this text, as witness the example of Gaston Cleric. Are we then to assume that Ántonia herself comprises an entire category, no other earth mother existing, all these men being the sons of women who are something other than earth mothers? Yet whom has Ántonia nourished? Not her father certainly. Cuzak?—"a crumpled little man" who lifts "one shoulder higher than the other . . . under the burdens of life" and looks "at people sidewise, as a work-horse does at its yokemate" (pp. 356, 358). Jim, who seems to have no life at all? Where are Ántonia's tall, straight sons?

If there are no well-fed sons, no end products to validate Jim's assertion of nourishment, there is evidence to suggest that when women feed men they poison them. Female nourishment is linked to death. Wick Cutter's viciousness, which culminates in his wife's murder and his own suicide, runs on the energy generated by Mrs. Cutter's outrage: "he depended upon the excitement he could arouse in her hysterical nature" (p. 253). Mrs. Harling feeds Mr. Harling: "Before he went to bed she always got him a lunch of smoked salmon or anchovies and beer. He kept an alcohol lamp in his room, and a French coffee-pot, and his wife made coffee for him at any hour of the night he happened to want it" (p. 157). She feeds him ego food too: "Mr. Harling not only demanded a quiet house, he demanded all his wife's attention.... Mrs. Harling paid no heed to anyone else if he was there" (pp. 156–7). The result of this feast is an arrogant imperialism which stops life: "We had jolly evenings at the Harlings' when the father was away" (p. 156). And what are the consequences of Antonia's whipping up cakes for "Charley"? Charley/Larry doesn't seem to have benefitted much from her hot lunches. He is last seen disappearing toward Mexico where he may get rich, "collecting half-fares off the natives and robbing the company," and where he may just as easily get killed (pp. 312–313). And Charley/Jim? The most elaborate exposure of the dangers of female nourishment occurs in a scene which involves Jim, the architect of the earth mother image. In Book I, Jim kills a snake and Antonia is unrelenting in her praise of his courage; singlehandedly she creates monster and hero, dragon and George, feeding Jim's ego until "I began to think that I had longed for this opportunity, and had hailed it with joy.... Her exultation was contagious. The great land had never looked to me so big and free. If the red grass were full of rattlers, I was equal to them all" (pp. 47–48). Back at the ranch, Otto, the cowboy, succinctly punctures Ántonia's windy distortion: "Got him in the head first crack, didn't you? That was just as well" (p. 49). Later Jim learns how lucky he really was: "A snake of his size, in fighting trim, would be more than any boy could handle. So in reality it was a mock adventure; the game was fixed for me by chance, as it probably was for many a dragon-slayer. I had been adequately armed by Russian Peter; the snake was old and lazy; and I had Ántonia beside me, to appreciate and admire" (pp. 49–50). But what if there were no Otto? What if Ántonia's was the only voice Jim ever heard? Might he not, thus stuffed with heroic imagery, set off on other adventures where, not so lucky, he would return on his shield rather than with it?

The point here is not to suggest that Cather is writing an anti-feminist text which demonstrates how bad women are for men, a position implicit if not explicit in Blanche Gelfant's truly provocative and insightful essay[5] and one which finally reinforces the apotheosis of the earth mother. Rather it is to suggest that the text of My Ántonia radically undercuts the premises of the image which occupies its center, thus calling into question the value of the very conventions it asserts. Women are not under attack here for failing to be earth mothers. Nor are earth mothers under attack for failing to fulfill their promises or, more insidiously, for masquerading as nourishers while enacting emasculation. Rather under attack is the apotheosis of the earth mother image. The pressure the text resists is the pressure embodied in the voice of the Widow Steavens with her easy assurance of good and bad and it resists this pressure by undermining the bases of the earth mother image. Like a system responding to the implantation of a foreign body, My Ántonia surrounds Antonia with anti-stories.

One such features as heroes Russian Peter and Pavel who, for daring to act out a powerful though non-conventional truth, have suffered banishment and stigmatization. Can the apotheosis of the earth mother work without a positive attitude toward heterosexual marriage? For the Widow Steavens, Lena's badness is directly connected to her resistance to marriage; yet much of the text of *My Ántonia* supports Lena's badness, not Tony's goodness. The significance of the Russians' story may be taken, as Gelfant suggests, from its mode of presentation.[6] Like any highly explosive material it is carefully contained. Dying, Pavel tells his story to Mr. Shimerda; Ántonia overhears it and, translating first from Russian to Bohemian and then from Bohemian to English, she repeats it to Jim who tells it to us. And what is the content of this highly explosive tale? A hatred of marriage as pure as the snow onto which the bride and bridegroom are thrown and as intense as the hunger of the wolves who consume them. Pavel and Peter's priorities are ratifed by a text whose hostility to marriage would be hard to exceed. Examples of destructive marriages abound: Cutters, Shimerdas, Harlings, Crazy Mary and just as crazy Ole, Jim and the woman who "for some reason" wishes to remain Mrs. Burden. Good marriages exist only when essential to maintaining the surface tone of the text, as is the case with Jim's family. Note, however, that Jim's parents are conveniently dead; his family is his *grand*parents, safely distanced by a generation from his generation. Further, we see very little of the actual texture of this relationship. That necessarily good relationship whose texture we do partially witness in fact confirms, though more moderately, the vision of marriage as a structure of mutually conflicting interests: "It did rather seem to me that Cuzak had been made the instrument of Ántonia's special mission. This was a fine life, certainly, but it wasn't the kind of life he had wanted to live. I wondered whether the life that was right for one was ever right for two!" (p. 345).

Attitudes toward sexuality obviously inform the attitude toward marriage. While more complex, they are equally hostile. Ántonia's extraordinary fecundity finds neither resonance nor reinforcement in a text whose sexual emblems are Crazy Mary, Wick Cutter and Lena with the reaping-hook. The act required for the "rich mine of life" motif is fraught with danger and repugnance. Mr. Shimerda's dalliance with the servant girl who comes to work for his mother terminates in the gruesome scene in a Nebraska barn, a frozen corpse on the floor and "bunches of hair and stuff" stuck to the roof (p. 98). Like father, so daughter, whose brief moment of eroticism, those nightly trips to the dancing tent, finds an equally painful conclusion in the house attached to the barn. Haunting the landscape of sexual passion is the figure of Crazy Mary, whose jealousy of Lena reduces her to a caricature with a corn knife in danger of being recommitted. The pathetic object of her passions is no more fortunate in his relation to sexual longing; having married his Mary to keep him steady, he finds the remedy insufficient and himself wandering the prairies looking for Lena.

Though the sexual impulse in *My Ántonia* dooms men as well as women, a loathing of male, not female, sexuality informs the negative context. Emblematic here is Wick Cutter, whose name reveals at once his phallic identity and the narrative attitude toward it. In Wick male sexuality emerges as unrestrained, unre-strainable and rapacious, preying on those women who must serve him to survive. Through him is articulated the hidden, and shameful, sexual history of Black Hawk, a history of exploitation and abuse which spawns an endless series of pregnant "Marys," some of whom return to town after being "forced to retire from the world for a short time" and some of whom do not return but move on to Omaha and Denver where they are "established in the business" for which they have been "fitted" (pp. 203, 210). Though less obvious than the abuse of the hired girls, the anemia, paralysis and unlived lives of the "white," middle-class town girls must also be laid in part at the door of a sexuality which requires "purity" in wives and mothers and vents its lust on the bodies of servants. Yet there is in *My Ántonia* a loathing of male sexuality that transcends the presumably political. The disgust which Wick Cutter's flesh elicits, "his pink, bald head, and his yellow whiskers, always soft and glistening" (p. 210), is adumbrated in the nausea elicited by the extraordinarily phallic snake of Book I: "His abominable muscularity, his loathsome, fluid motion, somehow made me sick. He was as thick as my leg, and looked as if millstones couldn't crush the disgusting vitality out of him. . . . He seemed like the ancient, eldest Evil" (pp. 45–47).

Up to this point in the analysis, we have a paradigm which, while somewhat complicated, is nevertheless easy to grasp: the conventional enshrinement of the conventional image of the earth mother undermined by a critique of the premises upon which the convention is based; or, if you will, a patriarchal story co-existing with a feminist story. We must now move to a level of analysis which is more complex, one which engages the contradictions within the two stories as well as those between them and one which understands the two stories not simply as co-existing but as coinciding, both inevitably present because dynamically related. For surely neither sexual politics nor phallic loathing, though richly informative of the attitude toward marriage, is adequate to explain the aura of fear which encircles sexual experience in *My Ántonia* and creates a radical contradiction within the conventional story between the romanticization of earth mother fecundity and the attribution of "goodness" to her stance of asexuality. The key rests with the figure of Lena Lingard, whose "badness" is related to her sexuality and whose sexuality reveals the erotic asymmetry at the heart of the novel. If Wick Cutter's flesh elicits loathing and disgust, Lena's elicits desire—in crazy Ole; in the Polish musician who lives across the hall; in old Colonel Raleigh, her landlord; in Jim himself; and in the narrative voice which describes her. The fear Lena arouses can only be understood as a response to the desire she has first aroused. And most certainly she arouses fear. The landscape of Ántonia's "rich mine of life," the fruit cave whose veritable "explosion of life" dizzies Jim temporarily, finds no complement in the erotic land-scape of Jim's dream life. Rather this landscape is bare, cut and full of shocks. In the dream Jim dreams "a great many times," Lena appears to him as the grim reaper, armed with the hook which he, at least, never forgets. Though Jim says he wished he could have this "flattering" dream about Ántonia, it is obvious that his ability to idealize her, like the Widow's ability to define her as "good," is directly connected to her refusal to appear to him in the imagery of sexual desire. Moreover, it is connected to the fact that she serves him as the agent of sexual repression and prohibition, reinforcing that part of him which needs to set the erotic in the landscape of dream and surround it by an aura of fear. Shortly before Jim tells us about his dream, he records an equally significant exchange between himself and Ántonia. Attempting to kiss Tony as "Lena Lingard lets me kiss her," Jim experiences a sharp rebuff (p. 224). Tony gasps with indignation and snarls protectively, "If she's up to any of her nonsense with you, I'll scratch her eyes out!" (p. 224). To which Jim responds with an outburst of pride and the avowal that now he knows "where the real women were, though I was only a boy; and I would not be afraid of them, either!" (p. 225).

It would be a thankless, if not hopeless, task to attempt to unravel the contradictions and confusions of this particular bit of textual sequence. But it would be irresponsible to fail to note their existence or to fail to observe that this abundance of confusion coincides precisely with the most overtly sexual moment in the text. Surely, if not answers, questions are being forced upon us. Why is Jim's pride in Ántonia tied to her protecting him from Lena? How can an earth mother be idealized both for her fecundity and for her asexuality? And behind these, and the welter of similar questions, is the overriding issue of the source of the imperative against responding to female sexuality. Women's resistance to male sexuality is adequately explained by sexual politics and phallic loathing. But why can't Jim have erotic dreams about Tony or see Lena without her reaping-hook?

In Book III, Jim, accompanied by Lena, attends the theatre and on one particular afternoon encounters for the first time the transcendant power of art. The initiating play is *Camille* whose theme, significantly enough, is renunciation. Why, we may well ask, is Jim so transfixed by the dream of renunciation and why does this drama enable him to grasp the meaning and function of art? What, we might equally well ask, is being renounced here and who is doing the renouncing?

IV

Jim Burden has presented a problem to many readers of *My Ántonia*.[7] Indeed, Cather's own uneasiness on the subject of her point of view is apparent, not simply in her various explanations/rationalizations of her narrative choice but also within the text itself.[8] How else can one understand the "Introduction" save as an effort to substantiate Jim Burden, explain his relation to story and character, and make him credible as a narrator? "Unlike the rest of the book," Brown tells us, Cather found the introduction "a labor to write."[9] Her difficulty may well suggest something false in the nature of the task, an inability to say what needs to be said, an unwillingness to explain where explanation is essential. Her discomfort was such that for the 1926 reissue of *My Ántonia* she revised the introduction, improving the effect, according to Brown, and most particularly by removing from "the reader's mind a question that could do the book no good—whether in fact it would not have been better told by another woman, the query Miss Jewett had raised about

'On the Gull's Road'."[10] Cather's revisions may indeed have improved the "Intro-duction," but not because they solved its problems. Rather her revisions re-focus the questions which the "Introduction" will inevitably raise so as to more accurately reflect and engage these problems. The ultimate effect of the revised "Introduction" is to focus the reader's attention on the problematic nature of the narrative voice in the text, for instead of explaining Jim Burden the "Introduction" leaves us won-dering who has made the attempt. The "I" who introduces our "eye" is not now Willa Cather who, as a "little girl" had watched Ántonia "come and go" and who has made a feeble attempt to write Ántonia's story herself, but is rather a nameless, faceless, sexless voice. Three pages into the story and we itch for definition, crave knowledge of who is speaking to us. Neither itch nor craving is satisfied here or later and this, I would propose, is precisely the point of Cather's excisions and final "solution." While putatively existing to solve a problem, the "Introduction" in fact serves to identify a problem and to indicate that the problem is the point. Indirect in its strategy, the "Introduction" further reveals that the inability to speak directly is the heart of the problem which is the point.

In revising the "Introduction" Cather removed all references to herself. Dra-matized in the act of revision and embedded thus in the revision itself, palimpset sub-text informing the super-imposed surface text, is the renunciation of Cather's own point of view and of the story that could be told from that point of view. To return to the motif of *Camille*, I would suggest that the renunication at issue is Cather's own. In *My Ántonia* Cather renounces the possibility of writing directly in her own voice, telling her own story, and imagining herself in the pages of her text. Obviously autobiographical, the obvious narrator for *My Ántonia* would be Cather herself. Yet for Cather to write in a female voice about Antonia as an object of intense and powerful feelings would require that she acknowledge a lesbian sen-sibility and feel comfortable with such a self-presentation—a task only slightly easier to do now than then.[11] Indeed, in the context of early 20th century self-consciousness of sexual "deviance" and thus of the potentially sexual content of "female friendships,"[12] Jewett's directive to Cather to avoid the "masquerade" of masculine impersonation and write openly in her own voice of women's love for women—("a woman could love her in that same protecting way—a woman could even care enough to wish to take her away from such a life, by some means or other"[13])—seems faintly specious. In fact, it was not "safer" for Cather to write "about him as you did about the others, and not try to be he!"[14] Her "safety" lay precisely in her masquerade.

Yet *My Ántonia* is not simply "safe." Choosing to transpose her own expe-rience into a masculine key, Cather nonetheless confronts us with a transposition which is radically incomplete. At the end of Book IV, Jim confesses to Ántonia, "I'd have liked to have you for a sweetheart, or a wife, or my mother or my sister—anything that a woman can be to a man" (p. 321). Why, then, does he not so have her? No reader of *My Ántonia* can avoid asking this question because Cather makes no attempt to answer it and thus prevent us. For the contradiction between speech and act cracks open the text and reveals the story within the story, the story which can't be told directly, the essence of whose meaning is the fact that it can't be told.

Though nominally male, Jim behaves in ways that mark him as female. From the start he is anomalous. On the farm, he rarely leaves the kitchen; he inhabits women's space: "When grandmother and I went into the Shimerdas' house, we found the women-folk alone.... The cold drove the women into the cave-house, and it was soon crowded" (pp. 114, 115). Yet Cather can't have him doing women's work; thus Jim does virtually nothing, a fact which at once contributes to his insubstantiality and provides a context for understanding its source. Jim's most active moment comes, not surprisingly, when he is left alone. With no one to observe him and with responsibility for all tasks of both sexes, he throws himself into housework and barn work with equal vigor. There is a moment in Book II which similarly defines his ambiguity. Realizing that he is about to leave Black Hawk, Jim delivers a reminiscent tribute to his life as a Black Hawk boy: "For the first time it occurred to me that I should be homesick for that river after I left it. The sandbars, with their clean white beaches and their little groves of willows and cottonwood seedlings, were a sort to No Man's Land, little newly created worlds that belonged to the Black Hawk boys. Charley Harling and I had hunted through these woods, fished from the fallen logs, until I knew every inch of the river shores and had a friendly feeling for every bar and shallow" (p. 233). To which peroration we can only murmur, "really?" For we have seen no part of this boys' world. Instead, we have seen Jim hanging out at the Harlings, participating in female-centered family life; Jim playing with the hired girls and getting a reputation for being "sly" and "queer" (p. 216); Jim studying his books at home alone; Jim walking the streets at night and sneering at the cowardice and hypocrisy of these very Black Hawk boys who are supposedly his fishing and hunting buddies. Nor does Jim identify with Black Hawk men. Toward an obvious role model, he manifests the most intense dislike. How are we to explain Jim's hatred of Mr. Harling, a figure who represents his own possibilities for future power, dominance, self-assertion and self-gratification? It is particularly significant that Jim's hostility focuses precisely on those aspects of Mr. Harling which are most patriarchal—the subservience of his wife and children, their absolute catering to his every whim, his ownership of time and space; in short, his "autocratic" and "imperial" ways, the ways of a man "who felt that he had power" (p. 157). Jim's hostility, reminiscent of his earlier contempt for the arbitrary predominance accorded Ambrosch, though unintelligible in a male, is thoroughly intelligible in a female who understands patriarchal privilege as tyranny.

Equally revealing of gender ambiguity is Jim's sexual self-presentation. With Harry Paine, the town boy who loses Tony her job by forcing her to kiss him on the Harlings' back porch, as the "norm" for adolescent male sexuality, Jim's behavior stands out as "queer" indeed. Attempting to kiss Tony himself and meeting with a similar rebuff, he responds not with force but with petulance and then support. "Lena Lingard lets me kiss her," he weakly asserts, disclosing thus his essential sexual passivity and foreshadowing the postures of his erotic dream. After listening to Tony's lecture on the dangers of playing with Lena, Jim capitulates completely, submerging his dissent in a rush of pride at the "true heart" of his Ántonia. The conflict produced by the oppositional nature of male and female sexual interests collapses at this point; it cannot survive the stronger pull of Jim's implicit sympathy for and identification with Tony's position. As Ántonia knows, sexuality can be dangerous for women. It is she who has paid the price of Harry Paine's desire and it is she who will be left with child and without money at the end of her affair with Larry Donovan. Jim's pride in Ántonia's warning is worthy of a mother or a sister or a friend, but not of a suitor whose interest lies in undermining her perceptions and making her ashamed of her resistance.

There are two scenes in *My Ántonia*, both explicitly about sex and gender, which define unmistakably the essential femaleness of Jim Burden. In Book I Jim tells us of an incident which made a change in his relationship with Ántonia, a change which he claims to have welcomed and relished. Through this event Ántonia presumably learns that gender means more than age; thus taught, she abandons her tone of superiority and assumes her appropriately subservient place: "Much as I liked Ántonia, I hated a superior tone that she sometimes took with me. She was four years older than I, to be sure, and had seen more of the world; but I was a boy and she was a girl, and I resented her protecting manner. Before the autumn was over, she began to treat me more like an equal and to defer to me in other things than reading lessons. This change came about from an adventure we had together" (p. 43). Jim's sexism here is so unlike anything we know of him before or after that, for this reason alone, the snake episode would invite our closer scrutiny. Yet even a cursory glance reveals an agenda very different from the one Jim asserts. Not masculine superiority and the validity of masculine privilege but the fraudulence of male heroics and hence of the feminine worship that accompanies and inspires it are the subjects of this episode. Jim responds to the sudden appearance of the snake with sheer terror and he kills it by sheer luck. From his experience he learns that a stacked deck makes heroes and a chorus of female praise obscures the sleight of hand. The aura of the impostor colors the scene and explains the absence of any sequel to it. Once again, the disjunction between speech and act points us in the direction of gender ambiguity. Jim's experience is far more intelligible as that of a girl, who, while temporarily acting a boy's part, discovers the fraudulence of the premises on which the system of sexism is based and thus comes to see all men as impostors; but who nevertheless recognizes that, though she may play male roles and sign herself William Cather, her signature is a masquerade and her identity a fake.

The second scene occurs in Book II when Tony, made nervous by the more than usually bizarre behavior of her employer, Wick Cutter, asks Jim to take her place. And take her place is precisely what Jim does. In theory, Ántonia's request ought to provide Jim with a golden opportunity, a chance to demonstrate that masculine superiority which is the putative lesson of the earlier scene by protecting the woman whom he continually tells us he loves. Further, since Cutter's intention is rape and since the whole town loathes the man, the situation carries with it the additional possibility of becoming a local hero. Knight in shining armor, defender of fair womanhood, Black Hawk avenger—Tom Sawyer would jump at it. Jim Burden turns and runs, straight home to grandmother where he puts his face to the wall and begs, "as I had never begged for anything before," that she allow no one else to see him, not even the doctor (p. 249). To her reiterated note of thankfulness "that I had been there instead of Ántonia," Jim responds with pure hatred: "I felt that I never wanted to see her again. I hated her almost as much as I hated Cutter. She had let me in for all this disgustingness" (p. 250). Surely Jim has literally taken Ántonia's place and experienced the rape intended for her. The physical repulsion, awareness of sexual vulnerability, sense of shame so profound as to demand total isolation—all are intelligible as the responses of a woman to an attempted rape. Jim's identification with Ántonia structures the scene, undermining his pretense to masculinity and maleness. Is it not obvious why Jim can't marry Ántonia?

At the end of his story, Jim returns to the landscape of his youth. Setting out, north of town, into "pastures where the land was so rough that it had never been ploughed up," Jim has "the good luck to stumble upon a bit of the first road that went from Black Hawk out to the north country; to my grandfather's farm, then on the Shimerdas' and to the Norwegian settlement. Everywhere else it had been ploughed under when the highways were surveyed; this half-mile or so within the pasture fence was all that was left of that old road which used to run like a wild thing across the open prairie, clinging to the high places and circling and doubling like a rabbit before the hounds" (pp. 369, 370–371). Formless, unploughed and unsurveyed, with possibilities for wildness, this landscape, so steeped in nostalgia, reflects a longing for a time before definition, before roads have been marked and set and territories rigidly identified. Not surprisingly, at the end of the book Jim has returned to a psychological state parallel to that of his beloved landscape. Reunited at last to Ántonia, he is also reunited with a past before the domination of sexual definition where one might be tomboy and love one's Ántonia to one's heart's content. The attendant spirit on the longing for gender ambiguity is a profound uneasiness in the face of actual manifestations of this desire. Like a threatened animal tracked to its lair, the text exudes the stench of trauma at those moments when gender crossing actually occurs—for example, when Ántonia begins to dress and act like a man and grandmother Burden determines to "save" her. This tension between impulse and repression, desire and renunciation determines the various trajectories described by the text of My Ántonia. "The Pioneer Woman's Story" is not the only tale this text is telling. Though My Ántonia may have at its center a massively romanticized earth mother, the surrounding context denies both condition and consequence of that role. Profoundly non-heterosexual in its view of men, male sexuality and marriage, the text embodies the feeding not of sons but daughters. In My Ántonia daughters, not sons, stand tall and straight for they alone have access to the shelves of jars, the barrels of food, stored in the fruit cave of the womb, the rich mine of life.

The text as a whole recapitulates the burden of narrative choice—a forced feeding only partially swallowed; a transposition only partially completed; a story, a sensibility, an eroticism only partially renounced. Emblematic of the unrenounced is the character of Lena Lingard. If the idealization of Ántonia in "the pioneer woman's story" requires the steady denial of her sexuality,[15] Lena remains convincingly sexual to the end. More significantly, her sexuality is neither conventionally female nor conventionally male but rather some erotic potential only possible outside the heterosexual territory of rigid definitions and polar oppositions. Characterized by a diffused sensuality rooted in a sense of self and neither particularly aggressive nor particularly passive, Lena represents a model of lesbian sexuality. Her presence in the text as a symbol of desire, felt as desireable and allowed to be desired, "flushed like the dawn with a kind of luminous rosiness all about her" (p. 226), provides occasional moments of pure sensual pleasure and indicates the strength of Cather's resistance to renouncing her lesbian sensibility.

V

In the foreword to his biography of Willa Cather, James Woodress writes: "Although Willa Cather wrote an old friend in 1945 that she never had any ambitions, the truth was just the opposite. Her entire career down to the publication of *O Pioneers!,* her first important book, shows a very ambitious young woman from the provinces, determined to make good."[16] Certainly that "determination" to "make good" must have played a large role in Cather's decision to renounce her own point of view, masquerade as a male, and tell a story which is not her own. As critics from Leslie Fiedler to Carolyn Heilbrun and, most recently, Nina Baym[17] have demonstrated, American literature is a male preserve; the woman who would make her mark in that territory must perforce write like a man. The pressure which converted Willa Cather into Jim Burden was not simply homophobic; equally powerful was the pressure exerted by the definition of the American "I" as male and the paradigm of American experience as masculine. Yet perhaps the ultimate irony of Cather's career lies in the fact that she is best remembered, not for her impersonations of male experience, her masculine masquerades, but rather for the strategies she evolved to maintain her own point of view and tell her own story within the masquerade. In a word, she is less remembered for the consequences of her renunciation than she is for the results of her resistance.

In *My Ántonia,* Cather reveals the face of that ambition which she later declared the book to have satisfied: "The best thing I've done is *My Ántonia.* I feel I've made a contribution to American letters with that book."[18] It is not surprising that the book in which Cather reveals her artistic ambitions should be her most powerful work. Nor is it surprising that this book is marked by the theme of renunciation and defined by the tension between the pressure to renounce and the equally imperative need to resist this pressure. Nor finally is it surprising that it is here, in this text, that Cather works out the terms of her compromise with her context—the context of an ambitious American writer who is also female and lesbian.

At the opening of Book III, Jim sits musing on the lines from Virgil's *Georgics:*

" 'Primus ego in patriam mecum deducam Musas'; for I shall be the first, if I live, to bring the Muse into my country' " (p. 264). He remembers that his teacher, Gaston Cleric, had explained "that 'patria' here meant, not a nation or even a province, but the little rural neighborhood on the Mincio where the poet was born"; and he wonders if "that particular rocky strip of New England coast about which he had so often told me was Cleric's *patria*" (pp. 264, 265). Surely Jim's musings illustrate Cather's ambition—to be, like Virgil, the first to bring the muse into her own country. But if Virgil's country is a *patria,* Cather's Nebraska is ardently female, envisioned and embodied in a lavishly feminine imagery, metaphor, and analogy, which culminates in the identification of the Bohemian girl with the American land.

Equally female is Cather's muse. Jim's musing on poets and poetry is interrupted by a knock at the door and the entrance of Lena Lingard. After she leaves, "it came over me, as it had never done before, the relation between girls like those and the poetry of Virgil. If there were no girls like them in the world, there would be no poetry" (p. 270). It would be hard to overestimate the significance of this moment for the career of Willa Cather or for the history of the woman artist in America. Locating the source of poetic inspiration in the figure of Lena Lingard— the unconventional, the erotic, the lesbian self retained against all odds—instead of in the figure of Ántonia—the conventional, the desexed, the self distanced and defined as Other (for Ántonia, unlike Lena, could never have written *My Ántonia*), the location one would expect if one read the entire text as "The Pioneer Woman's Story," Cather reverses the transposition which produced Jim Burden, drops her masquerade, and defines a woman's love for women as the governing impulse of her art. Lesbian eroticism is at the heart of her concept of artistic creation. Moreover, if muse and country are both female, and if the function of the writer is to bring muse and country together, then the textual act itself is in this formulation equally lesbian. Yet, in what sense does *My Ántonia* validate Cather's aesthetic theory? In what sense, beyond anything yet observed, is *My Ántonia* an expression of lesbian eroticism, a story of women's love for women—in other words, a lesbian book?

In the "Introduction" to *My Ántonia,* we hear a voice that is marked as neither male nor female. This voice recurs throughout the text. Often we forget that we are listening to Jim Burden—his masculinity, as suggested above, has been made easy to forget—and we assume instead that we are hearing the voice of Willa Cather. This slippage occurs most frequently and most easily when the subject of contemplation is the landscape. A woman's voice making love to a feminine landscape—here, I would suggest, is the key to Cather's genius and achievement. Unable to write directly of her own experience and to tell her own story in her own voice, and thus baffled and inhibited in the development of character and plot, Cather turned her attention elsewhere, bringing the force of her talent to bear on the creation of the land, her country, her *matria*. In the land, Cather created a female figure of heroic proportions, proportions adequate to both her lived experience as a woman and her imaginative reach as a woman writer. In the land, Cather successfully imagined herself; in the land, she imagined a woman who could be safely eroticized and safely loved. Thus the story she could not tell in terms of character and character is told in terms of narrator and country, and the flattening and foreshortening of personality which is the consequence of her renunciation of her own voice has as its corollary a complementary lengthening and enriching of landscape. Cather made her mark in the territory of American literature with her landscape; we remember her *matria* long after we have forgotten her masquerade. Though she may have sold her birthright, the price she got for it was gold.

NOTES

[1] See, for example, E. K. Brown and Leon Edel, *Willa Cather: A Critical Biography* (New York: Knopf, 1953; pb. rpt. New York: Avon, 1980), pp. 152–159; Blanche Gelfant, "The Forgotten Reaping-Hook: Sex in *My Ántonia*," *American Literature*, 43 (1971), 60–82; William J. Stuckey, "*My Antonia:* A Rose for Miss Cather," *Studies in the Novel*, 4 (1972), 473–483.

[2] In *Lesbian Images* (Garden City: Doubleday, 1975), Jane Rule explicitly denounces a lesbian approach to Cather's work, suggesting that it violates Cather's sense of herself as an artist and a person and fulfills her worst fears of the critical act as merely an effort to "reduce great artists to psychological cripples, explaining away their gifts and visions in neuroses and childhood traumas" (p. 74). Rule shares Cather's fears about the motives of critics; she presents a series of "readings" which she labels "grossly inaccurate" and which she claims "can only be explained by a desire of each of these men to imply that Willa Cather's 'basic psychology,' 'personal failure,' or 'temperament' negatively influenced her vision" (pp. 75, 76). Obviously Rule has reason to assume that masculinist critics will seek to find in Cather's lesbianism the "flaw" which explains what's "wrong" with her work. Rule's solution to this situation, however, is absurd. Reciting the biographical evidence for viewing Cather as a lesbian, she nevertheless severs the life from the work, refusing to imagine the possibility that Cather's lesbianism might have influenced her art and resolving the paradox she has thus created by resorting to a mystical mumbo-jumbo, as in the following statement, which means as far as I can tell, absolutely nothing: "What actually characterizes Willa Cather's mind is not a masculine sensibility at all but a capacity to transcend the conventions of what is masculine and what is feminine to see the more complex humanity of her characters" (p. 80). Rule's anxiety to protect Cather against the masculinist misreadings which result from patriarchal homophobia lead her, unfortunately if predictably, to commit similar atrocities, as when she calls *My Ántonia* Cather's "most serene and loving book," proving thereby that, though Cather was emotionally devastated by Isabelle McClung's marriage to Jan Hambourg, her personal torment as a lesbian in no way interfered with her ability to write a classic of heterosexual love. Homophobia can go no further. It is not surprising that David Stouck in his review essay, "Women Writers in the Mainstream," *Texas Studies in Literature and Language,* 20 (1978), 660–670, gleefully seizes on Rule's analysis as proof of the limits of feminist criticism for illuminating the work of Willa Cather.

[3] "The Defeat of a Hero: Autonomy and Sexuality in *My Ántonia*," *American Literature,* 53 (1982), 676–690.

[4] Willa Cather, *My Ántonia* (Boston: Houghton Mifflin, 1918; rev. 1926; pb. rpt. 1980), p. 313. All subsequent references are to this edition and will be included parenthetically in the text.

[5] See, for example, pp. 70, 74.

[6] See Gelfant, p. 74. Gelfant must be credited with first according this scene the attention it deserves. It is, however, interesting that in her interpretation of it as a "grisly acting out of male aversion" to women, she overlooks the fact that the groom as well as the bride gets eaten.

[7] See, for example, E. K. Brown and Leon Edel, pp. 153–154.

[8] See James Woodress, *Willa Cather: Her Life and Art* (Lincoln: University of Nebraska Press, 1970), p. 176: "She felt obliged to defend her use of a male point of view, however, when she wrote her old friend and editor Will Jones. Because her knowledge of Annie came mostly from men, she explained, she had to use the male narrator, and then she rationalized that she felt competent to do this because of her experience in writing McClure's autobiography." Or Mildred Bennett, *The World of Willa Cather* (Lincoln: University of Nebraska Press, 1961), pp. 46–47: "One of the people who interested me most as a child was the Bohemian hired girl of one of our neighbors, who was so good to me. She was one of the truest artists I ever knew in the keenness and sensitiveness of her enjoyment, in her love of people and in her willingness to take pains. I did not realize all this as a child, but Annie fascinated me and I always

had it in mind to write a story about her. But from what point of view should I write it up? I might give her a lover and write from his standpoint. However, I thought my Ántonia deserved something better than the Saturday Evening Post sort of stuff in her book. Finally, I concluded that I would write from the point of a detached observer, because that was what I had always been. Then I noticed that much of what I knew about Annie came from the talks I had with young men. She had a fascination for them, and they used to be with her whenever they could. They had to manage it on the sly, because she was only a hired girl. But they respected and admired her, and she meant a good deal to some of them. So I decided to make my observer a young man."

[9] Brown and Edel, p. 153.

[10] Brown and Edel, p. 153.

[11] For a fuller exploration and discussion of the issues involved in such a decision, see the first several pages of Deborah Lambert's essay.

[12] For a discussion of the emergence of this self-consciousness and of the loss of "innocence" attendant on it, see Lillian Faderman, *Surpassing the Love of Men: Romantic Friendship and Love between Women from the Renaissance to the Present* (New York: William Morrow, 1981), pp. 297–331.

[13] *The Letters of Sarah Orne Jewett,* ed. Annie Fields (Boston: Houghton Mifflin, 1911), p. 247.

[14] *Jewett,* p. 246.

[15] See Deborah Lambert's essay for a detailed analysis of the stages by which Ántonia is "reduced to an utterly conventional and asexual character."

[16] Woodress, p.13.

[17] "Melodramas of Beset Manhood: How Theories of American Fiction Exclude Women Authors," *American Literature,* 33 (1981), pp. 123–139.

[18] Bennett, p. 203.

Susan J. Rosowski

MY ÁNTONIA: THE CLOSING
OF THE CIRCLE

She . . . had that something which fires the imagination, could . . . stop one's breath for a moment by a look or gesture that somehow revealed the meaning in common things.[1]

It was as if everything Cather had written until now had been in preparation for *My Ántonia.* In her early essays and short stories she had told of imaginatively fusing two worlds—that of ideas and that of experience, of the general and the particular. She allegorically described the need to do so in *Alexander's Bridge,* then focused sequentially on each world, in *O Pioneers!* so celebrating the idea that she seemed to leave physical realities behind, and in *The Song of the Lark* so involved with particulars that they sometimes seem all there is. In *My Ántonia* she put the two together. The result was the single work that would insure Cather's place in literature.

One sign of Cather's achievement is that *My Ántonia* defies analysis, a quality critics often note when beginning a discussion of it. In 1918 W. C. Brownell said he did not "mind being incoherent" in writing of Cather's new book if he could "convey his notion in the least by [his] flounderings," compared its air to that of Homer, who lifted his subject "somehow," then concluded, "I don't know any art more essentially elusive."[2] Half a century later James Woodress wrote of the same quality in different terms. *My Ántonia* has passion, and though "one knows when he is in the presence of it, . . . the identification of it is somewhat intuitive. . . . it is difficult to explain."[3] More specific readings differ dramatically—David Stouck interprets it as a pastoral and Paul A. Olson as an epic; James E. Miller, Jr., as a commentary on the American dream and Blanche H. Gelfant as a drama of distorted sexuality—until one wonders how a single work can mean so many things to so many people.[4] Yet the greatness of the book lies in precisely this capacity. With *My Ántonia* Cather

From *The Voyage Perilous: Willa Cather's Romanticism* (Lincoln: University of Nebraska Press, 1986), pp. 75–91.

introduced into American fiction what Wordsworth had introduced to English poetry a century earlier—the continuously changing work.

By creating a narrator, Jim Burden, to recall Ántonia, a girl he knew while growing up in Nebraska, Cather for the first time in a novel used the narrative structure ideally suited to the romantic. She made the reacting mind a structural feature of her book. She then provided what E. K. Brown called a "very curious preface," in which she instructed her reader about what was to follow.[5] In that preface Cather anticipated major questions raised by critics. Is *My Ántonia* about Jim or about Ántonia? The question assumes mutually exclusive alternatives Cather rejected. Jim originally titled his story simply "Ántonia," then frowned, added "my," and seemed satisfied. As his title indicates, *My Ántonia* is about neither Jim nor Ántonia per se, but how the two, mind and object, come together, so "this girl seemed to mean to us the country, the conditions, the whole adventure of our childhood."[6]

Is it a novel, and has it any form? The impetus for Jim's story was his desire to recollect his emotions, so that he might understand the pattern that emerges from them. To speak Ántonia's name "was to call up pictures of people and places, to set a quiet drama going in one's brain," and in writing, Jim was true to his experience of remembering (xii). He didn't make notes, didn't arrange or rearrange, but "simply wrote down what of herself and myself and other people Ántonia's name recalls to me" (xiv). Thus his story is not structured by situation, as novels usually are, but by one person's feelings, in the manner of a lyric. Its meaning is as personal as its form; Jim specifies that his story won't be his reader's. When he presents his manuscript to Cather (and implicitly to each reader), he asks, "Now what about yours?" then cautions, "Don't let it influence your own story" (xiii, xiv). This is a book, then, that hasn't a settled form, but instead that sets in motion an ever-changing, expanding process of symbolic experience, "a quiet drama" in the mind of each reader.

That is not to say *My Ántonia* is formless. From the apparently episodic looseness of Jim's recollections emerges the classic romantic pattern of a dialectic between subject and object, momentarily resolved as a symbol. It consists of two major movements, followed by fusion: first, awakening to experience (Part I) and moving outward by its physicality (Part II), then awakening to ideas (Part III) and returning by them (Part IV); finally, fusing the two as symbol (Part V). By turning back upon itself, the pattern forms circles of expanding meaning. As Jim returned to scenes of his childhood, so the story returns the reader to the beginning, to recognize as symbols particulars once seen discretely. This is precisely the process Jim articulates at the conclusion (a misnomer, for here there is no conclusion; meaning is open-ended and ongoing), when he walks again along the first road over which he and Ántonia came together and realizes that man's experience is "a little circle" (372).[7]

That circle begins in and returns to childhood, "the fair seed-time" of the soul.[8] Part I, "The Shimerdas," tells of a child's awakening to nature. When he came to Nebraska as a ten-year-old orphan, Jim Burden felt he had entered a prairie that at night seemed the void predating creation. Awakening the next morning, Jim found himself in the beginning of a new world. It was a pastoral, Edenic world, in which his grandmother's garden seemed nature's womb. There Jim was warmed by the earth, nourished by fruit within arm's reach, entertained by acrobatic feats of giant grasshoppers, and comforted by the wind humming a tune. His was the unconscious sensation of "something that lay under the sun and felt it, like the pumpkins, and . . . [he] did not want to be anything more." As if one with the mother who holds him within her body, he feels the happiness of being "dissolved into something complete and great" (18).

The scene anticipates point of view throughout this section, in which Cather describes geographical and imaginative expanses from carefully defined vantage points, usually nestled within the earth. Jim is characteristically stationary, securely protected within a bed of one kind or another—a womblike garden, a prairie nest, a hay bed in Peter's wagon, his own bed beside the open window, even his grandmother's kitchen, "tucked away so snugly underground" (101). And Ántonia too is associated with a bed within the earth, dug into the wall of her family's cave and "warm like the badger hole" (75).

Stationary themselves, Jim and Ántonia are witness to the miraculous activity of nature. From it flowers grow as big as trees and cottonwoods shimmer with colors of a fairy tale; from it too come animal forms, astonishing in their variety. When Jim watched the Shimerdas emerge from a hole in the bank, it was as if the earth was giving birth to life itself. First appeared a woman with "an alert and lively" face and "a sharp chin and shrewd little eyes," then a girl of fourteen with eyes "full of light, like the sun shining on brown pools in the wood" and wild-looking brown hair. Following them came a foxlike son of nineteen, with sly, suspicious little hazel eyes, which "fairly snapped at the food" Jim's grandmother brought, and following him a little sister, mild, fair, and obedient. From behind the barn appeared another Shimerda son, unexpectedly with webbed hands and the speech of a rooster. Finally, most surprising of all, the father emerges, neatly dressed in a vest and a silk scarf, carefully crossed and held by a red coral pin. When he bends over Mrs. Burden's hand, he could be greeting her in the most formal of drawing rooms rather than on a wild prairie in an unsettled land (22–24).

The effect of a miracle recalls O Pioneers! Yet unlike that first Nebraska novel, where characters often seem more mythic than human, in My Ántonia the miraculous resides within the ordinary. The prairie Jim entered is the one a nine-year-old Cather had entered, and it has the depth of lived experience—the smells, textures, sounds, sights of the land itself. Autobiographical particularity continues throughout the book. In Black Hawk (Red Cloud transformed into art) Cather's childhood friends appear: the Miner family, neighbors to the Cathers, as the Harlings; Mrs. Holland, the hotel keeper, as Mrs. Gardener; two musicians—Blind Boone and Blind Tom—as Blind d'Arnault. In Lincoln, Herbert Bates, Cather's teacher at the University of Nebraska, appears as Gaston Cleric, Jim's teacher at the same school. Most important, Annie Sadilek Pavelka, the Bohemian girl whom Cather knew while growing up and whose friendship she renewed in middle age, appears as Ántonia Shimerda Cuzak.[9]

In *My Ántonia* particulars anchor the story, keeping it from floating away from this world. On their way to meet their new Bohemian neighbors, the Burdens pass through a natural paradise, with sunflowers making a gold ribbon across the prairie and one of the horses munching blossoms as he walked, "the flowers nodding in time to his bites" (20). The scene could easily seem a fantasy, yet the Burdens carry with them "some loaves of Saturday's bread, a jar of butter, and several pumpkin pies," and the everyday reality of the supplies, listed and identified by historical reality (the bread was baked on Saturday), keeps the scene within the here and now (19). The Shimerdas' dough has the fairy-tale mystery of a witch's brew, yet it is mixed "in an old tin peck-measure that Krajiek had used about the barn" (31), and a storybook storm, when snow "simply spilled out of heaven, like thousands of feather-beds being emptied," takes place on January twentieth, Jim Burden's eleventh birthday (92).

Thus the ideal and the real, the general and the particular, are fused by the synthetic power of the imagination, especially strong in childhood. The ten-year-old Jim Burden sees his grandparents' hired men as Arctic explorers, his grandfather as a biblical prophet or an Arabian sheik, and their lives in Nebraska as more adventurous than those of characters in *The Swiss Family Robinson* and *Robinson Crusoe*. When transformed by the imagination, nature, like the Burdens' Christmas tree, is "the talking tree of the fairy tale; legends and stories nestled like birds in its branches" (83).

From the beginning Ántonia embodies these connections; she is a coming together of man and nature, a mediator between them. Her wild-looking hair, her eyes like the sun shining on brown pools, her spontaneity, make her seem nature's child, able to direct Jim's awakening to beauty. Her first act with him is to take his hand and lead him into the prairie, not stopping "until the ground itself stopped— fell away before us so abruptly that the next step would have been out into the tree-tops"; then from a nest in the long prairie grass, she points to the sky (25–26). As she will later stand in an orchard and reach out to a fruit tree or look up at the apples, so she here draws Jim toward the horizon, where this world stops and another begins—the bourne of heaven. She brings the Old World into the New (when an insect's song reminds her of Old Hata, the beggar woman in her childhood Bohemian village comes close to the Nebraska prairie), and she changes hardship into joy (when she tells of it, a hole dug into the wall of a primitive cave becomes a warm burrow, and a frightening encounter with a rattlesnake becomes a heroic adventure).

Nature fosters "alike by beauty and fear"—Wordsworth's words might have been Cather's description of the childhood section of *My Ántonia,* in which she included as an undercurrent to joy reverberations of loss and death.[10] Two black shadows flit before or follow after the children, Mrs. Burden's garden conceals a snake, Mr. Shimerda's smile suggests profound sadness, and the fullness of autumn's beauty contains "a shiver of coming winter in the air" (38). This darker reality is conveyed especially by the story of Peter and Pavel, so powerful it is often the single episode people remember years after first reading *My Ántonia.* The story is simple. Returning home over snow, a wedding party is overtaken by wolves, and to lighten their load Pavel throws the groom and bride from his sledge. Even in the barest outline it is a powerful incident, for as the snake in Mrs. Shimerda's garden represents the oldest Evil, so the story does our most basic fears. Cather intensifies its effect in the telling.

As the context for Pavel's story Cather establishes the vastness of a wilderness, the darkness of night, and, especially, the emptiness of silence. No one talks during the ride to Peter and Pavel's house; there, Pavel is asleep, awakening only to tell his story, then returning to sleep; following the tale Ántonia and Jim scarcely breathe. As is life within a wilderness or light within darkness, sound which breaks silence is dramatic; it is a principle Cather uses throughout this episode. Pavel begins his story in a whisper which grows to a raging cry, cut short by convulsive coughing, then by sleep. Ántonia's translation to Jim similarly builds from the merriment of the wedding guests to the shrieks of people and screams of horses attacked by wolves, then stops short, for Pavel could remember nothing of throwing over the bride and groom. When this silence too is broken by another sound, the reader expects still other wolves to be pursuing the last members of the wedding party, then realizes these are monastery bells in Peter and Pavel's village calling people to early prayer. Like the knocking on the gate in *Macbeth*, the bells signal a more profound horror than any thus far realized—a reentry of the ordinary world from which Peter and Pavel will henceforth be outcasts.

Repetition evokes the sense of ongoing truth. Three times friends journey home together, and three times the tale is told. Peter, Mr. Shimerda, Ántonia, and Jim travel by wagon to Peter and Pavel's house, where they hear of other friends traveling by sledge to their village; afterwards, they return by wagon to the Shimerda farm. Similarly, Pavel first tells his story in Russian; Ántonia repeats it in English; then Jim and Ántonia tell it to one another. Russian merges with English; cries of coyotes are answered by a man, and both echo those of wolves; screams of horses and of people combine; the moans of the wind seem spirits to be admitted, answered by a dying man soon to be among them. Different voices combine to tell a truth so profound all of nature speaks of it, the tragedy of life in a wilderness.

The idea appears in various forms throughout this first section: during that first hard winter the Shimerdas faced starvation, Pavel died of consumption, Peter lost his land, and Ántonia's father committed suicide. Indeed, the childhood scenes contain such hardships that one wonders how a mood of joy survives. Again, Pavel's story suggests an explanation. Jim recalled that "for Ántonia and me, the story of the wedding party was never at an end. We did not tell Pavel's secret to anyone, but guarded it jealously—as if the wolves of the Ukraine had gathered that night long ago, and the wedding party been sacrificed, to give us a painful and peculiar pleasure" (61). This is the egocentricity of childhood, and it proves a saving protection.

Like Wordsworth, Cather recognized that nature ministers to the child, not literally, of course, but psychologically. Rowing late at night in a stolen boat and suddenly seeing the mountain uprear its head, the boy Wordsworth felt as if it were rising in response to him; in his recollection of the episode he is truthful to the childhood perception rather than to his adult understanding of the facts. Similarly, Cather presents a child's view of the outside world as if it existed for him. The wind hummed to Jim, a small frail insect sang for Ántonia, and people, like characters from a fairy tale, appear to tell their tales, then disappear. Not surprisingly, to Jim Russia seems as remote as the North Pole, and the personal lives of Peter and Pavel, strange men with unpronounceable names, are obscured in the distant realm of adulthood.

Through it all there is a child's belief that things will always be this way, made poignant by adult awareness of change. This is, after all, the middle-aged Jim Burden's recollection of his childhood, a retrospective Cather recalls by phrases repeated so often they become motifs—"I still remember," "they are with me still," and "I can see them now." Tension between innocence and experience increases with changes in Ántonia. By the end of their first year in Nebraska, Ántonia has left the security of childhood to work the land; she aches with exhaustion and, realizing other hardships lie ahead, wishes winter would not return. Meanwhile Jim, only eleven, is still reassured by the notion that it "will be summer a long while yet" (140).

"When boys and girls are growing up, life can't stand still. . . . they have to grow up, whether they will or no" (193). In recognition that Jim was getting older and needed to attend school in town, the Burdens moved from their homestead to Black Hawk, a small prairie town halfway between the country and the city, wilderness and civilization. Ántonia followed them, to work as a hired girl for the Burdens' neighbors, the Harlings. The move signals the transition from childhood to adolescence, from receptivity to irrepressible energy. In Black Hawk the beauty of the immigrant girls suddenly shines forth, stunning within the narrow confines of a small community, and the energy of boys and girls alike spills over.

Music announces the change in mood. In the childhood scenes music provided an elegiac background: an insect singing before winter, Mr. Shimerda removing his violin from its box but never playing it, Fuchs singing a hymn while making a coffin and the community singing another by Mr. Shimerda's grave. In Part II, "The Hired Girls," the people are eased from the harsh struggle of those first years, and they burst into song. Jim Burden is drawn to his neighbors' home by the notes which filter from it: there everyone plays the piano, Ántonia hums as she works, children sing, and Mrs. Harling conducts them all. As Jim recalled, "Every Saturday night was like a party" (175). With Mrs. Harling at the piano it seems inevitable that they begin to dance, Frances teaching the younger children.

From the Harlings the dancers begin a procession which wends its way through Black Hawk. They go next to Mrs. Gardener's hotel, where the tempo changes dramatically. When Mrs. Gardener is out of town one Saturday, her carefully ordered establishment erupts into revelry, inspired again by a piano player—no longer the motherly Mrs. Harling but Blind d'Arnault. Looking "like some glistening African god of pleasure, full of strong, savage blood," d'Arnault played barbarously, wonderfully, awakening in his listeners their own savage blood, which erupts in a wild, frenzied dancing that he will not allow them to stop (191). Like him, they are blind to the consequences.

When the setting again changes, so does the mood. Three Italians come to Black Hawk and look over the children, then set up a dancing pavillion that is "very much like a merry-go-round tent, with open sides and gay flags flying from the poles" (194). From it come siren sounds to which the youth are irresistibly drawn: "First the deep purring of Mr. Vanni's harp came in silvery ripples through the blackness of the dusty-smelling night; then the violins fell in—one of them was almost like a flute. They called so archly, so seductively, that our feet hurried toward the tent of themselves" (196). Upon hearing the music, Ántonia would hurry with her work at the Harlings, dropping and breaking dishes in her excitement, and "if she hadn't time to dress, she merely flung off her apron and shot out of the kitchen door. . . . the moment the lighted tent came into view she would break into a run, like a boy" (205). Energy until now barely contained spills over in animal heat. The iceman, delivery boys, young farmers, all come tramping through the Harlings' yard, and "a crisis was inevitable" (206). Told to cease attending the dances or to leave the Harlings' employ, Ántonia moves into the household of the notoriously dissolute Wick Cutter.

Still, the dancers do not stop. When the Vannises dismantle their tent and move away, the same people who attended it go to the Fireman's Hall Saturday dances. And as Ántonia earlier had broken from the Harlings, so now Jim breaks out, crawling from his grandparents' window on Saturday nights, kissing Ántonia as he has no right to do, and dreaming Lena Lingard turns to him saying, "Now they are all gone, and I can kiss you as much as I like" (226).

Two concluding episodes present two aspects of this energy, one pointing back, the other forward. In the first Jim and the hired girls return to the prairie for a picnic, feeling the idyllic contentment of childhood one last time. They play a game, then sit talking; it is one of the few scenes in this section in which they are physically still. The scene ends with one of the most famous images in Cather's writing, that of the plow momentarily transformed into heroic size by the blood-red energy of the sun, then fading into littleness. This is the passion of imaginative perception. The second episode points ahead ominously, to the dark side of passion that degenerates into debauchery. At Wick Cutter's, Ántonia is in danger of rape; and sleeping in her place, Jim is attacked. He emerges bruised and bitter, as if he had fallen and been trampled upon by the bacchanalian parade in which he had been dancing.

Having followed physicality to its darkest extreme, Jim turns away from it altogether. He moves from Black Hawk to Lincoln, where, at the university, he awakens to a world of ideas. Part III, "Lena Lingard," is complementary to Part I, "The Shimerdas": the two sections present two awakenings to two worlds, one of nature, the other of ideas. In this second awakening Jim again feels happiness so complete that it momentarily erases his past, for "when one first enters that world [of ideas] everything else fades for a time, and all that went before is as if it had not been" (258). Indeed, Jim jealously protects his new life from his former one, shutting his window when the prairie wind blows through it and begrudging "the room that Jake and Otto and Russian Peter took up in my memory, which I wanted to crowd with other things" (262). Not only Ántonia but nature itself seems remote; this is a time of interiors, and appropriately, it is set within Jim's rooms, Lena Lingard's workrooms, the theater.

Yet memories are there. As when he opened his window the earthy smell of the prairie outside wafted through, so "whenever my consciousness was quickened, all those early friends were quickened with it, and in some strange way they accompanied me through all my new experiences" (262). When Lena Lingard quietly but inevitably reenters Jim's life, she seems the physical form of the early memories accompanying him. And drawing upon those memories, Jim grasps the idea that great art arises from particulars: "If there were no girls like them in the world, there would be no poetry" (270).

During this period, however, Jim is far detached from those particulars in his own life. His first year at the university is as idyllic as was his first year in Nebraska— and as suspended from reality. Because Jim is totally absorbed in the mental world opening to him, his early friends are real only as ideas he holds within himself, "so much alive" *in* him that he "scarcely stopped to wonder whether they were alive anywhere else" (262). As Ántonia and Jim had once played in nature, so now Lena and Jim play with ideas; as innocence once protected Ántonia and Jim from suffering pains, so it now protects Lena and Jim from seeing reality. When they attend *Camille,* they are as innocent as "a couple of jack-rabbits, run in off the prairie," of what awaits them (272). And they are open to experience as only children can be. The curtain rises upon a brilliant world they have never before imagined, and they enter it so completely that they leave the real world behind. Dumas's lines alone are enough to convey the idea of tragic love, an "idea . . . that no circumstances can frustrate" (278), not an old, lame, stiff actress playing Marguerite or a disproportionately young, perplexed fellow playing her Armand, not faults in staging or weaknesses of the orchestra.

For a while Jim and Lena, luxuriating in newly discovered roles, are as oblivious to circumstances in their own lives as they had been to those in *Camille.* But when the school year comes to an end, so does their pastoral interlude. Gaston Cleric is offered a position at Harvard, and he proposes that Jim follow him in the fall. The return is comically abrupt. Jim goes to Lena with the rather self-serving but noble resolution that he has been standing in her way, "that if she had not me to play with, she would probably marry and secure her future," only to learn that she has no intention of marrying him or anyone else (289).

Thus closes Jim's chapter with Lena, and one of Cather's most interesting characters recedes from view. By temporarily moving Ántonia to the background of the narrative and the recesses of Jim's memory, Cather releases Jim to revel in ideas. Appropriately, he does so with Lena, the idea of sexuality without its threatening reality. She is sensuously beautiful, and not surprisingly, men cluster about her: in Black Hawk Ole Bensen, Sylvester Lovett, and Jim Burden; in Lincoln the Polish violin-teacher Ordensky, old Colonel Raleigh, and (again) Jim Burden. What is striking is the contrast between these men paying court to Lena and those clustering about Ántonia in Black Hawk. The courtship of Lena is conducted languidly, devoid of animal vitality, by old men and boys to whom she appeals because she knows they are only playing at love. Nobody needed to have worried about Ole Bensen, she recognized, because he simply liked to sit and look at her; similarly, she allows the old men of Lincoln to court her, for "it makes them feel important to think they're in love with somebody" (290). Implicitly she has a similar bemused affection for the schoolboy Jim Burden.

Even while Jim is most detached from Ántonia, however, the memory of her remains, awaiting a return. Part IV, "The Pioneer Woman's Story," tells of beginning that return. Ántonia has continued to live her own life, following Larry Donovan to Denver, becoming pregnant, and returning alone and unmarried to give birth to a daughter. Bitterly disappointed in her, Jim has tried to shut her out of his mind until, seeing a crayon enlargement of her daughter displayed prominently in a Black Hawk photographer's window, he feels he must see her again. He goes first to the Widow Steavens, the Shimerdas' neighbor who assisted Ántonia in the preparations for her marriage and in the delivery of her baby; from her, Jim learns Ántonia's story. Only then does he go to the Shimerdas' homestead, where he sees Ántonia. Their brief meeting builds to Jim's declaration of faith: "Do you know, Ántonia, since I've been away, I think of you more often than of anyone else in this part of the world. I'd have liked to have you for a sweetheart, or a wife, or my mother or my sister—anything that a woman can be to a man. The idea of you is a part of my mind; you influence my likes and dislikes, all my tastes, hundreds of times when I don't realize it. You really are a part of me" (321).

The moment is important in Jim's imaginative return, as interesting for what it does not include as for what it does. Jim here affirms his idea of Ántonia as archetypal woman—that much is clear: he sees her face "under all the shadows of women's faces, at the very bottom of my memory" (322). But this is *his* idea only, and when he imagines linking that idea to the real world, he rather indiscriminately wishes she could be whatever a woman can be to a man—sweetheart, wife, mother, sister—apparently it doesn't matter. There is strikingly little of Ántonia in this meeting; the scene is almost wholly centered upon Jim, with only perfunctory references to Ántonia's life or child. Because he has not yet grasped her particularity, he is as yet unable to conceive of Ántonia as apart from him; and without the yoking of the idea with the particular that enables the romantic to unite subject and object in symbolic perception, Jim's return is incomplete.

Part V, "Cuzak's Boys," is the closing of the circle. Allegiance to his idea has kept Jim away from Ántonia for twenty years, for he has heard that she had married an unsuccessful man and lived a hard life. Perhaps it was cowardice, he recalled, but "I did not want to find her aged and broken; I really dreaded it. In the course of twenty crowded years one parts with many illusions. I did not wish to lose the early ones. Some memories are realities, and are better than anything that can ever happen to one again" (328). Again, Lena Lingard acts as an intermediary. As she had appeared in Jim's student rooms and brought with her memories of his past, so years later she gives Jim a cheerful account of Ántonia and urges him to see her.

When the middle-aged Jim returns to the scenes of his childhood, it is to fuse the idea and the particular by seeing what Coleridge called "the universality in the individual, or the individuality itself."[11] First Jim sees Ántonia in all her physical reality, an aging woman with grizzled hair, missing teeth, and hands hardened from work; then he realizes the timeless truth that resides within that reality. For the first time it is her identity rather than his idea of her that he affirms.

As if "experience . . . repeated in a finer tone," scenes from childhood recur, metamorphosed.[12] Jim enters by wagon (then as a boy, now as an adult) and looks about a kitchen (then Jim's grandmother's sunny one, now Ántonia's); Jim at first sees Ántonia and especially her eyes (then of a girl, now a woman), and they talk alone on the prairie (then a wild spot, now planted with an orchard); Jim witnesses an unexpected explosion of life from the earth (then the Shimerdas' cave, now Ántonia's fruit cellar), and he lies down in nature, feeling great contentment (then in the garden, now a hayloft). Even the most apparently ordinary detail resonates with childhood memories: Ántonia's white cats sunning among yellow pumpkins echo Jim's first morning in his grandmother's garden, sunning himself among other pumpkins.

With each scene there is the familiarity of recognition coupled with an explosion of meaning, as the particular is fused with an idea and experienced as a symbol. This is the return of the romantic sensibility, now refined and able to understand the emotional pattern that emerges from the experience:

> Ántonia had always been one to leave images in the mind that did not fade—that grew stronger with time. In my memory there was a succession of such pictures, fixed there like the old woodcuts of one's first primer: Ántonia kicking her bare legs against the sides of my pony when we came home in triumph with our snake; Ántonia in her black shawl and fur cap, as she stood by her father's grave in the snowstorm; Ántonia coming in with her work-team along the evening sky-line. She lent herself to immemorial human attitudes which we recognize by instinct as universal and true. I had not been mistaken. She was a battered woman now, not a lovely girl; but she still had that something which fires the imagination, could still stop one's breath for a moment by a look or gesture that somehow revealed the meaning in common things. She had only to stand in the orchard, to put her hand on a little crab tree and look up at the apples, to make you feel the goodness of planting and tending and harvesting at last. All the strong things of her heart came out in her body, that had been so tireless in serving generous emotions.
>
> It was no wonder that her sons stood tall and straight. She was a rich mine of life, like the founders of early races. (352–53)

Here is the peace of resolution. When Jim leaves the Cuzak farm, he feels a sense of loss, yet reassures himself with the possibility of return. Ántonia—and her children after her—will endure, and the memories of her are "spots of time" by which he can renew himself.

The overall pattern of *My Ántonia,* with its separation, resolution, and return to separation, is familiar to readers of romantic literature: one need think only of Wordsworth's "Tintern Abbey," Coleridge's conversation poems, and Keats's odes. Like her predecessors in romanticism, Cather uses that pattern to write of the individual imagination perceiving the world symbolically. Unlike them, however, she uses gender assumptions to heighten tension between her subject and object. As her early essays make clear, Cather was acutely aware that our culture assigns to men the position of subject and to women that of object, and she incorporates those assumptions into her novel. Jim Burden expresses conventionally male attitudes: he assumes the subject position, moves outward, engages in change and progress, and writes possessively about *his* Ántonia as the archetypal woman who provides an anchorage for his travels and a muse for his imagination. Through Jim, Cather presents myths of male transcendence, of man as a liberating hero, romantic lover, and creative genius; of women to be rescued, loved, and transformed into art. In Ántonia, however, Cather contradicts these assumptions by creating a woman who works out her individual destiny in defiance of her narrator's expectations.[13]

My Ántonia is Jim's account of all that Ántonia means to him, or more precisely, of his youthful attempt to *make* her "anything that a woman can be to a man" (321). By his account Ántonia seeks primarily to nurture by giving—to give her ring to the ten-year-old Jim and to admire his exploits, to give her love to Larry Donovan, and to give to her children a better chance than she had. As important, she makes no demands upon the world or upon others in it. Even after becoming pregnant, Ántonia does not press Larry Donovan to marry her, for "I thought if he saw how well I could do for him, he'd want to stay with me" (313). Her husband, Cuzak, affirms "she is a good wife for a poor man" because "she don't ask me no questions" (365–66). Ántonia offers unconditional love; both her strength and her weakness are that she could never believe harm of anyone she loved (344; see also 268, 343). Through her love, Ántonia, like the orchard she tends, offers "the deepest peace" of escape from worldly demands (341). To Jim, Ántonia is a wellspring for male activity in the larger world. On a physical level she bears sons. Jim titles his final chapter "Cuzak's Boys," and he concludes, "It was no wonder that her sons stood tall and straight." On a spiritual level she is a muse to Jim, for she "had that something which fires the imagination" (353).

At the same time that Cather uses Jim to present "the collective myths" about women,[14] she builds tension against his account. There emerges a certain ruthlessness about Jim's affection for Ántonia that belies his stated affection for her. His love, unlike hers, is conditional. He is proud of Ántonia when he believes her to be "like Snow-White, in the fairy tale" (215); he turns from her when she asserts her individuality. He resents her protecting manner toward him, is angered over her masculine ways when she works the farm, is bitter when she "throws herself away on . . . a cheap sort of fellow" and, once pregnant, falls from social favor. Jim's allegiance is consistently to his ideas; when they conflict with reality, he denies the reality.

The world and the people in it just as consistently belie the myths Jim attempts to impose upon them. Otto Fuchs is not a Jesse James desperado but a warm-hearted ranchhand; Lena Lingard is not a wild seductress but a strong-minded girl who becomes an independent businesswoman; Jim himself is not the adventurer, the lover, or the poet he pretends to be. By contrasting the boast and the deed, Cather suggests comic, self-serving, and ineffectual dimensions of male gallantry. Picturing himself as a dragon slayer, Jim kills an old, lazy rattlesnake. Drafted by his grandmother into service as Ántonia's rescuer, Jim sleeps at the Cutters, saving Ántonia from rape but feeling something close to hatred of her for embarrassing him. Resolving to "go home and look after Ántonia" (268), Jim returns to her only twenty years later, after being assured that he will not have to part with his illusions. Finally, Ántonia and Lena, the objects of Jim's benevolence, react to his promise with smiles (322–23) and "frank amusement" (268). They get on with their lives basically independently from men, whether by design, as when Lena resolves that she will never marry, or by necessity, as when Ántonia proceeds to rear her daughter alone.

Tension against Jim's account increases as his narrative role changes. In the initial sections Cather presented Ántonia through Jim's point of view. Jim measured Ántonia against his idea of women, approving of her when she assumed a role he expected of her. But in Book IV, "The Pioneer Woman's Story," Cather moved Jim aside, to the position of tale recorder, and made the midwife who attended Ántonia the tale teller. The Widow Steavens provides a woman's account of a woman's experience, and with it a significant change in tone toward Ántonia. She relates her story with understanding and sympathy rather than with Jim's shocked and bitter insistence that Ántonia play her part in his myth.

By Part V, Jim and Ántonia have reversed roles. Jim began the novel as the story teller in several senses, telling the account he titles *my* Ántonia, and also telling it in terms of stories he has read or heard—*The Life of Jesse James, Robinson Crusoe, Camille,* the *Georgics.* But the child Jim grew into a man who followed the most conventional pattern for success: he left the farm to move to town, then attended the university, studied law at Harvard, married well, and joined a large corporation. In the process, his personal identity seems to have faded. Ántonia, who began the novel as a character rendered by Jim, in the fifth section breaks through myths Jim had imposed upon her and emerges powerfully as herself. With her children around her, she is the center of "the family legend" (350), to whom her children look "for stories and entertainment" (351). Ántonia's stories, unlike Jim's, are not from literature. They are instead domestic ones drawn from life, "about the calf that broke its leg, or how Yulka saved her little turkeys from drowning . . . or about old Christmases and weddings in Bohemia" (176).

As Jim leaves the Cuzak farm in the last paragraphs, Ántonia recedes into the background. One of a group standing by the windmill, she is waving her apron, as countless women have said goodbye to countless men. Returning to the larger male world, Jim spends a disappointing day in Black Hawk, talking idly with an old lawyer there. Finally, he walks outside of town to the unploughed prairie that remains from early times. There Jim's mind "was full of pleasant things," for he intended "to play" with Cuzak's boys and, after the boys are grown, "to tramp along a few miles of lighted streets with Cuzak" (370). But these plans seem curiously empty, irrelevant to the center of life represented by the female world of Ántonia. The early male myths of adventure have led to pointless wandering and lonely exile, and the women, originally assigned roles of passivity, have become the vital sources of meaning.

NOTES

[1] *My Ántonia* (1918; Boston: Houghton Mifflin, Sentry Edition, 1961), 353. Unless otherwise indicated, all references are to this text.

[2] Quoted by E. K. Brown, *Willa Cather: A Critical Biography*, completed by Leon Edel (New York: Knopf, 1953), 204–5.

[3] James Woodress, *Willa Cather: Her Life and Art* (1970; Lincoln: University of Nebraska Press, 1982), 180.

[4] David Stouck, *Willa Cather's Imagination* (Lincoln: University of Nebraska Press, 1975), 46–58; Paul A. Olson, "The Epic and Great Plains Literature," *Prairie Schooner* 55 (Spring/Summer 1981): 263–85; James E. Miller, Jr., "*My Ántonia* and the American Dream," *Prairie Schooner* 48 (Summer 1974): 112–23; Blanche H. Gelfant, "The Forgotten Reaping-Hook: Sex in *My Ántonia,*" *American Literature* 43 (March 1971): 60–82.

[5] Brown, *Willa Cather: A Critical Biography*, 199.

[6] Quotations in this and the following paragraph are to the 1918 introduction, *My Ántonia* (Boston: Houghton Mifflin, Cambridge: The Riverside Press, 1918), xii. Cather was to shorten her introduction for the 1926 edition, but she did not alter meaning in it.

[7] For a discussion of *My Ántonia* as the story of "Jim Burden's success in converting [Ántonia] into a symbol of a way of life he approves of," see William J. Stuckey, "*My Ántonia*: A Rose for Miss Cather," *Studies in the Novel* 4 (Fall 1972): 473–83. Stuckey is quite right in stressing tension between Jim Burden's "desire to convert Ántonia into a beautiful image of agrarian life and Ántonia's resistance to that conversion" (474).

[8] William Wordsworth, *The Prelude of 1805*, Book First, line 305, in *The Prelude, 1799, 1805, 1850*, ed. Jonathan Wordsworth, M. H. Abrams, and Stephen Gill (New York: 1979).

[9] For discussions of ways in which Cather drew upon life for *My Ántonia*, see Bennett, *The World of Willa Cather*, and Woodress, *Willa Cather: Her Life and Art*.

[10] Wordsworth, *The Prelude of 1805*, Book First, line 305.

[11] Coleridge, "On Poesy or Art," in *English Romantic Writers*, ed. David Perkins (New York: Harcourt, Brace, Jovanovich, 1967), 494.

[12] John Keats to Benjamin Bailey, 22 November 1817, *The Complete Poetical Works and Letters of John Keats*, Cambridge Edition (Cambridge: The Riverside Press, 1899; distributed by Houghton Mifflin, Boston), 274.

[13] This discussion on Cather's use of gender for narrative tension is adapted from my essay, "Willa Cather's Women," *Studies in American Fiction* 9 (Autumn 1981): 261–75.

[14] Ellen Moers, *Literary Women* (1976; Garden City, N.Y.: Doubleday, Anchor Books, 1977), 350.

Hermione Lee

THE ROAD OF DESTINY

And the end of all our exploring
Will be to arrive where we started
And know the place for the first time.   —T.S. Eliot, 'Little Gidding', 1942

At the end of *My Ántonia,* the story-teller Jim Burden says that he has retraced his 'road of Destiny' and come back full circle to take possession of his past (in the 'figure' of Ántonia), recognizing as he does so that this circular journey has been a predetermined one. Back at the beginning of the book, there is a double entrance to this 'road of Destiny'. The novel begins, not with Jim's story, but with an Introduction, a conversation on a train journey. The speaker of this Introduction, a neutral and asexual voice standing for Cather, travelling either towards or away from Nebraska (it's not clear which), with Jim, an old childhood friend, says: 'During that burning day when we were crossing Iowa, our talk kept returning to a central figure, a Bohemian girl whom we had both known long ago'. Jim's subsequent narrative reduplicates this entrance: it too begins on a train journey, with Jim arriving as a child in Nebraska. 'I first heard of Ántonia', he starts, 'on what seemed to me an interminable journey across the great midland plain of North America'.

Because the frame journey of the Introduction covers the same ground as the novel's first journey, the book straight away establishes the feeling it will end with, of circular infinity, renewable time. In its end is its beginning. Jim's wry introductory word for the journey, 'interminable', is tied by affinity and by opposition to the solemn, concluding word 'predetermined', like the sun and the moon Jim sees on one of his return journeys, confronting each other 'across the level land, resting on opposite edges of the world'.[1] The journey — ours, Cather's, Jim's — doesn't close, it 'keeps returning' (Jim and Ántonia, we are made to feel, are still living as we read it). But it has a point, which is to understand what the journey has been for. These concepts of renewal and purpose are consolatory: *My Ántonia* is an exceptionally heartening and affirmative book. But to be on an interminable and predetermined

From *Willa Cather: A Life Saved Up* (London: Virago Press, 1989), pp. 133–34, 138–44, 150–58.

journey is also a source of anxiety; and the novel is 'burdened' too with the difficulty and strangeness of returning, and the shadowy presence of what the circle might exclude. ⟨. . .⟩

In the first part of My Ántonia, 'The Shimerdas', Jim, secure in his well-run Protestant grandparents' home, grows up alongside Ántonia, who is doing her best in her struggling, poor, ill-adapted Bohemian family. Together, they make sense of the 'materials' to hand: he teaches her language, she tells him stories. Their mutual discoveries keep pace until after the suicide of Mr Shimerda, the central event of the first section. Then they begin to move apart. In the second section, 'The Hired Girls', Jim's family moves into the town, Black Hawk, and Ántonia soon follows, to work for his neighbours, the attractive Harlings. As Jim becomes increasingly restless, the narrative opens out into the life of the town, in particular of Jim's friends, the immigrant 'hired girls'—Ántonia, Lena, Tiny, and the others. In the third section, 'Lena Lingard', he is at university. A visit from Lena, now a smart Lincoln dressmaker, starts a subdued flirtation (coloured by their emotional response to a performance of Camille) which they renounce in the interests of his future. The fourth section, ambiguously named 'The Pioneer Woman's Story', is set two years after Jim, now in training as a lawyer, has gone East. He comes back to hear from the Widow Steavens (his grandparents' tenant on their old farm) the story of what has been happening to Ántonia: deserted by a selfish, unscrupulous railroad man, she has come back home with an illegitimate baby. She and Jim meet again, 'like the people in the old song, in silence, if not in tears', and speak of their old friendship. In 'Cuzak's Boys', twenty years on, much-travelled Jim comes back once more (after seeing Lena and Tiny, prospering in San Francisco) to find Ántonia married to a Bohemian, on a thriving farm, with ten or eleven children. He is given an emotional welcome, spends the night there, and promises himself a renewal of the friendship. Black Hawk disappoints him, but he retraces his steps over the country where Mr Shimerda was buried, recognizing his 'predetermined' road.

This apparently bare, inconsequential narrative, which notably fails to fulfil the title's promise of a love affair or a heroine's life story, gives up its meaning through the shape it takes. And the shape of the book is the making of Jim's memory. Its 'formless' structure — two long and three short sections spread over about forty years — is, in fact, very carefully formed to represent the process of memory-making. In the first two sections the material accumulates for retrospection. 'I can remember exactly how the country looked to me' Jim says. [MA, p. 16] Or: 'All the years that have passed have not dimmed my memory.' [MA, p.28][2] In the last three the past is gone away from, returned to, and made sense of. So the book's shape enacts the relation between Cather's early life and her writing. But by using Jim as an equivocal, limited, reserved surrogate, she avoids the unmediated autobiographical literalness of The Song of the Lark. Jim is and is not 'her', just as Ántonia is and is not 'his'.

Jim, unlike Cather, is an orphan, when he makes his journey (like Cather) from safe Virginia into the 'utter darkness' and undifferentiatedness of Nebraska, where there seem at first to be no whereabouts: 'There seemed to be nothing to see'; 'not a country at all, but the materials out of which countries are made'. [MA, p. 7] We recognize this dark negative space, like chaos before the Word, from the beginning of *O Pioneers!* As in the earlier pastoral, this blank stuff is going to be created and ordered through speech, love, endurance, and the making of shapes.

From the moment Jim emerges from the train, and sees Ántonia and her huddled, 'encumbered' family also emerging, the shape of his narrative replicates the process of growth from infancy to adulthood. Like a child's book, the first section has simple, coloured, apprehensible things standing out on every page —food, clothes, animals, plants — in a primary environment of smells, warmth, light, space, snow, sky. Useful objects have their uses explained; grandfather's silver-rimmed spectacles for reading prayers, grandmother's hickory cane tipped with copper for killing rattlesnakes, Mrs Shimerda's feather quilt for keeping her food warm. (Sometimes the usefulness is untranslatable, like Mrs Shimerda's *cèpes* from the Bohemian forests, thrown on the fire by Jim's suspicious grandmother.) The child's perspective sees things either very close or very far. This, as Eudora Welty says, is Cather's usual perception of the world:

> There is the foreground, with the living present, its human figures in action; and there is the horizon of infinite distance ... but there is no intervening ground ... There is no recent past. There is no middle distance.[3]

So Jim, taking possession of his Nebraska, is at once investigative child and retrospective author. On his first day, Jim comes out of his grandmother's warm basement kitchen and moves up through the farmyard, the sea of red prairie grass his own height, the cattle corral, the garden set away from the house, towards 'the edge of the world'. His impulse is towards 'the horizon of infinite distance': 'I had almost forgotten that I had a grandmother'. But there she is, very real and close, digging potatoes and warning him against rattlesnakes. She leaves him in a sheltered spot in the garden:

> The earth was warm under me, and warm as I crumbled it through my fingers. Queer little red bugs came out and moved in slow squadrons around me. Their backs were polished vermilion, with black spots. I kept as still as I could. Nothing happened. I did not expect anything to happen. I was something that lay under the sun and felt it, like the pumpkins, and I did not want to be anything more. I was entirely happy. Perhaps we feel like that when we die and become a part of something entire, whether it is sun or air, or goodness and knowledge. At any rate, that is happiness; to be dissolved into something complete and great. When it comes to one, it comes as naturally as sleep. [MA, p.18]

Jim could be another Thoreau or Emerson ('I am nothing, I see all')[4] or Whitman loafing at his ease, 'observing a spear of summer grass',[5] as the narrator contemplates his 'intimations of immortality' in the language of American transcendentalism.

But at the same time he seems tiny and animal, a vivid microscopic part of the natural scene.

This pull between earth and space, near and far, solidity and dissolution, is the constant factor in Jim and Ántonia's childhood. They are always coming out from underground (Jim from his secure kitchen, Ántonia from her dark constricting cave) into infinite space.

Jim's response to the death of Mr Shimerda is at the heart of this movement. Jim imagines the old man's spirit resting in his grandparents' kitchen before his long journey home: 'Outside I could hear the wind singing over hundreds of miles of snow'. Through his intense re-imaginings of everything Ántonia has told him about her father's life, Jim encloses him inside a protected space, before his memory 'fades out from the air', and dissolves. His crossroads burial on 'a very little spot in that snow-covered waste', which will be preserved as 'a little island' in the changing landscape, sums up the movement between enclosure and dissolution which makes the whole shape of the book.

As Jim and Ántonia grow up, this shape is cross-cut with other patterns, as in the confusing, complicating growth from childhood into adolescence and adulthood. In the town scenes, there is still an attraction towards safe enclosures, like the grandparents' Black Hawk house, a 'landmark' for country people coming into town, or the Harlings' convivial kitchen, or the town laundryman's pleasant prospect, like a framed Degas:

> On summer afternoons he used to sit for hours on the sidewalk in front of his laundry, his newspaper lying on his knee, watching his girls through the big open window while they ironed and talked in Danish. [MA, p.221]

But the town's spaces — the hotel with its partition between parlour and dining-room, the temporary dance-pavilion on the vacant lot, the school, the Fireman's Hall, the depot, the Opera House — are more ambiguous enclosures, where social and sexual partitions take complex shape. And Jim's relation to these enclosures is less accepting: he climbs out of his bedroom window at night, resenting, now, his grandparents' security; he paces the streets feeling that 'the little sleeping houses' are places of 'evasions and negations', producing nothing but waste. [MA, p.219] (In a parallel but subordinated movement, Ántonia is also breaking out from the enclosures of her home and the Harlings' protection, into more dangerous spaces.)

Once, towards the end of the section, they rediscover the essential, childhood relationship between the close and the infinite, in an extended Arcadian idyll by the river. It begins with Jim swimming alone and naked in the river, then dressing in a 'green enclosure' under a growth of grapevines. As he leaves, he repeats his possessive childhood gesture of crumbling the earth in his fingers: 'I kept picking off little pieces of scaly chalk from the dried water gullies, and breaking them up in my hands'. [MA, p.234] He finds Ántonia under the side of the river bank, grieving over the memories aroused by the smell of the elderflowers. Consolingly, crouched under the bank and looking at the sky, they retrace the story of Mr Shimerda. Then, with the other girls, they move up the chalk bluffs, with a view of the town and the prairie, and lie about in the sun, their talk opening out through their personal history and desires (it is a feminine version of 'The Enchanted Bluff') to the history of the first pioneers. The long, imperceptibly shaped scene concludes with their momentary sighting of the plough on the horizon, magnified in the frame of the setting sun. Though the whole passage is adult, socialized, sensual, historically conscious, it re-enacts the shape of the childhood scenes.

Jim's adult life is made up of dislocation and absence. He inhabits or looks in on makeshift, improvised spaces, like his awkwardly furnished college room. After he moves East, he seems an absentee in his own narrative, coming back in from long disappearances to catch up on the old stories. His first return to Ántonia, in her troubles, goes back over the familiar routes, to his childhood bedroom, to Mr Shimerda's grave, to the 'old pull of the earth' at nightfall, to Ántonia's face 'at the bottom of my memory'. But these items seem recapitulated as a prelude to leave-taking. It's not until the very end of the book (which is balanced against the whole weight of the long first part) that Jim refinds the shape of childhood so as to keep it. Ántonia's innumerable children re-enact (but with more energy and vigour than Jim and Ántonia) the original processes. They too keep rushing up and out from underground hidden places to the outside:

> We were standing outside talking, when they all came running up the steps together, big and little, tow heads and gold heads and brown, and flashing little naked legs; a veritable explosion of life out of the dark cave into the sunlight. It made me dizzy for a moment. [MA, pp.338–9]

With Ántonia in her orchard, Jim feels himself back in a protected place, the town and America and the world kept out:

> There was the deepest peace in that orchard. It was surrounded by a triple enclosure; the wire fence, then the hedge of thorny locusts, then the mulberry hedge which kept out the hot winds of summer and held fast to the protecting snows of winter. The hedges were so tall that we could see nothing but the blue sky above them . . . [MA, p.341]

But appeasing and consolatory though this is, this is not Jim's place, or his childhood; it's as though he is trying to reinsert himself into the womb. Trying to get back inside is what memory does. Memory grafts together the close and the far, making scenes of the past 'so near that I could reach out and touch them with my hand'—like the earth he crumbled through his fingers—and so distant as to be 'incommunicable'. ⟨. . .⟩

Jim's summing-up of the Ántonia who 'fires his imagination', in another of Cather's much-quoted, transcendent passages, is like his vision of the plough. 'His' Ántonia—mother of sons, rich mine of life—is a 'figure' which he now, definitively, reads for us: one who leaves 'images in the mind that did not fade', who stays in the mind in 'a succession of pictures, fixed there like the old woodcuts of one's first primer', who 'lent herself to immemorial human attitudes which we recognize by instinct as universal and true'. [MA, p.353] Just so, the lamp falls on the pot in the centre of the table, or the plough stands out against the sun, or the 'figures' of the naked land are superimposed on the classical pastoral. It is a moving conclusion to the narrative's process of reading and remembering. All the same, Ántonia is a woman, not a plough. She is not as 'fixed' as Jim would have her.

Jim's elegiac pastoral expresses Cather's deepest feelings: it would be perverse to argue that his reading of Ántonia is meant to be distrusted.[6] But his imagination is only 'fired' within limits. Figures which do not speak to his sense of what is 'immemorial' or 'universal' or 'true' (Lena Lingard, or Tiny Soderball) are relegated to the edges of his circle of memory, like the awkward items of furniture pushed out of the way in his college room. And what might have been powerful emotions in Ántonia's story—the aftermath of sexual betrayal, for instance—are muted in the interests of Jim's memorializing.

But the presence of alternative possibilities makes itself felt inside Jim's narrative from the first. As in Twain's *Huckleberry Finn,* where the made-up bookish adventures of Tom Sawyer look dubious against Huck's real emergencies, Jim's childhood reading of *Robinson Crusoe* or *Swiss Family Robinson* is always being outdone by realities. When he gets up after the blizzard, eager for new excitements—'perhaps a barn had burned; perhaps the cattle had frozen to death; perhaps a neighbour was lost in the storm' [MA, p.94]—what he gets is the suicide of Mr Shimerda. A deflation of romance goes on throughout. Jim weeps his heart out over *Camille*, but he has 'prudently' remembered to bring his umbrella with him for going home.

Cather's version of American pastoral may not be as brutal or jovial as Mark Twain's or Bret Harte's, but she can go in for a tough Western humour which brings us down with a bump from Jim's heroic sunsets. ' "I don't see how he could do it!" ' the grandmother laments over Mr Shimerda, to which Otto replies: ' "Why, ma'am, it was simple enough; he pulled the trigger with his big toe." ' [MA, pp.96–7] The reunion with the Cuzaks is full of benign memories, but the high point of the dinner is the horrible story of the money-lender Wick Cutter's murder of his wife. ' "Hurrah! The murder!" the children murmured, looking pleased and interested.' [MA, p.361]

It's the ogre-like Wick Cutter (the ugly name sounding both brutal and sexual) who makes the two most startling irruptions into Jim's Arcadia. 'The Hired Girls' does not end, as might have been expected, with the transcendent vision of the plough on the horizon, but with the grotesque story of the money-lender's attempt to rape Ántonia. Cutter is a vividly horrid small-town character, a gambler and lecher masquerading as a good clean-living American (he is always quoting 'Poor Richard's Almanack' and talking about the 'good old times'). His vicious treatment of his wife, whom he loves to make jealous, and whose frenzied reactions excite him more than the sex itself, is horrifyingly convincing. Ántonia goes to work for the Cutters in rebellion against Mr Harling's strictures on her dance-hall evenings, but comes back in a fright when Cutter tells her he is off on a journey, hides all his valuables under her bed, puts a heavy Yale lock on the door, and orders her to stay alone in the house. Jim takes her place for the night, and Cutter, having tricked his wife onto the wrong train, creeps back, thinking to find Ántonia, and assaults him. The scene makes an extremely disconcerting conclusion to Jim's childhood memories; why has Cather placed it there?

It is partly that Wick Cutter, like his Yale lock, is the future (he will come back as Ivy Peters in *A Lost Lady*). He stands for the debased American currency which Cather saw buying out the pioneers' values. Benjamin Franklin's *Poor Richard's Almanack* is all about thrift; Cutter's attempted assault on Ántonia is like a miser's theft. He tries to make her as debased as the usurer's notes under the bed. The golden figure of the plough against the sun was like a glorious stamp on a coin; Cutter's licentious hoarding, by immediate contrast, introduces another system of valuation. (His wife is just as 'base': 'I have found Mrs Cutters all over the world; sometimes founding new religions, sometimes being forcibly fed.' [MA, p.214] This is one of Cather's most disagreeable moments, but there's no avoiding it as part of her feeling about changing values.) When Cutter finally murders his wife so that she won't get his property, and then kills himself, the 'spiteful' suicide is set, at the end of the book, against Mr Shimerda's at the beginning, that of a man who had nothing, and died of a broken heart.

But Wick Cutter is also a priapic monster who fills Jim with revulsion. His fantasies of protecting Ántonia like a chivalric knight are obliterated by the 'disgustingness' and ignominy of the event, and, very revealingly, Cather has Jim blame Ántonia: 'I felt that I never wanted to see her again. I hated her almost as much as I hated Cutter. She had let me in for all this disgustingness'. [MA, p.250] It feels like Adam blaming Eve after the fall. And the next thing we know Jim has left his Arcadia, and never *does* see Ántonia again until she has really lost her sexual innocence and become, not the child of Mr Shimerda he always wants to remember, but an adult woman, capable of being lover, wife and mother.

Jim's squeamishness is an interesting element in his ambivalent sexuality. Cather was somewhat defensive about her first extensive use of a male narrator. She may still have been thinking of Sarah Orne Jewett's criticism of an earlier story, that a male 'masquerade' was not necessary for expressing emotions towards a female character.[7] She tended to explain Jim away by saying that he came out of her experience of ghosting McClure's autobiography, or seemed appropriate because most of her original stories about 'Ántonia' were told her by men.[8] What she does not say is that he allows her free entry into male literary traditions of pastoral and epic, and enables her to speak from her own sexual identity and express her own emotions for women.

To read Jim Burden, however, simply as a mask for lesbian feelings, is a narrowing exercise.[9] He is more complicated than that, an androgynous narrator who mediates between male and female worlds like those Shakespearean pastoral hero/ines, boys dressed as girls dressed as boys. In childhood, he is attracted to the male outdoor pioneering of Otto and Jake — their Wild West exploits, their tackling of bulls and blizzards. No tough pioneer himself, as a young adult he finds male companionship in scholarship; his friendship with Gaston Cleric is like the

pastoral brotherhood of male poets and singers. But he also participates in the
female world, sitting indoors with his grandmother, or with the motherly and
sisterly Harlings, or the hired girls, a privileged pet and a listener. (This is like a
contemporary androgynous narrator, also engaged in refinding his past, Proust's
Marcel in *Á l'ombre des jeunes filles en fleurs.*)[10] He is privy to the women's stories,
those matriarchal narratives which so inspired Cather in her childhood: stories of
women giving birth on the immigrant ships, or of the Swedish and Norwegian and
Bohemian mothers, or Widow Steavens' female account of Ántonia's disasters.
Adolescent Jim, reading his Latin for university, spending his evenings with the
telegrapher and the cigarmaker, and making a May-basket for Nina Harling, is both
boyish and girlish.

Being androgynous makes Jim an empathetic narrator, but he is not allowed
a love affair, either with Ántonia or Lena, and his marriage is an offstage failure.
(There is a definite prejudice here: all the marriages in the book give ammunition
to Jim's exclamation: 'I wondered whether the life that was right for one was ever
right for two!' [MA, p.367]) Yet, in its way, *My Ántonia* is a very sexy book. Those
alluring foreign girls who cluster around Jim are written up in pleasurably erotic
language, whether they are dancing, dressing, lying around, or ironing:

> their white arms and throats bare, their cheeks bright as the brightest wild
> roses, their gold hair moist with steam or the heat and curling in little damp
> spirals about their ears. [MA, p.222]

At the centre of this pagan bacchanal (over which Blind d'Arnault at one point
presides 'like some glistening African god of pleasure, full of strong, savage blood'
[MA, p.191]) is seductive Lena, who seems sensual to Jim in a passive, cat-like way
quite unlike the energetic, 'outdoor' Ántonia. Dancing with Lena is like sinking into
'a soft, waking dream' on a 'soft, sultry summer day'. [MA, p.222] On their hot day
out by the river she is 'panting' and 'supine'; she is always touching and tempting him.
Her flirtation with Jim in Lincoln is subtle and uncommitted; she leads him on and
holds him off at once, even in her farewells, made from a typically 'supine' position
on her couch: 'At last she sent me away with her soft, slow, renunciatory kiss'. [MA,
p.293] It is no accident that *Camille*, which makes them both cry so much, and for
which Cather allows so much space (she wanted their naive wallowing in it to be
comical, but couldn't resist a wallow herself)[11] is a play about renunciation as much
as about seduction.

Lena's later history as a plump successful businesswoman in partnership with
Tiny Soderball in San Francisco is pointedly placed at the margin of the last three
parts of the novel, as though her independence from the past and her assimilation
into America disconnect her from Jim's imagination. This marginalizing is even more
noticeable in the narrative treatment of Tiny, whose amazing life story is briefly
fitted into the section called 'The Pioneer Woman's Story'. The title refers to
Widow Steavens' account of Ántonia (both are pioneer women) but it would suit
Tiny even better. This neat, slender Norwegian girl makes a dramatic journey (like
Carl Linstrum, and again offstage) to the Klondike in the gold rush, sets up a hotel

for the gold miners, inherits a claim romantically from a dying Swede, makes a fortune in the wilds, is lamed in the arctic weather, and comes back a rich, 'hard-faced', grimly ironic woman. Jim catches up with her in Salt Lake City 'in 1908'. That '1908' is the only date in the book, and shows how Jim associates her, and Lena, with contemporary American life. 'This is what actually happened to Tiny', [MA, p.299] her story begins: it may sound like a tall tale, but it is 'actually' a slice of life, like a story in a newspaper. Tiny and Lena are modern; they have cut off the past. Their relationship, asexual, dry, companionable, fails to inspire him. Jim describes Tiny as someone 'in whom the faculty of becoming interested is worn out', [MA, p.302] but he also means, of becoming interesting.

Ántonia's peculiar place in his imagination is contrasted with Lena throughout. Whenever Lena tries to seduce him, Ántonia is censorious; she wants to keep Jim's innocence as much as he wants to keep hers. His revealing erotic dreams of the two girls spell this out:[12]

> I used to have pleasant dreams: sometimes Tony and I were out in the country, sliding down straw-stacks as we used to do; climbing up the yellow mountains over and over, and slipping down the smooth sides into soft piles of chaff.
>
> One dream I dreamed a great many times, and it was always the same. I was in a harvest-field full of shocks, and I was lying against one of them. Lena Lingard came across the stubble barefoot, in a short skirt, with a curved reaping-hook in her hand, and she was flushed like the dawn, with a kind of luminous rosiness all about her. She sat down beside me, turned to me with a soft sigh and said, 'Now they are all gone, and I can kiss you as much as I like'.

'Tony' and he are like boys together; but they also keep slipping back down into a soft, protected womb-like place. Lena appears as threatening erotic, a reminder of his (unused) potency, but also a figure of mortality. Sex is death: the only way he can preserve Ántonia from simply growing old is to censor his sexual feeling for her. He must never have *that* dream about her. His love scenes with Ántonia are carefully controlled. When, as an adolescent, he tries to kiss her like a grown-up, she insists on treating him 'like a kid', and he welcomes it. It means that 'she was, oh, she was still my Ántonia!' [MA, p.225] Their most passionate scene is a valedictory renunciation:

> 'I'd have liked to have you for a sweetheart, or a wife, or my mother or my sister—anything that a woman can be to a man. The idea of you is a part of my mind; you influence my likes and dislikes, all my tastes, hundreds of times when I don't realize it. You really are a part of me.'

To which she replies:

> 'Ain't it wonderful, Jim, how much people can mean to each other? I'm so glad we had each other when we were little. I can't wait till my little girl's old

enough to tell her about all the things we used to do. You'll always remember me when you think about old times, won't you?' [MA, p.321]

Jim renounces the possibility of an active relationship with her ('I'd have liked to have you') so that she can take her place in his mind as a generalized female inspiration for his memory. Following his lead, she promises to inspire it ('You'll always remember me'). The point of motherhood seems, here, to be the opportunity it gives her of recalling their past.

Another kind of story could have been written about Ántonia: a bright immigrant girl, shattered by her father's suicide, living in abject poverty with her mean, grim mother and brother, working in the fields like a man, her attempt to upgrade herself in service wrecked by her seduction and abandonment, shamed (like Hardy's Tess) by having to return home pregnant, surviving the terrible times of the Nebraska depression, finding satisfaction, in the end, only in interminable childbearing and domestic work. That this harsh realist pastoral does make itself felt inside the novel is one of its strengths. In its light, Cather's conclusion for Ántonia may look sentimental. The lavish associations with breeding, nourishment, milk, preserves, harvest, life itself, might seem uncomfortably like an idealization of maternity. But the associations do work as metaphors for 'home'. Ántonia's destiny, in the end, is to fire Jim's — and Cather's — imagination, to be the 'home' to which they return from their exile in time and space.

My Ántonia, like all Cather's great novels, powerfully gives the sense that 'the thing not named', in her famous phrase, is the myth underlying the fiction. My Ántonia is not a religious book, but it has religious feelings. It would be quite plausible, if your mind worked along those lines, to make Mr Shimerda into the Fisher King of the Waste Land, Jim into the Questing Knight of the Grail, and the Cuzak home into the place of redemption. This pilgrimage points us towards death. Jim's 'predestined road' takes him, finally, back to Mr Shimerda's grave. Though the last paragraph tries to suggest that there will be a future for him and Ántonia ('the road was to bring us together again') — a future rather feebly gestured to in the Introduction — it feels much more as if Jim's return home is his preparation for oblivion. As in O Pioneers!, the reunion at the end of My Ántonia is coloured by a deeply melancholy determinism. Jim recognizes 'what a little circle man's experience is'; that 'all we can ever be' (not much, perhaps) is predetermined, that the past makes up for 'whatever we had missed'. It sounds more like a lament than a celebration; a heavy burden is being placed on the past to make it console us for, even replace, the present. The present — and the future — are kept out of the circle of return, by a very strong process of elimination which gives this beautiful novel its aura of simplicity and containment. But what is eliminated presses on it. Now it would have to come in.

NOTES

[1] My Ántonia (Boston and New York: Houghton Mifflin, 1918; Virago, 1980), p. 322. Subsequent page references will occur in the text. All page references are to the Virago edition.

[2] Susan J. Rosowski, *The Voyage Perilous: Willa Cather's Romanticism* (Lincoln and London: University of Nebraska Press, 1986), p. 81, draws attention to this.
[3] Eudora Welty, 'The House of Willa Cather', *The Eye of the Storm: Selected Essays and Reviews* (New York: Vintage, 1979; London: Virago, 1987), p. 44.
[4] Ralph Waldo Emerson, 'Nature', Ch. 1, 1836.
[5] Walt Whitman, 'Song of Myself', 1855.
[6] Rosowski, pp. 89–91, is more distrustful of Jim.
[7] Sarah Orne Jewett to Willa Cather, Nov. 27, 1908, in *Letters of Sarah Orne Jewett*, ed. Annie Fields (Boston: Houghton Mifflin, 1911), p. 246.
[8] Letter to Will Owen Jones, May 20, 1919, The Clifton Waller Barrett Library, University of Virginia, Charlottesville, Virginia.
[9] Deborah G. Lambert, in 'The Defeat of a Hero: Autonomy and Sexuality in *My Ántonia*', *American Literature*, vol. 53, no. 4, January 1982, pp. 676–90, makes a simplistic decoding of Cather in terms of her lesbianism. Sharon O'Brien writes more subtly on the same theme in 'The Thing Not Named: Willa Cather as Lesbian Writer', *Signs: Journal of Women in Culture and Society*, vol. 9, no. 4, 1984, pp. 576–99.
[10] *Á l'ombre des jeunes filles en fleurs*, Part Two of *Á la recherche du temps perdu*, was published the year after MA, in 1919. Cather later makes occasional reference to Proust in letters and speeches (e.g. Letter to Dorothy Canfield Fisher, 1 Dec. 1930, The Bailey/Howe Library, The University of Vermont, Burlington, Vermont).
[11] Letter to Helen Seibel, Feb. 2, 1919, The Nebraska State Historical Society, Lincoln, Nebraska.
[12] Blanche Gelfant, 'The Forgotten Reaping-Hook: Sex in *My Ántonia*', *American Literature*, vol. 43, no. 1, March 1971, pp. 60–82, reads the novel in terms of Jim's fear of sex and his inability to accept 'the nexus of love and death'.

CONTRIBUTORS

HAROLD BLOOM is Sterling Professor of the Humanities at Yale University and Henry W. and Albert A. Berg Professor of English at the New York University Graduate School. He is a 1985 MacArthur Foundation Award recipient, served as the Charles Eliot Norton Professor of Poetry at Harvard University (1987–88), and is the author of nineteen books, the most recent being *The Book of J* (1990). Currently he is editing the Chelsea House series Modern Critical Views and The Critical Cosmos, and other Chelsea House series in literary criticism.

JOHN H. RANDALL III is Professor of English at Boston University. He has written *The Landscape and the Looking Glass: Willa Cather's Search for Value* (1960).

RICHARD GIANNONE, Professor of English at Fordham University is the author of *The Shapes of Fiction* (1971), *Vonnegut: A Preface to His Novels* (1977), and *Flannery O'Connor and the Mystery of Love* (1989), and editor of *John Keats: A Thematic Reader* (1971).

WILLIAM J. STUCKEY has written *The Pulitzer Prize Novels: A Critical Backward Look* (1966; rev. ed. 1981) and *Caroline Gordon* (1972). He is Professor of English at Purdue University.

EDWARD J. PIACENTINO is Professor of English at High Point College (High Point, North Carolina). He is the author of *T. S. Stribling: Pioneer Realist in Modern Southern Literature* (1988).

MARY KEMPER STERNSHEIN is a librarian at J.C. Harmon High School, Kansas City, Kansas, and teaches English at Kansas City Community College. She has written on Cather, the American West, and Middle English.

PATRICK W. SHAW is Professor of English at Texas Tech University in Lubbock, Texas. He has written articles on many nineteenth- and twentieth-century American novelists.

JUDITH FETTERLEY is Professor of English at SUNY at Albany. She has written *The Resisting Reader: A Feminist Approach to American Literature* (1978) and edited *Provisions: A Reader from 19th-Century American Women* (1985) and Alice Cary's *Clovernook Sketches and Other Stories* (1987).

SUSAN J. ROSOWSKI is Professor of English at the University of Nebraska. She is editor, with Helen Stauffer, of *Women and Western American Literature* (1982), and has written many articles on Cather and other writers in academic journals.

HERMIONE LEE is Senior Lecturer in English at the University of York. She has written *The Novels of Virginia Woolf* (1977), *Elizabeth Bowen: An Estimation* (1981), and *Philip Roth* (1982), and has edited works by Anthony Trollope (1982), Stevie Smith (1983), and Elizabeth Bowen (1986).

BIBLIOGRAPHY

Arnold, Marilyn. *Willa Cather: A Reference Guide*. Boston: G. K. Hall, 1986.

Bailey, Jennifer. "The Dangers of Femininity in Willa Cather's Fiction." *Journal of American Studies* 16 (1982): 391–406.

Bennett, Mildred R. *The World of Willa Cather*. New York: Dodd, Mead, 1951.

Bloom, Edward A., and Lillian D. Bloom. *Willa Cather's Gift of Sympathy*. Carbondale: Southern Illinois University Press, 1962.

Bloom, Harold, ed. *Willa Cather*. New York: Chelsea House, 1986.

———, ed. *Willa Cather's* My Ántonia. New York: Chelsea House, 1987.

Bohling, Beth. "The Husband of *My Ántonia.*" *Western American Literature* 19 (1984): 29–39.

Brown, E. K. "Homage to Willa Cather." *Yale Review* 36 (1946–47): 77–92.

———. *Willa Cather: A Critical Biography*. Completed by Leon Edel. New York: Knopf, 1953.

———. "Willa Cather and the West." *University of Toronto Quarterly* 5 (1935–36): 544–66.

Brown, Marion Marsh, and Ruth Crone. *Willa Cather: The Woman and Her Works*. New York: Scribner's, 1970.

Chadbourne, Richard. "Two Visions of the Prairies: Willa Cather and Gabrille Roy." In *The New Land: Studies in a Literary Theme,* ed. Richard Chadbourne and Hallvard Dahlie. Waterloo, Ontario: Wilfrid Laurier University Press, 1978, pp. 93–120.

Charles, Sister Peter Damien. "*My Ántonia*: A Dark Dimension." *Western American Literature* 2 (1967): 91–108.

Colby Library Quarterly Series 8, No. 2 (June 1968). Special Willa Cather issue.

Crane, Joan. *Willa Cather: A Bibliography*. Lincoln: University of Nebraska Press, 1982.

Dahl, Curtis. "An American Georgic: Willa Cather's *My Ántonia.*" *Comparative Literature* 7 (1955): 43–51.

Daiches, David. *Willa Cather: A Critical Introduction*. Ithaca: Cornell University Press, 1951.

Edel, Leon. *Willa Cather: The Paradox of Success*. Washington, DC: Library of Congress, 1960.

Feger, Lois. "The Dark Dimension of Willa Cather's *My Ántonia.*" *English Journal* 59 (1970): 774–79.

Gelfant, Blanche H. "The Forgotten Reaping-Hook: Sex in *My Ántonia.*" *American Literature* 43 (1971): 60–82.

[Grant, Douglas.] "The Frontier Dream." *Times Literary Supplement,* 27 July 1962, p. 540.

Gregory, Robert, "Cather in the Canon." *Modern Language Studies* 15 (1985): 95–101.

Haller, Evelyn H. "The Iconography of Vice in Willa Cather's *My Ántonia.*" *Colby Library Quarterly* 14 (1978): 93–102.

Harris, Richard C. "Renaissance Pastoral Conventions and the Ending of *My Ántonia.*" *Markham Review* 8, (1978–79): 8–11.

Helmick, Evelyn. "The Mysteries of Ántonia." *Midwest Quarterly* 17 (1975–76): 173–85.

Hinz, Evelyn J. "Willa Cather's Technique and the Ideology of Populism." *Western American Literature* 7 (1972): 47–61.

Kroetsch, Robert. "The Fear of Women in Prairie Fiction: An Erotics of Space." In *Crossing Frontiers: Papers in American and Canadian Western Literature,* ed. Dick Harrison. Edmonton: University of Alberta Press, 1979, pp. 73–83.

Lewis, Edith. *Willa Cather Living: A Personal Record.* New York: Knopf, 1953.

McFarland, Dorothy Tuck. *Willa Cather.* New York: Ungar, 1972.

Martin, Terence. "The Drama of Memory in *My Ántonia.*" *PMLA* 84 (1969): 304–11.

Miller, James E., Jr. "*My Ántonia:* A Frontier Drama of Time." In *Quests Surd and Absurd: Essays in American Literature.* Chicago: University of Chicago Press, 1967, pp. 66–75.

———. "*My Ántonia* and the American Dream." *Prairie Schooner* 48 (1974–75): 112–23.

Morgan, H. Wayne. "Willa Cather: The Artist's Quest." In *Writers in Transition: Seven Americans.* New York: Hill & Wang, 1963, pp. 60–81.

Murphy, John J. My Ántonia: *The Road Home.* Boston: Twayne, 1989.

———. "The Respectable Romantic and the Unwed Mother: Class Consciousness in *My Ántonia.*" *Colby Library Quarterly* 10 (1973): 149–56.

———. "Willa Cather: The Widening Gyre." in *Five Essays on Willa Cather: The Merrimack Symposium,* ed. John J. Murphy. North Andover, MA: Merrimack College, 1974, pp. 51–74.

———, ed. *Critical Essays on Willa Cather.* Boston: G. K. Hall, 1984.

Nelson, Robert J. *Willa Cather and France: In Search of the Lost Language.* Urbana: University of Illinois Press, 1988.

Nyquist, Edna. "The Significance of the Locale in the Nebraska Fiction of Willa Cather, Especially in *My Ántonia.*" *Wisconsin Studies in Literature* No. 2 (1965): 81–89.

O'Brien, Sharon. "'The Thing Not Named': Willa Cather as a Lesbian Writer." *Signs* 9 (1983–84): 576–99.

———. *Willa Cather: The Emerging Voice.* New York: Oxford University Press, 1987.

Popken, Randall L. "From Innocence to Experience in *My Ántonia* and *Boy Life on the Prairie.*" *North Dakota Quarterly* 46 (1978): 73–81.

Robinson, Phyllis C. *Willa: The Life of Willa Cather.* Garden City, NY: Doubleday, 1983.

Romines, Ann. "After the Christmas Tree: Willa Cather and Domestic Ritual." *American Literature* 60 (1988): 61–82.

Rose, Phyllis. "The Case of Willa Cather." In *Writing of Women: Essays in a Renaissance.* Middletown, CT: Wesleyan University Press, 1985, pp. 136–52.

Rosowski, Susan J. "Willa Cather—A Pioneer in Art: *O Pioneers!* and *My Ántonia.*" *Prairie Schooner* 55 (1981–82): 141–54.

———. "Willa Cather and the Fatality of Place: *O Pioneers!, My Ántonia,* and *A Lost Lady.*" In *Geography and Literature: A Meeting of the Disciplines,* ed. William E. Mallory and Paul Simpson-Housley. Syracuse: Syracuse University Press, 1987, pp. 81–94.

———. "Willa Cather's Frontier Women: A Feminist Interpretation." In *Where the West Begins: Essays on Middle Border and Siouxland Writing, in Honor of Herbert Krause,* ed. Arthur R. Huseboe and William Geyer. Sioux Falls, SD: Center for Western Studies, 1978, pp. 135–42.

Rucker, Mary E. "Prospective Focus in *My Ántonia.*" *Arizonia Quarterly* 29 (1973): 303–16.

Rule, Jane. "Willa Cather." In *Lesbian Images.* Garden City, NY: Doubleday, 1975, pp. 74–87.

Schroeter, James, ed. *Willa Cather and Her Critics.* Ithaca: Cornell University Press, 1967.

Schwind, Jean. "The Benda Illustrations to *My Ántonia:* Cather's 'Silent' Supplement to Jim Burden's Narrative." *PMLA* 100 (1985): 51–67.

Slote, Bernice, and Virginia Faulkner, ed. *The Art of Willa Cather.* Lincoln: University of Nebraska Press, 1974.

Stegner, Wallace. "Willa Cather: *My Ántonia.*" In *The American Novel: From James Fenimore Cooper to William Faulkner,* ed. Wallace Stegner. New York: Basic Books, 1965, pp. 144–53.

Stouck, David. "Marriage and Friendship in *My Ántonia.*" *Great Plains Quarterly* 2 (1982): 224–31.

―――. "Perspective as Structure and Theme in *My Ántonia.*" *Texas Studies in Literature and Language* 12 (1970–71): 285–94.

―――. *Willa Cather's Imagination.* Lincoln: University of Nebraska Press, 1975.

Thorberg, Raymond. "Willa Cather: From *Alexander's Bridge* to *My Ántonia.*" *Twentieth Century Literature* 7 (1961–62): 147–58.

Van Ghent, Dorothy. *Willa Cather.* Minneapolis: University of Minnesota Press, 1964.

Wasserman, Loretta. "The Lovely Storm: Sexual Initiation in Two Early Willa Cather Novels." *Studies in the Novel* 14 (1982): 348–58.

Watkins, Floyd C. "*My Ántonia:* 'Still, All Day Long, Nebraska.' " In *In Time and Place: Some Origins of American Fiction.* Athens: University of Georgia Press, 1977, pp. 73–101.

Women's Studies 11, No. 3 (December 1984). Special Willa Cather issue.

Woodress, James. *Willa Cather: A Literary Life.* Lincoln: University of Nebraska Press, 1987.

―――. *Willa Cather: Her Life and Art.* New York: Pegasus, 1970.

ACKNOWLEDGMENTS

"Willa Cather: Lady in the Wilderness" by Maxwell Geismar from *The Last of the Provincials: The American Novel 1915–1925* by Maxwell Geismar, © 1943, 1947, 1949 by Maxwell Geismar, renewed 1975 by Maxwell Geismar. Reprinted by permission of Houghton Mifflin Co. and Russell & Volkening, Inc.

"The Frontier Isolation" by Edwin T. Bowden from *The Dungeon of the Heart: Human Isolation and the American Novel* by Edwin T. Bowden, © 1961 by Edwin T. Bowden. Reprinted by permission of Macmillan Publishing Co.

"Hope and Memory in *My Ántonia*" by Robert E. Scholes from *Shenandoah* 14, No. 1 (Autumn 1962), © 1962 by Washington and Lee University. Reprinted by permission of *Shenandoah*.

"Willa Cather" by Louis Auchincloss from *Pioneers and Caretakers: A Study of 9 American Women Writers* by Louis Auchincloss, © 1961, 1964, 1965 by the University of Minnesota. Reprinted by permission of the University of Minnesota Press.

"Willa Cather: The Home Place, Stultification and Inspiration" by Anthony Channell Hilfer from *The Revolt from the Village 1915–1930* by Anthony Channell Hilfer, © 1969 by The University of North Carolina Press. Reprinted by permission.

"Rich Mine of Life: *My Ántonia*" by Philip Gerber from *Willa Cather* by Philip Gerber, © 1975 by G. K. Hall & Co. Reprinted by permission.

"The Central Androgynous Characters in *My Ántonia*" by Clara B. Cooper from *Indian Journal of American Studies* 9, No. 2 (July 1979), © 1979 by American Studies Research Center (Hyderabad, India). Reprinted by permission.

"The *Bildungsroman*, American Style" by C. Hugh Holman from *Windows on the World: Essays on American Social Fiction* by C. Hugh Holman, © 1979 by The University of Tennessee Press. Reprinted by permission.

"The Epic and Great Plains Literature: Rølvaag, Cather, and Neihardt" by Paul A. Olson from *Prairie Schooner* 55, Nos. 1/2 (Spring–Summer 1981), © 1980 by University of Nebraska Press. Reprinted by permission.

" 'The Good Game': The Charm of Willa Cather's *My Ántonia* and W. O. Mitchell's *Who Has Seen the Wind*" by Michael Peterman from *Mosaic* 14, No. 1 (Spring 1981), © 1981 by *Mosaic*. Reprinted by permission.

"Willa Cather: Between Red Cloud and Byzantium" by Michael A. Klug from *Canadian Review of American Studies* 12, No. 3 (Winter 1981), © 1981 by *Canadian Review of American Studies*. Reprinted by permission.

"The Defeat of a Hero: Autonomy and Sexuality in *My Ántonia*" by Deborah G. Lambert from *American Literature* 53, No. 4 (January 1982), © 1982 by Duke University Press. Reprinted by permission.

"The Virginian and Ántonia Shimerda: Different Sides of the Western Coin" by John J. Murphy from *Women and Western American Literature*, edited by Helen Winter

Stauffer and Susan J. Rosowski, © 1982 by Helen Winter Stauffer and Susan J. Rosow-ski. Reprinted by permission of the editors.

"Mothers, Daughters, and the 'Art Necessity': Willa Cather and the Creative Process" by Sharon O'Brien from *American Novelists Revisited: Essays in Feminist Criticism,* edited by Fritz Fleischmann, © 1982 by Fritz Fleischmann. Reprinted by permission.

Willa Cather: Writing at the Frontier by Jamie Ambrose, © 1988 by Berg Publishers. Reprinted by permission.

"The Golden Girl of the West: *My Ántonia"* by Susie Thomas from *Willa Cather* by Susie Thomas, © 1990 by Susie Thomas. Reprinted by permission of Macmillan & Co., London & Basingstoke.

"The Evolution of Modernism" by Linda Wagner-Martin from *The Modern American Novel 1914–1945: A Critical History* by Linda Wagner-Martin, © 1990 by Linda Wagner-Martin. Reprinted by permission of G. K. Hall & Co.

"The World of Nature" by John H. Randall III from *The Landscape and the Looking Glass: Willa Cather's Search for Value* by John H. Randall III, © 1960 by John H. Randall III, renewed 1988 by John H. Randall III. Reprinted by permission of Houghton Mifflin Co.

"My Ántonia" by Richard Giannone from *Music in Willa Cather's Fiction* by Richard Gi-annone, © 1968 by The University of Nebraska Press. Reprinted by permission.

"My Ántonia: A Rose for Miss Cather" by William J. Stuckey from *Studies in the Novel* 4, No. 3 (Fall 1972), © 1972 by North Texas State University. Reprinted by permission.

"Impressionistic Character Portraiture in *My Ántonia* (originally titled "Another Angle of Willa Cather's Artistic Prism: Impressionistic Character Portraiture in *My Ántonia"*) by Edward J. Piacentino from *Midamerica* 9 (1982), © 1982 by the Society for the Study of Midwestern Literature. Reprinted by permission.

"The Land of Nebraska and Ántonia Shimerda" by Mary Kemper Sternshein from *Heritage of the Great Plains* 16, No. 2 (Spring 1983), © 1983 by *Heritage of the Great Plains,* Emporia State University. Reprinted by permission.

"My Ántonia: Emergence and Authorial Revelations" by Patrick W. Shaw from *American Literature* 56, No. 4 (December 1984), © 1984 by Duke University Press. Reprinted by permission.

"My Ántonia, Jim Burden and the Dilemma of the Lesbian Writer" by Judith Fetterley from *Gender Studies: New Directions in Feminist Criticism,* edited by Judith Spector, © 1986 by Bowling Green State University Popular Press. Reprinted by permission.

"My Ántonia: The Closing of the Circle" by Susan J. Rosowski from *The Voyage Perilous: Willa Cather's Romanticism* by Susan J. Rosowski, © 1986 by University of Nebraska Press. Reprinted by permission.

"The Road of Destiny" by Hermione Lee from *Willa Cather: A Life Saved Up* by Hermione Lee, © 1989 by Hermione Lee. Reprinted by permission of Virago Press and the author.

INDEX